Anselm of Havelberg

CISTERCIAN STUDIES SERIES NUMBER TWO HUNDRED THIRTY-TWO

Premonstratensian Texts and Studies, 1

Anselm of Havelberg

Anticimenon:
On the Unity of the Faith and the Controversies with the Greeks

Translated by
Ambrose Criste, OPRAEM, and Carol Neel

α

Cistercian Publications
www.cistercianpublications.org

LITURGICAL PRESS
Collegeville, Minnesota
www.litpress.org

A Cistercian Publications title published by Liturgical Press

Cistercian Publications
Editorial Offices
Abbey of Gethsemani
3642 Monks Road
Trappist, Kentucky 40051
www.cistercianpublications.org

1	2	3	4	5	6	7	8	9

Library of Congress Cataloging-in-Publication Data

Anselm, Bishop of Havelberg, d. 1158.
    [Dialogi. English]
    Anselm of Havelberg, Anticimenon : on the unity of the faith and the controversies with the Greeks / translated by Ambrose Criste and Carol Neel.
        p.   cm. — (Cistercian studies series ; no. 232) (Premonstratensian texts and studies ; 1)
    Includes bibliographical references.
    ISBN 978-0-87907-106-6
    1. History—Religious aspects—Christianity.   2. Church—Unity.
I. Criste, Ambrose.   II. Neel, Carol.   III. Title.

BR115.H5A513 2010
280'.209021—dc22

                                       2009034791

Contents

Preface

As president of the editorial board of Premonstratensian Texts and Studies, I introduce the reader to the first volume of our new series with great excitement and pleasure. This series seeks to bring to light primary works and scholarly studies on the history of the religious order founded in the twelfth century by Norbert of Xanten. Our endeavor joins together the work of regular religious maintaining the vital Norbertine tradition with the efforts of professional academics in historical and theological studies, thus affirming the mutual contribution of a lived spirituality and scholarly investigation in bringing to a wide English-speaking audience monuments of European spiritual and religious life that have been little known until now.

That so many of the foundational texts of Premonstratensian history and spirituality have never been translated into English is a serious and unfortunate lacuna, given the prominence of the Order in the articulation of the ideals of the Gregorian reform. The canons regular, among them the Premonstratensians, played a crucial role in the theology and devotional life of the High Middle Ages, and indeed continued to do so until the devastations of the French Revolution. While the most important writings of the canons of the abbey of St. Victor have long been available in English, the same is not true for their fellow Augustinian canons, the Premonstratensians.

This first volume of Premonstratensian Texts and Studies, the *Anticimenon* of Anselm of Havelberg, represents one of the most interesting and important texts of the whole medieval period, by an author whom the translators rightly name "Norbert's most devoted, proximate, and successful disciple and most articulate apologist." Anselm's treatment of the issues dividing Roman Catholic and Orthodox Christians is unparalleled until, perhaps, the twentieth century in its attempt to offer a fair and thorough presentation of the theological and indeed psychological premises for each side. As Carol Neel and Fr. Ambrose Criste, OPraem, demonstrate in their introduction, Anselm's nuanced treatment of issues dividing Latin and Greek Christendom is an outgrowth and application of his equally compelling treatment of the issue of historical development and diversity in the church. In stressing the fundamental unity of the argument of the three books that comprise the *Anticimenon*, the translators eloquently demonstrate how Anselm's attempt to point the way forward in Roman Catholic and Orthodox dialogue is part of his larger goal to "illuminate for his contemporaries the agency of the Holy Spirit in human time."

Anselm's belief is that variety and diversity among Christians sharing the common core of faith is actually a strength and sign of the continuous work of the Holy Spirit among the Christian people rather than being necessarily divisive and problematic. This perspective was hardly typical of his era, but it is a profoundly hopeful message that may well find a receptive audience in our own time. Who can disagree that Christians, divided both within and between the churches, need more than ever to listen to one another in charity and engage one another, eager to discern the works of the Holy Spirit in each other's midst? This first volume of Premonstratensian Texts and Studies thus is an auspicious occasion for which we owe a debt of gratitude to Dr. Neel and Fr. Criste and to our collaborators at Cistercian Publications and Liturgical Press. It is truly a moment full of hope that Anselm's voice as an advocate of reform and renewal in the church, fully accessible now in English translation for the first time, will provide both an appropriate inauguration and continuing inspiration to all those who will come to seek wisdom from the deep well that is Premonstratensian tradition.

William P. Hyland, PhD
Director, Center for Norbertine Studies
St. Norbert College, De Pere, Wisconsin
September 29, 2008
Michaelmas

Foreword

This translation has brought together interests and contacts extending over many years. Carol Neel first read Anselm of Havelberg's *Anticimenon* in the course of her graduate studies in the late 1970s. Ambrose Criste and Neel began working together while the former was a student at Colorado College in the 1990s, but Criste did not himself encounter Anselm's great work until after he had entered the author's own religious order, the Premonstratensians, several years later. As a novice, Criste read elements of *Anticimenon*'s Book 1 as translated by Fr. Hugh Barbour, O.Praem., for the novices' instruction at St. Michael's Abbey. His interest so piqued, Criste then completed his own translation of Books 1 and 2. Subsequently, during one of Criste's annual visits to Colorado College, he noticed a typewritten translation of *Anticimenon*'s Book 3 on Neel's desk. We had been discussing contributions we might respectively make to a planned new series, Premonstratensian Texts and Studies. Development of a polished, publishable English version of this twelfth-century text of mutual interest seemed to us both topically appropriate and a happy opportunity to work together again. Our collaboration on this text has been in this instance at long distance, since Neel was in the United States while Criste continued his own graduate studies in Rome.

We are grateful for the support to Neel, during her 2007–2008 residency at the Collegeville Institute for Ecumenical and Cultural Research, of the monastic community of St. John's Abbey for their hospitality; the reference and interlibrary loans staffs of St. John's University's Alcuin Library, especially Stefanie Weisgram, OSB, and Janine Lortz, for their seamless helpfulness; the staff of St. John's

Hill Monastic Museum and Library for access to their rich reference collection and other medievalists' tools; colleagues and staff at the Institute for their companionship and interest; Fr. Kilian McDonnell, OSB, the Institute's guiding spirit, for his scholarly and personal model. The Definitory of the Order of Prémontré, Daylesford Abbey, St. Michael's Abbey, St. Norbert's Abbey, St. Norbert College, and the Paul Sheffer Memorial Fund for Roman Catholic Studies of Colorado College have supported this project and the initiation of the series in which it is the inaugural volume. To these institutions and the encouragement of the persons who form them we are again grateful.

Rozanne Elder, long-term editor of Cistercian Studies, and the editors of Cistercian Publications have fostered this work at crucial moments in its development; the translators thank Dr. Elder, in particular, for sharing with us the typescript translation made in the course of graduate study many years ago by the late Fr. Raymond Bierlein, her student. Although we have nowhere followed the Bierlein translation closely, it has been of invaluable help in sharpening our sense of Anselm's meaning. This translation is therefore a tribute to Fr. Bierlein's pioneering work on the text of *Anticimenon* and to Dr. Elder's commitment to both his and his medieval subject's work. We add here our appreciation of the editors of Premonstratensian Texts and Studies for enabling and improving the publication of this important medieval work in a language accessible to many interested in its author's period and concerns; William Hyland of St. Norbert College and Theodore Antry, OPRAEM, of Daylesford Abbey have greatly facilitated this book not only in their advocacy of our project but in their expert, meticulous, and generous attention to its detail. Finally, we express our gratitude to our respective religious and scholarly communities, and to our families, for their consistent interest, assistance, and patience with our engagement with Anselm of Havelberg.

Ambrose Criste, OPRAEM, and Carol Neel
Rome/Colorado Springs
June 6, 2008
Feast of Saint Norbert, Founder of the Order of Prémontré

Introduction

Anselm and his *Anticimenon*

Anselm of Havelberg's *Anticimenon*, written in 1149/50 on medieval Europe's northeastern frontier, addresses differences among Christian communities and divisions among Christian peoples as troubling to moderns as to his work's immediate medieval readership.[1] This twelfth-century author's discourse on doctrinal and ritual variation across time and his representation of dialogues based on his own historical encounter with a Greek theologian nearly fifteen years earlier offer an authentic portrayal of controversy within European Christianity and separation from the Greek-speaking East. His work nonetheless concludes with a hopeful call for a universal council to reaffirm the unity of the faith. Anselm's *Anticimenon*—both ecumenical and, broadly speaking, conciliarist—is thus important for the study of historical theology, but also for contemporary interchange among Christian communions. The author's belief that the Holy Spirit

---

[1] On the date of *Anticimenon*'s text see Jay T. Lees, *Anselm of Havelberg: Deeds into Words in the Twelfth Century*, Studies in the History of Christian Thought 79 (Leiden: Brill, 1998), 91, 164–65; Sebastian Sigler, *Anselm von Havelberg: Beiträge zum Lebensbild eines Politikers, Theologen und königlichen Gesandten im 12. Jahrhundert* (Aachen: Shaker, 2005), 130, 152. Lees' biography, the first book-length attention to Anselm's career and written works, is fundamental to subsequent commentary; Sigler's generally responds to it. Both recent volumes depend, especially with regard to *Anticimenon*, on the basic study of Anselm's text: Johann Wilhelm Braun, "Studien zur Überlieferung der Werke Anselms von Havelberg I: Die Überlieferung des *Anticimenon*," *Deutsches Archiv für Erforschung des Mittelalters* 28 (1972): 133–209; on *Anticimenon*'s composition see pp. 135–36.

militates toward the concord of all believers even as it renews the church through continual change is deeply grounded in his own period's spiritual revival. Although Anselm's conviction that the faith's unity is paramount is a profoundly medieval perspective, it nonetheless challenges more recent times' weary acceptance of Christianity's fragmentation.

Anselm's Latin work in three books, despite its interest as a historical source and ecumenical charge, has until now been among the most important of medieval European works unavailable in English.[2] Indeed, although a French translation of the first book was completed in the 1960s, the entire text has never been published in any modern language.[3] Meanwhile, despite abundant recent scholarship on Anselm's period—especially on the twelfth century's reformation of European Christianity—this author's own religious order, the Premonstratensians, has received less attention both inside and outside the academy than its historical extent and influence merit. Further, while Anselm's thought with respect to the shape of time and the development of the church in expectation of the apocalypse has been much discussed in scholarly literature, the relationship between his historical and ecumenical interests has

---

[2] This translation adopts Anselm's Latinate spelling, *Anticimenon* (*Anticymenon* in some manuscript exemplars) rather than the standard Greek transliteration *Antikeimenon* used in some modern scholarship, notably Lees', because Braun establishes the former as the likely title of an eventual critical edition: see Lees, *Deeds into Words*, 4 and *passim*; Braun, "Studien"; see also Berlin, Staatsbibliothek Preussischer Kulturbesitz, Ms. theol. fol. 80, fol. 208r: *"Incipit prolog(us) Anselmi havelbergens(is) ep(iscopi) in anticymenon i(dest) libru(m) cont(ra)positor(um) sub dialogo (con)scriptum ad ven(er)abiliem papa(m) Eugenium secundu(m)."* A later copyist identified the wrong Eugenius; Anselm in fact addressed Eugenius III.

[3] The available edition is a faulty nineteenth-century Latin version: *Dialogi*, Patrologiae Latinae cursus completus, series Latina, ed. Jacques-Paul Migne (Paris, 1841–64), 188, cols. 1138–1252. This edition is itself based on a seventeenth-century redaction: *Antikeimenon*, ed. Luc d'Achéry, in *Spicilegium sive collectio veterum aliquot scriptorum*, vol. 13 (Paris, 1677), 88–252; this early edition was emended in the following century: *Antikeimenon*, ed. Étienne Baluze et al., *Spicilegium sive collectio veterum aliquot scriptorum*, vol. 1 (Paris, 1723), 161–207. The first book of d'Achéry's Latin text is reprinted with facing French translation as *Dialogues, Livre I: Renouveau dans l'église*, trans. Gaston Salet, Sources Chrétiennes 118 (Paris: Cerf, 1966). Salet adds notes but makes no new contribution to establishing the text. Reference below to the Migne editions of Anselm's *Anticimenon* and related texts are as PL.

been little investigated. The connection between Anselm's written works and his life as a member of the new, dynamic religious order founded by Norbert of Xanten has meanwhile received little serious exploration.[4] The present volume aims to redress the unevenness of

---

[4] Lees, in particular, minimizes the importance of Premonstratensian identity to Anselm's thought: see esp. *Deeds into Words*, 30. Sigler, by contrast, notes that Anselm was consistently loyal to his Premonstratensian "roots" and Norbert's model while furthering the interests of the white canons within his diocese; Sigler does not, however, develop this discussion with extensive reference to *Anticimenon*: compare Sigler, *Beiträge*, iii, 238–43, 259, 282, 317. The fullest recent scholarly attention to Anselm as Premonstratensian is by Werner Bomm, "Augustinusregel, *professio canonica* und Prämonstratenser im 12. Jahrhundert. Das Beispiel der Norbert-Viten, Philipps von Harvengt und Anselms von Havelberg," in Gert Melville and Anne Müller, eds., *Regula Sancti Augustini: Normative Grundlage differenter Verbände im Mittelalter* (Paring: Augustinerchorherren-Verlag, 2002), esp. 276–92; Bomm's focus, however, is on Anselm's earlier *Apologetic Letter*, not the *Anticimenon* centrally at issue here. For an older, still-useful discussion of Anselm's engagement in the contemporary conflict among religious orders in relation to his Premonstratensian identity see Georg Schreiber, "Studien über Anselm von Havelberg zur Geistesgeschichte des Hochmittelalters," *Analecta Praemonstratensia* 18 (1942): 46–87.

Among the lengthy bibliography of older works on Anselm's place among the historical theorists of the High Middle Ages the following elements are central: Herbert Grundmann, *Studien über Joachim von Floris*, Beiträge zur Kulturgeschichte des Mittelalters und der Renaissance 32 (Leipzig: Teubner, 1927), esp. 92–94; Johannes Spörl, *Grundformen hochmittelalterlichen Geschichtsschreibung: Studien zum Weltbild der Geschichtsschreiber des 12. Jahrhunderts* (Munich: M. Hueber, 1935), 18–113; Horst Dieter Rauh, *Das Bild des Antichrist im Mittelalter: Von Tyconius zum deutschen Symbolismus*, Beiträge zur Geschichte der Philosophie und Theologie des Mittelalters, n.s. 9 (Münster: Aschendorff, 1979), 268–99. Of German studies focusing on his ecumenical thought see esp. Georg Schreiber, "Anselm von Havelberg und die Ostkirche," *Zeitschrift für Kirchengeschichte* 60 (1941): 354–411; Hermann Josef Sieben, *Die Konzilsidee des lateinischen Mittelalters (847–1378)* (Paderborn: Schöningh, 1984), 153–67.

For studies in English focusing on Anselm's theology of history see Walter Edyvean, *Anselm of Havelberg and the Theology of History* (Rome: Catholic Book Agency, 1972); Bernard McGinn, *Visions of the End: Apocalyptic Traditions in the Middle Ages* (New York: Columbia University Press, 1979), 109–17; Karl F. Morrison, "Anselm of Havelberg: Play and the Dilemma of Historical Progress," in Thomas F. X. Noble and John J. Contreni, eds., *Religion, Culture and Society in the Early Middle Ages: Studies in Honor of Richard E. Sullivan* (Kalamazoo, MI: Medieval Institute Publications, 1987), 219–56; Morrison, "The Exercise of Thoughtful Minds: The Apocalypse in Some German Historical Writings," in *The Apocalypse in the Middle Ages*, ed. Richard K. Emmerson and Bernard McGinn (Ithaca: Cornell

modern responsiveness to both Anselm's work and his confrères' role in the medieval reformation by presenting his *Anticimenon* as a major artifact of twelfth-century thought and a principal source on the early Order of Prémontré. Although the present volume's introduction outlines major trends in prior scholarship on this twelfth-century author and advances some fresh interpretation of his place in his period's intellectual and spiritual life, its principal goal is to enable a wider readership to engage with Anselm, so inviting further exploration of his place in the medieval religious revival and among the early followers of the Premonstratensian founder Norbert.

Anselm's work is often known as *Dialogi,* "dialogues," in the Latin in which its text is written. The Greek *Anticimenon* means, more strictly, "controversies." This translation maintains the latter title—although the term is less familiar to English-speaking readers than "dialogues"—because it is the author's own and is generally accepted in European scholarly literature. *Anticimenon,* moreover, reflects the interest in Greek language and Greek-speaking Christians memorialized in Anselm's work. Although several important writers of his and prior generations wrote theological dialogues, most notably Anselm of Canterbury—and although this genre had been modeled for medieval Christians by the greatest of the Latin Fathers, Augustine—the choice of a Greek title for such a work was virtually unique in the medieval West.[5] The seventh-century Spanish bishop Julian of Toledo used the Greek title *Anticimenon* or *Antikeimenon* for his own commentary in two books on the Old and New Testaments respectively.[6] Anselm, however, seems to have chosen the same exceptional title in recognition of his own en-

---

University Press, 1992), 352–73. On Anselm's dialogues with the Greeks see esp. Gillian R. Evans, "Anselm of Canterbury and Anselm of Havelberg: The Controversy with the Greeks," *Analecta Praemonstratensia* 53 (1977): 158–75; Norman Russell, "Anselm of Havelberg and the Union of Churches," *Sobornost* 1 (1979): 19–41; 2 (1980): 29–41.

[5] Lees discusses patristic and medieval models in relation to Anselm's use of the dialogue form: *Deeds into Words,* 232–33. Sigler notes likeness to Abelard's dialogue with a Jew, in which the non-Roman voice has no possibility of winning the day: *Beiträge,* 311.

[6] Julian of Toledo, *Antikeimenon,* PL 96, cols. 586–706. On the unusual Greek title see cols. 585–86.

gagement with his Byzantine contemporaries and his intention to communicate their perspectives to a Latin readership rather than in reference to Julian's exegetical model. The title *Dialogi* assigned to the work's three books in the widely available nineteenth-century *Patrologia Latina* edition thus seems ill-advised, and is corrected here.

Translation of Anselm's *Anticimenon* is necessarily informed by awareness that the author was himself attentive to the difficulty of the translator's enterprise. In the proem to *Anticimenon*'s second book, as its text begins to recount the author's conversations with a Greek interlocutor, Nicetas of Nicomedia, the speaker Anselm notes that word-for-word translation often distorts meaning. He petitions his Greek counterpart and the audience assembled to hear their discourse that the three translators facilitating their discussion focus on tone and meaning rather than on individual words. Close literal translation might, Anselm fears, create needless conflict through inexact representation of respective terms. As the author records, the dialogues' Greek interlocutor had first suggested literal translation: Nicetas remarks, "It seems to me that the appointed interpreter should translate what we are about to say word for word, because in this way we can better understand each other, and he can easily do this." The Latin speaker Anselm then counters, "But I do not speak in this way and such translation is suspect, in my view, because I can be misunderstood word by word if the translation is inexact, and we should not quibble over words. Rather the translation between us should gather and then set forth our respective speech as it develops, in its full meaning. In this way of speaking and translating we shall examine thoughts rather than be fixed on their expression."[7] The *Anticimenon* text thus represents its author's confidence that his literary interlocutors' respective understandings of Christian doctrine and practice are proximate, but emphasizes that language can be an obstacle to Christian concord. The Greeks who are present accede to the speaker Anselm's request; the dialogue goes forward with principals, interpreters, and audience alike committed to appreciation of the speaker's full contextual meaning. In this spirit, as two days

[7] *Anticimenon* 2.1.

of discussion ensue, according to Anselm of Havelberg's account the interlocutors achieve the rhetorical concord toward which they aim.[8] The present translation of this 850-year-old work responds to its author's concern, expressed through the figures of his theological dialogue, that translation attend to holistic meaning. This English version therefore privileges the tone and nuance of both the author and the interlocutors he represents while reflecting as closely as possibly their precise, sometimes technical usages.

Anselm of Havelberg's *Anticimenon* is effectively a primer on the principal issues it addresses—the shape of Christian time and the variety of Christian doctrine. Book 1, in form a discourse rather than a dialogue, discusses the variety of doctrine and religious practice across Christian time, mostly in the Latin West. Book 2 relates a discussion—unlike Book 1's, indeed, in dialogue form—ostensibly solicited by the Greeks in their eagerness to engage with an emissary from Latin Christendom. The second book focuses closely on the procession of the Holy Spirit, the most important of theological controversies between Greek and Roman communions. As the author's description makes clear, the dialogue it represents purports to bear a close relationship to his own actual conversations with the Greek archbishop Nicetas of Nicomedia in 1136, during the first of the German prelate's two diplomatic missions to Constantinople.[9] Book 3 continues with a second dialogue between Anselm, the author's own *persona*, and his opponent Nicetas on three matters of ritual difference between Greeks and Romans. First the interlocutors take up the Greeks' practice of leavening eucharistic bread, second their consecration of wine without water, and finally their custom of unction of Catholic Christians as a symbol of passage into Orthodox culture and belief—a practice Western princesses in particular had often undergone before the

---

[8] At the conclusion of Book 2 (*Anticimenon* 2.27) and again at the end of Book 3 (*Anticimenon* 3.22) the interlocutors together call for an ecumenical council, to the acclamation of the dialogues' assembled audience.

[9] *Anticimenon* 2.1. On the relationship between written text and historical dialogues see Lees, *Deeds into Words*, 232–33. Much scholarly debate about the historicity of Anselm's record of his dialogues with Nicetas has led to consensus that, while they are based on a historical encounter, their content is much enriched and edited: see esp. Sieben, *Konzilsidee*, 167.

celebration of their marriages to members of Byzantine imperial dynasties. Anselm was no doubt interested in this matter of unction upon marriage not only because it might seem a form of rebaptism, deemed heretical since the patristic period, but because the German emperors for whom he served as a councilor continually sought Byzantine marriage alliances for diplomatic and dynastic ends.[10]

All three books were written—and here are translated—to engage and inform readers who might lack prior experience of analogous theological material. Indeed, the tendentiousness of Book 1 and the lively give-and-take of Books 2 and 3 offer such expository clarity that recapitulation of their content here would not enhance it. Instead, the present introduction aims to provide useful background for its twelfth-century author's lucid, compelling text in terms of his historical and biographical circumstances, to outline modern scholarly perspectives, and to suggest pathways for further investigation. Anselm's goal in crafting the work at hand was ambitious: to illuminate for his contemporaries the agency of the Holy Spirit in human time. Modern readers will be supported, in their response to this cosmic and metahistorical enterprise, by awareness of Anselm's career as at once a magnate of the German empire and a member of a religious order at the heart of the twelfth century's reformation of European religious life, and also by his period's experience of separation from Eastern Christians and the tumult within European religious life.

East and West in the Twelfth Century

Ironically, Anselm of Havelberg wrote the optimistic, even triumphant account of his own conversations with a Byzantine theologian translated here only a little more than half a century before hope of concord between Roman and Greek churches was deeply undercut by European Crusaders' sack of Constantinople in 1204 AD.[11] This event was a dark consequence of the twelfth-century

---

[10] Sigler emphasizes Anselm's role as a marriage broker: *Beiträge*, 133–35.

[11] On the abortive Fourth Crusade condemned by the papacy for its conquest of the Byzantine outpost, Zara, then the Greek capital, see Michael Angold, *The*

Western kingdoms' extraordinary economic and political expansionism. The same period had been the most transformative in the history of European religion with respect not only to its literature and doctrinal development but also to its phenomenology. Since the foundation of the new monastery at Cîteaux in 1098, regular religious life—that is monks, nuns, and clergy living together according to ancient rules for common life and liturgical practice— had been convulsed by challenges to the predominant monastic pattern, Benedictinism. Religious communities were the heart of the Latin church and in many ways the most important unifying force in European culture, so that their reformation had impact across European society far beyond the monastic houses governed by the sixth-century Rule of St. Benedict. Meanwhile, the secular polity of the church was at once invigorated and threatened by the epic conflict with the German empire resulting from the reformist pontificate of Gregory VII. Inextricable from all these developments was the rapid increase in the proportion of lay Europeans, including great numbers of women, non-elites, and townspeople, who demanded the opening of spiritual practices previously inaccessible to them.[12]

What Charles Homer Haskins famously called the "renaissance of the twelfth century" in the 1920s, historians now take to have been much more—a refashioning of Europeans' social and economic frameworks, political culture, and spiritualities.[13] In this multilayered transformation, the people of Latin Christendom began vigorously to define themselves and expand their borders against a series of previously little-known others: the pagan, Slavic northeast; the Muslim east and southwest; the Orthodox and Greek-speaking south and east. East-West schism had been foreshadowed in late antiquity during the controversies surround-

---

Fourth Crusade: Event and Context (London: Pearson, Longman, 2003); on Innocent III's reaction see pp. 113–14.

[12] On the transformation of European monastic life and popular spirituality in the generations immediately around Anselm's see Giles Constable's magisterial account: *The Reformation of the Twelfth Century* (Cambridge: Cambridge University Press, 1996), esp. 296–328.

[13] See Charles Homer Haskins, *The Renaissance of the Twelfth Century* (Cambridge, MA: Harvard University Press, 1927), vii–ix.

ing the many heresies of the fourth and fifth centuries, accelerated by the collapse of the Roman Empire in the same period, then exacerbated by the ecclesiological conflicts of the ninth century in which the idea of empire was revived in the West by the Frankish ruler Charlemagne in his alliance with the Roman papacy. Theological difference, emphasized for the political ends of the Frankish monarchs, then separated Greek- from Latin-speaking churches, but this division had little practical effect—given the political and ecclesiastical confusion of the following two centuries—until the mid-1000s, when in the prelude to the twelfth-century revival the emissaries of a reformist Roman hierarchy made schism explicit. The papal legate Humbert, in Constantinople to negotiate a military and political alliance against the Norman invaders of southern Italy, instead took up theological and ritual difference, and in 1054 anathematized the patriarch Michael Cerularius for various heresies. The patriarch responded provocatively from the perspective of Orthodoxy's own assertive ecclesiology, with the general support of the Eastern churches, although without excommunicating the pope. Humbert had represented Leo IX, who in fact had died before his legate excommunicated the patriarch, so that little of real legal importance had actually happened. The repute and the effects of these events were nonetheless definitive. Humbert's action and Michael Cerularius' response were subsequently viewed as marking East-West schism.[14]

Although the occasion of 1054 was fortuitous, the theological distance between Greek and Roman communions now emerged as profound. The primary issue involved the procession of the Holy Spirit, which the Greeks understood to be solely from God the Father while the Latins believed to be from the Son as well. In the West the term *filioque*, meaning "and the Son," was conventionally added to the credal text established at Nicea in 325 in its description of the Holy Spirit. This insertion of *filioque* had been widely accepted in Europe since the Carolingian ninth century, in part in expression of the western kings' and bishops' claim of independence from

---

[14] For a compelling outline of the events of 1054 and their etiology see Henry Chadwick, *East and West: The Making of a Rift in the Church from Apostolic Times until the Council of Florence* (Oxford: Oxford University Press, 2003), esp. 193–221.

Byzantine imperial authority; *filioque* then became a verbal tool for separating Roman purity of belief from the heresies with which the Frankish kings and the popes feared the East was rife. This very doctrinal addendum or—as the Roman Church had it—clarification of the meaning of the Nicene Creed was rejected as abhorrent and itself heretical by Byzantine Christians. *Filioque* then became both pretext and irritant in the essentially political conflict that led to the more definitive schism of Orthodoxy and Catholicism in 1054. But this Trinitarian matter was not the only issue delimiting East-West difference in the eleventh century. Lesser but still important matters of ritual practice, especially involving the elements of the Eucharist, separated Greeks from Roman Christians. Complicating their discussion was the issue of Petrine supremacy; the Eastern church acknowledged the special prestige of the see of Peter but failed to accept that its leadership might elide the authority of the great Eastern sees, especially Constantinople, within their jurisdictions, or that its example or teaching might supersede Greek tradition on doctrine and sacred rites.[15]

Throughout the following century popes and other eminent Latins attempted to win the Greeks by argument to acquiescence in the central Roman theological positions. Urban II, the pope who summoned the First Crusade, convened a synod at Myra, appropriately at the shrine of Nicholas of Bari, a saint whose relics had only lately been brought to Italy from their original site in Asia Minor. At this meeting Anselm of Canterbury was the chief representative of the Roman side. His subsequent work *On the Procession of the Holy Spirit* reflects his argument there.[16] But no resolution ensued, nor did any other Westerners conduct formal

---

[15] Again for general background see Chadwick, *East and West*, 27–39, 77–94, 200–18,

[16] On Anselm of Canterbury at Bari and in his related texts see Chadwick, *East and West*, 224–27. See also Anselm of Canterbury, *The Incarnation of the Word*, in *Anselm of Canterbury*, ed. and trans. Jasper Hopkins and Herbert Richardson (Toronto: Edwin Mellen, 1976), 7–37, and Anselm of Canterbury's later, more extensive discussions relevant to the second and third books of the later Anselm's *Anticimenon*, beginning with direct reference to the errors of the Greeks: *The Procession of the Holy Spirit*, in *Anselm of Canterbury*, 183–230, esp. 183–84; *The Sacrifice of Unleavened and Leavened Bread*, in *Anselm of Canterbury*, 233–240, esp. 233.

dialogues with the Greeks until the later Anselm's mission of the 1130s, although East-West theological difference continued to be both a rhetorical device and a real subject in increasingly rationalist discussion of theology within Latin Christendom, for instance in the various redactions of Peter Abelard's *Christian Theology*.[17] Anselm wrote in a context of wide European awareness of active conflict with Greek Christians in the imperial politics of Italy as well as in theological discourse.[18]

Among the documents of these relations, the bishop of Havelberg's *Anticimenon* holds unique importance as the one major twelfth-century work representing dialogue between Roman and Greek communions, looking hopefully, moreover, to the healing of the rift in the church. Some scholars have understood Anselm's position in this work to be a partisan defense of the Catholic theological perspective and of Petrine supremacy rather than a balanced or sympathetic representation of the Orthodox point of view, while others have emphasized the accuracy and open-mindedness with which the author sets forth the arguments of the Greek speaker Nicetas.[19] Anselm's literary representation of a Westerner's dialogue with the Greek theologian supports both interpretations to an extent. The author indeed portrays Nicetas of Nicomedia as a powerful apologist for Greek viewpoints on all the important theological, ritual, and ecclesiological matters. His own namesake speaker, the Roman advocate, nonetheless prevails, consistently winning Nicetas' agreement. Repeatedly, however, the two interlocutors call for a universal ecumenical council summoned by the pope to bring all European and Mediterranean Christians to concord. *Anticimenon*'s author was surely aware that the hope his

---

[17] See, for instance, Abelard's discussion of the procession of the Holy Spirit, which responds to Anselm of Canterbury's and in turn to the Greeks' perspectives: *Opera Theologica II: Theologia Christiana* 4.83–94 and 4.116–57, ed. Eligius M. Buytaert, Corpus Christianorum Continuatio Medievalis 12 (Turnhout: Brepols, 1969), 304–10, 323–42.

[18] On Anselm of Havelberg in the contemporary context of East-West conflict, see Chadwick, *East and West*, 228–32.

[19] See, for instance, Chadwick's emphasis on Anselm's evenhandedness: *East and West*, 232. Lees concurs regarding *Anticimenon*'s sympathetic portrayal of Nicetas: *Deeds into Words*, esp. 237–38; see, on the other hand, Sigler, who accounts Anselm a thoroughgoing papal partisan: *Beiträge*, esp. 189.

literary figures expressed in their conciliarist appeal was not immediately realistic, but the text of their dialogues nonetheless testifies
to his sense of that eventual possibility and his appreciation of the
value of carrying forward such discussion. Essential to sensitive interpretation of Anselm's ecumenism and conciliarism as expressed
in the later books of *Anticimenon*, however, is the relationship of
Book 2 and Book 3 to the work's equally engaging first book on
the variety of religious life within the Catholic West. Book 1 of
Anselm's *Anticimenon* is the best-known and most-studied part of
his *oeuvre* and requires historical introduction, in which Anselm's
biographical context and regular religious affiliation will clarify
his vision of both European and world Christianities.

The European Reform and the Bishop of Havelberg

Anticimenon's author was an important historical actor quite apart
from the literary and theological achievement documented in the
work's three books. Anselm's distinguished ecclesiastical and diplomatic career was rooted in his relationship with the guiding force
of the Order of Prémontré, Norbert of Xanten. That charismatic
reformer, itinerant preacher, community founder, and eventually
prince-bishop of Europe's eastern frontier had been a secular canon
and imperial courtier when in 1115 he experienced a conversion
to ascetic penance and reformist preaching. Thereafter Norbert
self-consciously modeled himself on the Latin father Augustine
as the paradigm of a religious vocation blending active and contemplative visions of ideal Christian life. In that imitation Norbert
founded the Premonstratensians, the most rapidly proliferating of
the many new twelfth-century regular religious movements after
the Cistercians.[20] This preacher-founder was a friend and traveling

---

[20] For a summary of Norbert's career see *Norbert and Early Norbertine Spirituality*,
ed. and trans. Theodore J. Antry and Carol Neel (New York: Paulist Press, 2007),
7–12. The definitive biography of the reformer is in Dutch and focuses on his
archiepiscopal career: Wilfried Grauwen, *Norbertus Aartsbisschop van Maagdenburg
(1126–1134)*, Verhandelingen van de Koninklijke Academie voor Wetenschappen,
Letteren en Schone Kunsten van België, Klasse der Letteren, Verhandeligen 40, no.
86 (Brussels: Paleis der Academiën, 1978); Grauwen's work is, happily, available in
German translation: *Norbert, Erzbischof von Magdeburg (1126–1134)*, 2d ed., trans.

companion of Bernard of Clairvaux, the most important figure in the early Order of Cîteaux, whose white-clad monks advocated a return to strict, primitive Benedictinism and embraced simplicity and manual labor in their pursuit of a life modeled on that of early Christians. Norbert too sought for himself and his followers such apostolic life, *vita apostolica*, so becoming Christ's poor, *pauperes Christi*.[21] Unlike the first Cistercians, however, Norbert adopted the Rule of St. Augustine as his followers' pattern of life. This text, which had a complex history, was grounded in the instructions for religious community of the greatest of the Latin Fathers of the church, who himself lived a common life with other clerics while

---

Ludger Horstkötter (Duisberg: Prämonstratenser-Abtei St. Johann, 1986). The best one-volume treatment of Norbert's role in his period and as Premonstratensian founder is a collection of German essays: Kaspar Elm, ed., *Norbert von Xanten: Adliger, Ordensstifter, Kirchenfürst* (Cologne: Wienand, 1984).

Christopher Brooke offers a provocative introduction to Norbert in his survey of medieval religious life: *The Age of the Cloister: The Story of Monastic Life in the Middle Ages* (Mahwah NJ: HiddenSpring, 2003), 217–22. Lees' chapter on Norbert and Anselm also offers a useful biographical summary on the reformer: *Deeds into Words*, 22–39. Ernest W. McDonnell's discussion of the *vita apostolica* in the twelfth century, with special reference to Norbert and Anselm, retains usefulness: "The *Vita Apostolica*: Diversity or Dissent," *Church History* 24 (1955): 15–31. Among recent works see the source collection and commentary by Antry and Neel, *Norbert and Early Norbertine Spirituality*, esp. 23–27, and on Anselm specifically pp. 29–37. On the spirituality of regular canons, especially the Premonstratensian Philip of Harvengt, see also Caroline Walker Bynum, *Docere verbo et exemplo: An Aspect of Twelfth-Century Spirituality*, Harvard Theological Studies 31 (Missoula, MT: Scholars Press, 1979), esp. 48–55; eadem, *Jesus as Mother: Studies in the Spirituality of the High Middle Ages* (Berkeley: University of California Press, 1982), 36–40; Giles Constable, *Three Studies in Medieval Religious and Social Thought: The Interpretation of Mary and Martha, the Ideal of the Imitation of Christ, the Orders of Society* (Cambridge: Cambridge University Press, 1995), esp. 71–72, 263–64.

  [21] On the Premonstratensians as "poor men" see Ernst Werner, *Pauperes Christi: Studien zu sozial-religiösen Bewegungen im Zeitalter des Reformpapsttums* (Leipzig: Koehler and Amelang, 1956), 19. On the order's place in the contemporary pursuit of apostolic life see again Brooke, *Age of the Cloister*, 219–22. On the Premonstratensians in their Augustinian context and in relation to the reform of Benedictinism see R. W. Southern, *Western Society and the Church in the Middle Ages* (New York: Penguin, 1970), 240–59. Antry and Neel discuss Premonstratensian spirituality in general: *Norbert and Early Norbertine Spirituality*, 23–27. The only monographic study of the spirituality of the order remains, however, the work of François Petit, *La spiritualité des Prémontrés aux XIIe et XIIIe siècles* (Paris: J. Vrin, 1947), esp. 11–124.

serving as a bishop in north Africa.[22] The Rule of St. Augustine therefore differed from the Benedictine rule in that it assumed its adherents might serve churches and persons outside their own circle, as Augustine himself did in his work in Hippo. It was thus appropriate for canons (clergy living in community), as opposed to monks, who might receive priestly ordination but whose central calling was prayerful separation from the secular world.

Norbert's clerical reform had immense immediate success. He founded his first community on Christmas of 1121. Three hundred houses of his white canons—for he chose for them entirely white garments symbolizing their purity of life—spread across Europe by 1200, falling behind the many hundreds of houses of the white monks in their explosive growth, but not by far.[23] Yet the ever-active and mobile Norbert, who died in 1134 as archbishop of Magdeburg on Europe's eastern edge eight years after leaving behind Prémontré in northern France and his other early foundations in the Low Countries and the Rhineland, left behind no written word. Bernard's abundant, mellifluous prose had brought immense notoriety to the Cistercian way of life in the twelfth century. That quantitative difference between the respective foundational writings of the two groups is a major root of the neglect of the Premonstratensians in modern historiography.

Little evidence survives about the early years of Norbert's follower Anselm. He seems likely to have come from the same general Rhineland region as his master Norbert, and like him to have been well educated in a cathedral school, probably at Liège.[24] Even before he became associated with Norbert, Anselm had in the course

---

[22] See George Lawless, *Augustine of Hippo and His Monastic Rule* (Oxford: Clarendon Press, 1987). Lawless summarizes the development of versions of the Augustinian rule on pp. 121–54; he offers an edition with English translation of both *Ordo monasterii* and *Praeceptum* chosen by Norbert as his followers' governing text: see pp. 74–103.

[23] See, for instance, Southern, *Western Society,* 312–18; Antry and Neel, *Norbert and Early Norbertine Spirituality,* 1–7, 11–15.

[24] Sigler argues against Lees that Anselm studied with the great Benedictine Rupert at Liège: *Beiträge,* 4. Lees agrees that Anselm studied in that city, but believes that—unlike his friend Wibald—he was uninfluenced by Rupert: *Deeds into Words,* 14–18. That Anselm ended up a regular canon and so in opposition to Rupert's advocacy of Benedictinism need not, however, mean that he was not informed by Rupert's

of his schooling made lifelong friends of two other ecclesiastics of eventual European influence, Arnold of Wied and Wibald of Corbie; his correspondence with Wibald sheds valuable light on his later career.[25] But Anselm's formation as a religious and a servant of church and empire was principally in Norbert's hands from at least his early twenties. As Norbert's principal biographer Wilfried Grauwen has pointed out, Anselm was Norbert's most devoted, proximate, and successful disciple.[26] In 1126, when the reformer assumed the archbishopric of Saxon Magdeburg, Anselm accompanied him. Anselm was present during the multiple crises of Norbert's leadership in this important and tumultuous frontier region, where his prosecution of clerical reform and installation of canons in the cathedral church of Our Lady met with bitter, sometimes violent resistance. Anselm accompanied Norbert on a variety of missions on the emperor's behalf, including expeditions to Italy in the course of papal-imperial conflict and diplomacy.[27]

In 1130, perhaps at the moment of Anselm's earliest canonical eligibility at age 30, Norbert appointed his young friend to one of Magdeburg's suffragan sees, Havelberg. This office then existed in exile and, for the most part, in name alone; the diocese established east of the Elbe in Slavic, pagan territory in the tenth century had been long since overrun and would be secured for settlement and conversion only through Anselm's own great effort, in the course of the so-called crusade against the Wends of the late 1140s.[28]

---

teaching; on Rupert and the conflict among the orders see John Van Engen, *Rupert of Deutz* (Berkeley: University of California Press, 1983), 306–34, esp. 323–34.

[25] Lees emphasizes the lifelong importance of Anselm's early friendships: *Deeds into Words*, 14, 21. Wibald's and Anselm's letters are published in the records of the Benedictine's abbey: Philippe Jaffé, ed., *Monumenta Corbeiensia*, Bibliotheca rerum germanicarum 1 (Berlin: Weidmann, 1864), letters 159 (263–66), 211 (330), and 221 (339–41).

[26] Grauwen, *Norbert*, 164.

[27] Lees, *Deeds into Words*, 29–38; Sigler, *Beiträge*, 5–28.

[28] On the date of Anselm's elevation see Lees, *Deeds into Words*, 13 and n. 5. On the establishment of the diocese of Havelberg and its vicissitudes see A. P. Vlasto, *The Entry of the Slavs into Christendom: An Introduction to the Medieval History of the Slavs* (Cambridge: Cambridge University Press, 1970), 147–54. Vlasto believes that Havelberg was not secured until 1184 (p. 153), but as Sigler points out, Anselm was able to assume residency in 1147: *Beiträge*, 111. See also Franz Winter, *Die*

Recent biographies by Jay Lees and Sebastian Sigler have alike emphasized that Anselm—in his own multiple, complex roles— was not only chosen for ecclesiastical leadership by his master Norbert but framed on Norbert's personal model.[29] Among the most important reasons for studying Anselm's career is the light it sheds on Norbert, among the most elusive of important twelfth-century religious figures.

For the purposes of attention to Anselm's *Anticimenon*, however, a general outline of Anselm's episcopal career suffices. In Norbert's shadow until the archbishop-founder's death in 1134, at which he was appropriately present, Anselm then emerged as a leading imperial councilor in his own right. In 1135 the Saxon emperor Lothar sent him on a diplomatic mission to Constantinople, the occasion for the debates he later represented in *Anticimenon*.[30] Thereafter Anselm clearly had special dignity in both imperial and papal courts as an expert on Byzantine politics and religious life; in the later 1130s and early 1140s Anselm was a frequent witness to imperial charters and participant in imperial diets, as well as being imperial representative to the papal court. His close association with Lothar, who was succeeded by Conrad III, a monarch of the rival Hohenstaufen family, led to some coolness between the bishop and the new king.[31] By the late 1140s Anselm was in such disfavor with Conrad that he experienced a period of isolation and inactivity. His letters to his old friend Wibald reveal that he deeply resented this forced retreat from influence and engagement with the affairs of church and empire.[32] But the initiation of the campaigns against the Slavic Wends, a secondary consequence of the Second Crusade to the Holy Land preached by Bernard of

---

Prämonstratenser des zwölften Jahrhunderts und ihre Bedeutung für das nordöstliche Deutschland: Ein Beitrag zur Geschichte der Christianisierung und Germanisierung des Wendenlandes (Berlin, 1865; repr. Aalen: Scientia, 1966), 154–68.

[29] Lees, *Deeds into Words*, esp. 38–39; Sigler, *Beiträge*, esp. 27–28.

[30] On Anselm's role as imperial ambassador see Lees, *Deeds into Words*, 42–45; Sigler, *Beiträge*, 30–35.

[31] Lees emphasizes Anselm's awkwardness in relations with Conrad and his subsequent "exile" in Havelberg: *Deeds into Words*, 53, 61, 72–97; compare Sigler, *Beiträge*, 64, 75, 141–48.

[32] Anselm's letters in *Monumenta Corbeiensia*, ed. Jaffé, 339–41.

Clairvaux, gave Anselm the opportunity to emerge from his eclipse in the role of papal legate, in which he seems to have militated toward evangelization of pagan peoples rather than their slaughter.[33] Meanwhile Anselm had been able to establish a church and residence in Havelberg in 1147, and from there he worked to found Premonstratensian houses whose activities might contribute to the conversion of the Slavs.[34] Finally, the reign of Conrad's successor, Frederick Barbarossa, brought Anselm renewed recognition, a further diplomatic mission to Constantinople, and eventually an archiepiscopate beyond the Alps. In 1154 the new emperor appointed this able servant of the German church and authority on Byzantine relations to the important see of Ravenna, with its complex position as an outpost of Greek authority and influence among the ever-rebellious urban centers of northern Italy.[35] Anselm died in Frederick's army in the summer of 1158, as some said smitten by God for his vehemence in urging the emperor to besiege and reduce Milan.[36]

Moderns unaccustomed to the interweaving of elites' religious and political roles may find the multiplicity of Anselm's activities improbable, even jarring: the same Anselm who followed the charismatic holy man Norbert was also an imperial magnate with

---

[33] Vlasto, *Entry of the Slavs*, 134–35. On Anselm's role, see Lees, *Deeds into Words*, 78–82; Sigler, *Beiträge*, 120–22.

[34] Lees, *Deeds into Words*, 70–73; Sigler, *Beiträge*, 75–81, 162. See also Winter, *Prämonstratenser*, 105–16, 148–54.

[35] Lees, *Deeds into Words*, 98–114, esp. 110. Sigler emphasizes that Anselm's success in representing Barbarossa in a second diplomatic mission to Byzantium in 1153/54 led to his archiepiscopal appointment: *Beiträge*, 192–96, 208. On Anselm's second embassy the bishop again conducted theological debates with the Greeks, this time in Thessalonica: Russell, "Anselm of Havelberg," 22–23; Lees, *Deeds into Words*, 109–10 and n. 42; Sigler notes that Anselm appears in the latter debates' records to be a less enthusiastic ecumenist than in *Anticimenon*: *Beiträge*, 202–3. Anselm's attentiveness to the Greek tradition is nonetheless attested in a further text: *De ordine pronuntiandae letaniae ad Fridericum Magdeburgensem archiepiscopum*, ed. Franz Winter, "Zur Geschichte des Bischofs Anselm von Havelberg," *Zeitschrift für Kirchengeschichte* 5 (1882): 144–55; here Anselm includes many Greek saints: see esp. 152–53. On the ecumenical emphasis of this treatise on the litany of the saints, see Sigler, *Beiträge*, 155.

[36] Vincent of Prague, *Annales*, Monumenta Germaniae Historica, Scriptorum 17 (Hannover, 1861), 671, 674.

the leisure to write theology or ecclesiology between episodes of high influence in the German court. As Jay Lees—whose meticulous work on Anselm is the first full biographical study and thus essential to further research—has usefully pointed out, however, Anselm shared with Norbert the intellectual and political ethos attributed by Stephen Jaeger to the northern cathedral schools, in which clerics of the generations immediately following the Investiture Controversy were committed to preserving the unity of Latin Christendom through service to church and secular empire alike.[37] Like Norbert's, Anselm's career in religious life and as imperial bishop demonstrated the profundity of this commitment and the efficacy of this preparation, and his work as bishop, writer, diplomat, crusader, both papal and imperial courtier—finally as ecumenist and conciliarist—consistently reflected this energetic ideal.

Anselm's Literary *Oeuvre*

In the course of his highly active administrative, religious, and military career, Anselm of Havelberg had, from the perspective of modern scholarship on the medieval reformation, become the twelfth-century Premonstratensians' most articulate apologist. His impassioned, startlingly original writings point to Norbert's inspiration. With the literary remains of other early white canons such as Philip of Harvengt, the written works of the bishop of Havelberg bespeak a distinctive Premonstratensian spirituality.[38] They show that in many ways the Augustinian communities inspired by Norbert were more innovative than the Cistercians and more prophetic of the pan-European Franciscanism of the following century with its huge popular following. Although Norbert understood himself to be returning to ancient ideals as did the Cistercian reformers of Benedictinism, his followers' expression of the apostolic life

[37] Lees, *Deeds into Words*, 18–19, 143–44, 285–86. Compare C. Stephen Jaeger, *The Envy of Angels: Cathedral Schools and Social Ideals in Medieval Europe, 950–1200* (Philadelphia: University of Pennsylvania Press, 1994), with emphasis on the regular canons in this context at pp. 76–87.

[38] Petit, *La spiritualité des Prémontrés*, 129–66; Antry and Neel, *Apologetic Letter*, 193–200.

was more a departure from prior medieval patterns of devotional practice and religious community than the white monks' return to monastic origins.[39] They were highly self-conscious of the inventiveness of their movement, and as their outstanding apologist Anselm responded vigorously to the criticisms of contemporaries decrying novelty in religious life.

Anselm's first major foray into the lively contemporary discussion of the status and merits of the many new European apostolic foundations of the early twelfth century came in the early 1140s, when he responded to a critique of the white canons by the Benedictine Ekbert of Huysburg.[40] The black monk's letter does not survive, but Anselm's powerful rejoinder suggests its content in harshly, persuasively refuting both Ekbert's argument and his scriptural exegesis. The tone Anselm adopts in his later *Anticimenon* is markedly gentler—and this difference bears careful independent scrutiny—but from the perspective of the later work this *Apologetic Letter* is important in its articulation of the character and historical significance of the white canons. Here, in the context of an invective against those who challenge the reform of clergy according to the Rule of St. Augustine, Anselm offers a positive account of regular canons' charism. Although he at no point names himself a Premonstratensian or speaks directly of the network of religious houses founded by Norbert of Xanten, for him to have done so would have been anomalous in the twelfth-century context, in which the notion of a religious "order" was still inchoate, and he and others of Norbert's followers understood themselves rather as in their master's spiritual filiation than as a formal category within the larger context of reformed Augustinians.[41] Yet Anselm here, in

---

[39] See again Brooke, *Age of the Cloister,* 217–32.

[40] Anselm, *Apologetic Letter,* in Antry and Neel, *Norbert and Early Norbertine Spirituality,* 38–62. Sigler has disputed Lees' (*Deeds into Words,* 54) dating of this text to 1138, arguing it cannot have been written earlier than 1143: *Beiträge,* 63, 235. Lees' analysis of the letter is nonetheless rich: *Deeds into Words,* 129–63.

[41] On the frequently anachronistic usage of the notion of "religious orders" among modern historians see Constance Hoffman Berman, *The Cistercian Evolution: The Invention of a Religious Order in Twelfth-Century Europe* (Philadelphia: University of Pennsylvania Press, 2000), esp. 221–36. On this issue in canon law, with special reference to Augustinians, see Peter Landau, "Der Begriff *ordo* in mittelalterlichen Kanonistik," in Irene Crusius and Helmut Flachenecker, eds., *Studien zum Prämonstratenserorden,*

the *Apologetic Letter,* treats the excellence of clerical as opposed to monastic callings, the fruitfulness of the contemporary reform, in particular the highly generative union of contemplation and active engagement in the secular church in terms of special resonance for the twelfth-century white canons.

This forceful apologetic work was then the by-product of Anselm's extraordinarily active years in service to the emperor Lothar, while *Anticimenon,* like many important works by busy public figures across time, owes its existence to a period of forced retirement. In his isolation in the late 1140s Anselm found greater focus on a still larger-scale literary effort than his polemic on behalf of the reformed Augustinians. He was still an apologist, although now more broadly the advocate of renewal and union in the church. Probably working in the library of the Premonstratensian canons established by his master Norbert in the cathedral church of Magdeburg, the bishop of frontier Havelberg sought to explain the tumultuous religious world he knew in the work translated in this volume.[42] Attention to *Anticimenon's* large and complex structure is a useful starting point for its content's analysis.

The first of this work's three books, despite its inclusion under a Greek title implying dialogical content, is not a dialogue, nor does it have much to do with the Greeks. Its historical material surveys Christian history to the time of the work's composition by building from biblical texts, later historical works, and a lively awareness of the discussion of the theology of history current in northern Europe in the author's period. The last two books are indeed dialogues between a speaker whom the author names as himself and a Byzantine called Nicetas, a real historical figure, the archbishop of Nicomedia when Anselm made his first diplomatic mission to Constantinople in the 1130s; these dialogues do not purport to be a transcription, but rather represent an imaginative reconstruction of actual dialogues held in Constantinople more

---

Veröffentlichen des Max-Planck-Instituts für Geschichte 185, Studien zur Germania Sacra 25 (Göttingen: Vandenhoeck & Ruprecht, 2003), 185–99. On Anselm's own usage see Gert Melville, "Zur Semantik von *ordo* im Religiosentum der ersten Hälfte des 12. Jahrhunderts: Lucius II., seine Bulle von Mai 1144, und der 'Orden' der Prämonstratenser," in *Studien zum Prämonstratenserorden,* 210–11.

[42] Sigler, *Beiträge,* 154.

than ten years before the author recounted them in writing. Overwhelmingly, scholars who have treated Anselm's work have emphasized that, while he may have had some record of his conversations of 1136—and while he certainly did conduct actual debates with the Greek Nicetas, as his *Anticimenon* asserts—his representation of their two dialogues in Books 2 and 3 reveals much literary craft. The dialogues' speaker Anselm, whom the author presents as his own voice, adduces patristic and more recent sources that cannot have been available to him on a diplomatic mission. Meanwhile the author attributes to his Greek opponent knowledge of sources accessible only in the West, even placing on Nicetas' lips a passage from the author Anselm's own *Apologetic Letter*, written a decade later than the dramatic date of *Anticimenon*'s dialogues.[43] Further, the Greek interlocutor and Greek audience seem occasionally to accept arguments against their own belief and practice to which, modern scholars agree, twelfth-century Greeks would have been loath to yield.[44]

Clearly, then, the exact course and content of the dialogues Anselm recounts are fictive, but that is not to say they might not suggest the general shape of their historical referent, the actual discussion between Anselm and Nicetas of Nicomedia in 1136. Since antiquity the dialogue form had been viewed as a literary device enabling the presentation of multiple perspectives without any intent to represent literal historicity. Indeed, from the perspective of a reading of *Anticimenon* aimed at appreciation of Anselm's own views, acknowledgment of his agency in shaping the dialogue adds to the interest of his text rather than diminishing it. Whether or not the historical Nicetas of Nicomedia was as enthusiastic about the prospects of an ecumenical council for resolving the *filioque* controversy, the issue of leavening in the bread of the Eucharist, or disagreement over the primacy of Rome, as the author Anselm here purports, the bishop of Havelberg clearly desired those resolutions.

---

[43] *Anticimenon* 2.14; compare *Apologetic Letter*, trans. Antry and Neel, 38.

[44] Lees summarizes the scholarship: *Deeds into Words*, 233 and n. 217, 253. Regarding important arguments see esp. Russell, "Anselm of Havelberg," 20, 39–40; Sieben, *Konzilsidee*, 157–67; Morrison, "Play," 237–41; Lees, *Deeds into Words*, 229–30, 244–45, 253.

Meanwhile, the text he left is the most important extant evidence for the circumstances under which he assembled these ideas, the audience he intended, and the specific reasons for which he undertook to address variety in European religion and conflict with the Greeks. Attention to the manner of *Anticimenon*'s composition therefore sheds light on Anselm's theology of history, ecclesiology, and ecumenical thought.

The whole of *Anticimenon*'s three books is dedicated to the Cistercian pope Eugenius III, disciple of Bernard of Clairvaux and proponent of religious reform in the pan-European context. In his general prologue Anselm claims that Eugenius, in whose company he had spent a long sojourn in the later 1140s, has asked him for help in understanding the pretensions and arguments of Byzantine ambassadors to the papal court.[45] But Book 1 itself, and indeed Book 2, present further comments on their respective audiences and occasions; effectively, the three books, taken together, have multiple beginnings: (1) a general prologue to all three books (here *Anticimenon* 1. Prologue); (2) a proem specific to Book 1's material on the theology of history (*Anticimenon* 1.1); (3) a covering prologue to Book 2, providing a transition to its ecumenical material (*Anticimenon* 2. Prologue); (4) a further historical proem to Book 2, with an explanation of the occasion and physical context of the dialogue with Nicetas (*Anticimenon* 2.1). Book 3 continues with no explanatory proem, only a clarification of the change of venue from the location of Book 2's discussion (*Anticimenon* 3.1). These repeated beginnings, each casting different light on the various books' contexts, suggest the author's multiple intentions in writing each of these books and unifying them under a title more appropriate, on first consideration, to its last two.

Although the general prologue emphasizes the pope's charge to Anselm to compose such a work, Book 1's proem states that Anselm has been compelled to expound his theory of history by the entreaties of those "brothers" who want to know their own place in the proliferation of contemporary religious movements— where they find themselves in the extension of human time be-

---

[45] *Anticimenon* 1. Prologue. On Eugenius's relationship to Anselm see Lees, *Deeds into Words*, 744–78; Sigler, *Beiträge*, 136–42.

tween Genesis and Apocalypse. Book 2's prologue then says that,
although his prior book has satisfied questioners and critics among
his brethren about variety and novelty in Latin Christendom, these
same confrères still wonder why and how the Greeks' beliefs differ.
Anselm thus directs his work to the pope and purports to write at
the papal behest, but acknowledges that Book 1 was a freestanding
earlier composition. As he suggests, he now recycles the justifica-
tion for novelty and diversity he has already drafted for the self-
understanding of his own order as Book 1's introduction to the
later dialogues on Greek otherness. But Anselm here in *Anticimenon*
1.1 confirms that all three books find an audience and rhetorical
purpose aside from the pope's Byzantine diplomacy. They are
written for the author's immediate canonical community and for
those wider communities of discourse about European religious
life in which they engaged. In all its parts, then, his *Anticimenon*
speaks to the twelfth-century religious reform—to its papal leader
but, more basically, to those who embrace its various charisms
and wish to comprehend their mutual relations, their historical
significance, and their providential meaning. While Books 2 and 3
concern controversy with the Greeks, they envision no Greek literary audience, but rather provide a Western readership with insight
about the Greeks' difference and—still more broadly—the role of
transhistorical difference in the one church.[46] The three books of
Anselm's *Anticimenon* are therefore integral both as a literary work
and in their representation of the scope of their author's thought.
Book 1 on the development of the western church is essential to
interpretation of Books 2 and 3 on East-West dialogue.

Interpreting Anselm's Vision of History

Despite *Anticimenon*'s evident rhetorical unity, however, modern
critics have overwhelmingly isolated the first book in their attention to Anselm of Havelberg's principal work.[47] Book 1 has been
treated more extensively than any other early Premonstratensian

[46] Lees assesses Anselm's audience in *Deeds into Words*, 167–72.
[47] Lees' careful argument that Book 1 is thematically bound to the later books by
its general goal of teaching by example is the culmination of this line of discussion:

text across several scholarly generations and in several languages, and its isolation from the later books has fundamentally misshaped interpretation of Anselm and his work. As that criticism has nonetheless demonstrated, Anselm is greatly indebted to patristic tradition for his fundamentally Augustinian notion of secular time as a mirror of providence. And he shares with other twelfth-century thinkers—notably his possible own early teacher Rupert of Deutz, the Cistercian Otto of Freising, the Calabrian visionary Joachim of Fiore, and the great Victorine Hugh—a vivid interest in emplotting the history of the church according to exegetically grounded stages of temporal development. Yet Anselm's thought is distinctive among the historiographical ideas of these other twelfth-century theorists, especially with regard to the meaning of doctrinal development. Hugh looked toward humankind's perfection through sacramental activity and advancements in secular knowledge. Joachim prophesied an apocalypse imminent in his own age, which he claimed for the Holy Spirit. But Anselm, more than any other medieval theologian of history, emphasized doctrinal and institutional development as the hallmark of Christianity's unfolding toward the apocalypse. In a period that most who cared about these matters saw as decline—in the words of Anselm's great contemporary Otto of Freising, a "world grown old"—Anselm of Havelberg saw the return of youth and vitality, the advancement of Christian doctrine and human possibility.[48]

Historians of medieval thought have thus assigned Anselm an important place in the development of the Christian theology of history. Johannes Spörl's *Grundformen mittelalterlichen Geschichtsschreibung* (1935), the foundational modern scholarly treatment

---

Deeds into Words, 164–77. Morrison, on the other hand, argues strongly for the essential unity of the three books: "Play," 236–45.

[48] For a summary of Anselm's relationship to the thought of twelfth-century theologians of history see Lees, *Deeds into Words*, 177–224; compare Edyvean, *Anselm*, 14–41. For emphasis on Anselm's appreciation of novelty see pp. 62–70 in this work, and Walter Berschin, "Anselm von Havelberg und die Anfänge einer Geschichtstheologie des hohen Mittelalters," *Literaturwissenschaftliches Jahrbuch*, n.s. 29 (1988): 229–32. On Otto's sense of a world in senescence see Otto of Freising, *The Two Cities: A Chronicle of Universal History to the Year 1146 A.D.*, 5, prologue, trans. Charles Christopher Mierow (New York: Columbia University Press, 1926), 322.

of the medieval understanding of the shape of time, privileged Anselm as a pioneer in his affirmation of the novelty of his own historical moment.[49] Subsequently many of the most acute students of medieval intellectual life have found him a startlingly original historical critic and theologian of time. Among scholarship in English, Bernard McGinn's *Visions of the End* (1977) describes Anselm as the most patently affirmative of novelty among medieval theorists of history.[50] Karl Morrison has more recently suggested that Anselm's writing bespeaks a historical theory and hermeneutics of interest from a postmodern critical perspective in its suggestion of the playfulness of providence in framing human experience.[51]

This rich critical tradition emphasizes that, like other medieval historical and theological authors, Anselm moved easily among a variety of patristic paradigms for the growth of the church in time: six days of creation as analogous to historical periods articulated in great biblical events, three ages analogous to the persons of the Trinity, four horsemen of the Apocalypse, seven apocalyptic seals. All these frameworks for historical interpretation are variously useful to Anselm's exposition of the variety of Christianity past and present in *Anticimenon*'s Book 1; none is original with him.[52] The distinctiveness of this author's thought lies rather in his unembarrassed acceptance of the diversity of Christian practice across time and his conviction that the Holy Spirit renews belief as historical ages follow upon each other. Both Book 1 and the later properly dialogical books consistently identify the Holy Spirit as the motive force behind secular developments and seek to discern the mechanisms of the Spirit's agency as means to time's interpretation. To study history, then, is to begin to understand the Spirit's will. Anselm writes:

> The one body of the church is . . . brought to life by the
> Holy Spirit, who is both singular in himself and manifold in

[49] Spörl, *Grundformen*, esp. 24–30.
[50] McGinn, *Visions*, 109–10.
[51] Morrison, "Play," esp. 220–23, 231–34, 245–46.
[52] Lees' outline of Anselm's use of various schemata for time and comparison with other major thinkers' is compact and useful: *Deeds into Words*, 177–91.

the multiform distribution of his gifts. This true body of the church—so unified by the Holy Spirit, divided and articulated among different members in different times and ages—began with Abel, the first just man, and will be consummated with the last of the elect. It is always one in the singularity of its singular faith but expressed in multiple forms by the manifold variety of its ways of life.[53]

Anselm resumes his identification of the role of the Spirit in the church's diversity throughout time in reference to his own century:

That Holy Spirit who governs the whole body of the church from the beginning, now and always, has recognized how to renew the sluggish souls of men, of faithful people cloyed by a long-familiar religious life, by the beginning of a new form of religion. The Spirit sees that, when such folk see others ascend to a higher form of religious life, they are the more inspired by new models. . . . So by God's wondrous design, since from generation to generation religious life always arises, the youth of the church renews itself like the eagle's, so that it may fly higher in contemplation, with the strength to gaze directly, unblinded, at the rays of the true sun.[54]

The eagle's youth, an image drawn from Psalm 102:5, had been the topic of much patristic and later exegesis, but Anselm alone among medieval theorists of time used it as a central figure for the development of belief and institutions.[55] In his reading of this image the

---

[53] *Anticimenon* 1.3.

[54] *Anticimenon* 1.10.

[55] Augustine's commentary—in which he iterated ancient natural philosophy describing the aging eagle as weighed down by the weight of its beak, then breaking off that burden on a high cliff—was normative: *Expositions on the Book of Psalms* 102.8, trans. A. Cleveland Coxe, Nicene and Post-Nicene Fathers (Grand Rapids: Eerdmans, 1956), 505–06. Anselm of Canterbury had used this image to suggest, characteristically, that understanding followed faith: *Incarnation* 1, trans. Hopkins and Richardson, 12. For Anselm of Havelberg's distinctive usage and its resonances among writings of other Premonstratensians see Carol Neel, "Philip of Harvengt and Anselm of Havelberg: The Premonstratensian Vision of Time," *Church History* 62 (1993): 488–90.

variety and innovation troubling to many in the twelfth-century church becomes instead the evidence of a vitality galvanized by the presence of the Holy Spirit. The church of Anselm's day soars like the eagle of mystical experience toward the sun of eternal truth. Anselm's image—and Anselm's view of the diverse and changing church—is eager, triumphant, and fearless.

In the context of the Middle Ages' well-known love of unity and uniformity and its consistently negative valorization of novelty, such a renewed church is indeed striking. It draws his reader's eye to an interpretive height from which all history may be viewed, as it were, from God's perspective. But this image is in no way discordant with the entire content of Book 1, which maps the stages, *status*, of the church from the creation to Anselm's own time. More emphatically than any other theologian of history of the twelfth century—in which theory of history was more at the center of western intellectual life than at any moment between Augustine and Foucault—Anselm lauds his own time. He praises Norbert of Xanten and Bernard of Clairvaux along with other contemporary spiritual leaders, but in contrast to twelfth-century preachers' and founders' generally meticulous self-description as revivalists of *vita apostolica*, he focuses on the Cistercians' and Premonstratensians' innovation.[56] *Quare tot novitates? Quare tot varietates?* Why so many new things, such variety?[57] Book 1's resounding answer is that novelty and variety are gifts of the Spirit. Anselm reemphasizes this theme with respect to differences between Latin and Greek communions in his Books 2 and 3.

While relatively few modern scholars have treated *Anticimenon* in its entirety, some have noted that the consistent theme of diversity constitutes its essential unity. Others have, with Lees, nonetheless stressed the different form and prior composition of Book 1 to the point that it seems a separate work.[58] Consideration of the centrality of the Holy Spirit to the three books assembled as *Anticimenon*

[56] On Norbert and Bernard see *Anticimenon* 1.10.

[57] *Anticimenon* 1.1.

[58] Lees argues that Book 1 effectively has a separate title, and that it is united with the other books only by a general rhetorical intent: *Deeds into Words*, 171–72. Again, the Salet translation, in its separate presentation of Book 1, effectively supports this view.

nonetheless sheds light on their common origin in Anselm's identity as a white canon. In Book 1 Anselm calls his reader to abandon a vision of religious life grounded in narrow historical precedent, to reread biblical and patristic texts courageously in the light of the Holy Spirit's fresh inspiration. The author scoffs at Benedictines who decry new movements such as the reform of the regular clergy promoted by his own master Norbert of Xanten. In a long and careful exposition of the seven seals of the apocalypse in terms of the unfolding of Christian history, Anselm responds vigorously to those who rail against the white canons and the white monks; their defense of conservative monastic models is the greatest danger to the vitality of faith. Conversely, then, those human souls willing to heed the Holy Spirit's call to spiritual progress are his most effective agents. Just as that Spirit is the protagonist of history, novelty and difference are evidence of his presence.[59]

The Holy Spirit reappears as the driving force of secular time and of human action in Anselm's second and third books of dialogue with the Byzantine theologian Nicetas. In Book 2 the third person of Trinity is directly, doctrinally at issue, because the Spirit's procession from the Son as well as the Father has been since the ninth century the central theological obstacle to East-West unity.[60] Thus Anselm's exegetical pilgrimage through scriptural and conciliar texts of significance for his debate with Nicetas builds on his first book's preoccupation with the historical role of the Holy Spirit. At the same time this treatment of the *filioque* controversy looks forward to Book 3's discussion of ritual practice, in which the Greeks' usage of leavened bread and consecration of pure wine again separates them from the Roman communion. But in Book 3 the Holy Spirit remains central to the discussion. Affirmed as historical agent in Book 1 and glorified in relation to both Father and Son in his procession in Book 2, that Spirit now summons all Christians to the same table. Again and again the speaker Anselm and his interlocutor Nicetas remind their throng of listeners and, by implication, their dialogue's readership, including ourselves, that to attend to the Holy Spirit is to listen to each other in *caritas,*

[59] *Anticimenon* 1.10.
[60] See again Chadwick's introduction to this problem: *East and West*, 89–94.

in charity or brotherly love.[61] Any doctrinal or ritual resolution in which Christian persons do not find concord is—for Anselm as author—objectionable, and we have failed each other and the Spirit alike if we do not, as members of Christ, heed this call to charity. As the speaker Nicetas reminds his Latin opponent in Anselm's text:

> The sacred host, whether of leavened or unleavened bread, is made of many grains gathered into one, so signifying the people of the whole church gathered into one and the same charity. . . . The rash perversity of the unfounded judgments with which we tear at each other seems to me a greater sin than the differences in sacramental practices occasioning that disagreement, for these rites make no matter to the Lord . . . [but our] discord offends God.[62]

Anselm's sympathy with Nicetas's perspective, according to *Anticimenon*'s representation of their debates, at last persuades the Greek archbishop that East and West must receive the Eucharist in like fashion—or openly tolerate each others' differing practices—because the Spirit's call to union is paramount.[63] So he and Nicetas join with the voices of all their listeners in calling for a council of all Greek and Latin Christians to reunify Mediterranean and European churches as Christ's singular body. This will be the Spirit's will and work.[64]

Anselm as a Premonstratensian Author

Nevertheless, twentieth-century and still more recent scholars have often considered the *Anticimenon* of Anselm of Havelberg a statement of Petrine supremacy more than an appeal for Christian

---

[61] See, for instance, *Anticimenon* 2.1. Morrison in fact finds charity the unifying theme of *Anticimenon*'s three books: "Play," 245.

[62] *Anticimenon* 3.19.

[63] *Anticimenon* 3.19–20.

[64] *Anticimenon* 3.22.

concord.[65] Indeed, Anselm is patently an advocate for papal
authority, but isolation of Books 2 and 3 from the prior, non-
dialogical book overemphasizes his investment in Petrine authority, downplaying the harmony between the openly developmental
emphasis of Book 1's discussion of the Western orders and the
later books' conversation with the Byzantines. Anselm transpar-
ently believes—as his namesake speaker argues cogently and as
the Greek Nicetas in the end concurs—that Peter's authority must
prevail, but at the same time his literary dialogue calls upon the
papacy to engage constructively and compassionately with the
Eastern church. Nicetas says to the speaker Anselm of his own
imagined contribution to an ecumenical council:

> With due humility and reverence I would call upon the Roman
> pontiff, pointing out how—with his help—we who have always
> been one in our catholic faith might again have unity in the ob-
> servance of the sacraments, so removing all occasion for enmity
> and discord. I hope that he might patiently hear me as I offered
> this humble counsel just as Peter, although he was foremost
> of the apostles, humbly listened long ago to Paul's frequent
> chastisement. In that reproach we commend Paul's firmness
> as confident, just rebuke and we praise Peter's patience in his
> gentle bearing. In this instance I would be far inferior to Paul,
> but the pontiff ought not to be inferior to Peter. Then the Roman
> pontiff might be a Latin to the Latins and to the Greeks a Greek,
> so *all things to all men* (1 Cor 9:22). He might gain all, settling
> all matters on which we disagree by the humble authority of his
> apostolic see, either taking away the one practice and instituting
> the other universally or, removing all scandal, authorizing both
> indifferently."[66]

Anselm of Havelberg here places a moving laudation of Petrine
authority in a Greek voice, in the context of the pope's unique potential to be *all things to all people*, so appealing for an ecclesiastical
unity appropriately affirmative of the oneness of Christian faith.

<hr>

[65] Sigler especially emphasizes Anselm's advocacy of papal primacy: *Beiträge*, 189; compare Lees, *Deeds into Words*, 259–61, 265.
[66] *Anticimenon* 3.19.

Notably, *Anticimenon*'s interlocutors mention imperial leadership only in passing in their appeal for a general council of Eastern and Western Christians. Here, for the author Anselm who so gives Nicetas voice, the primary explicit audience of the *Anticimenon* text is pope, not emperor. Therefore, one useful reading of Anselm's governing intention in assembling these three books on the theology of history and on ecumenical dialogue might indeed be encouragement of the papacy to adopt a less conflictual attitude with the Byzantines than the prior century's popes and their legates—a position of authority enabled by conviction of the solidity of the papal claim of primacy. Here Anselm's training as a court bishop underlay his position. As Lees has argued, so confident a paradigm of the essential unity and, by extension, hegemony of Latin Christendom was integral to the ideology of ecclesiastical leaders such as Norbert and this foremost of his disciples.[67] Recent scholarship, in acknowledging the importance of Norbert's personal model in shaping Anselm's career, nonetheless characterizes that influence principally according to the two canons' ecclesiastical, administrative roles. Lees thus minimizes the role of Norbert's spirituality for Anselm's career in his work, noting that the bishop of Havelberg "never identifies himself as a Premonstratensian."[68] Sigler acknowledges that the bishop of Havelberg indefatigably supported the work of Norbert's reformed canons on the Slavic frontier, but with Lees presents Anselm essentially outside the context of the religious vocation, to which he reveals passionate loyalty in his description of the eagle's youth.[69] Both omit what this twelfth-century figure himself attests in all his writing as most important to his own understanding of both history and his own time—the changing spirituality of the twelfth-century reform as the imprint of God's hand.

That Lees' and Sigler's, the first extensive scholarly treatments of this major author, should describe him as an essentially secular figure, however, comes as no surprise among the analogous general

---

[67] Again, see Lees, *Deeds into Words*, esp. 18–19.

[68] Lees, *Deeds into Words*, 30.

[69] Notably, Sigler's title makes no reference to Anselm as a white canon among his multiple roles as "politician, theologian, and royal emissary."

neglect of his Premonstratensian confrères. Anselm of Havelberg has been seen as an isolate because even a rich and well-developed scholarship on twelfth-century spirituality has until lately accorded the followers of Norbert disproportionately little attention. Even Rachel Fulton's brilliant and compelling study of the growth of feeling in medieval piety, *From Judgment to Passion*, which centers on the highly affective Marian devotion of Anselm's confrère and contemporary Philip of Harvengt, treats this other prominent disciple of Norbert outside the context of his role in articulating a Premonstratensian charism.[70] Nonetheless, consideration of these white canons from the perspective of the way in which their master Norbert shaped their sensibility—and the way in which life according to the Rule of St. Augustine influenced their sense of the church in time—opens a potentially useful perspective on Anselm's challenging and innovative *Anticimenon*, as to other works of the twelfth-century white canons. The distinctive theology and earnest ecumenism of Anselm in particular call for explanation in their relationship to the distinctive charism of Norbert and his early followers. Anselm's particular allegiance to Norbert, his centering of his master's language in his own literary works, and his direct praise of Norbert in his extant writings suggest that further aspects of his *Anticimenon* are reflective of Norbert's spiritual legacy.

Anselm of Havelberg's use of the image of the eagle's flight as a figure for the trajectory of human time was directly borrowed from the preaching of Norbert of Xanten. The founder Norbert called his followers his little eagles, urging them to fly with him toward divine truth.[71] Norbert was not a writer, so far as we know, but he was an exegete, and his preaching—as documented in the works of his first-generation followers—was strewn with imagery binding them and him with Augustine as the first founder of the regular canons and the apostle John as their scriptural archetype. The evangelist and author of Revelation was, for Norbert and his

---

[70] See Fulton, *From Judgment to Passion: Devotion to Christ and the Virgin Mary, 800–1200* (New York: Columbia University Press, 2002), 295–96, 351–404.

[71] *Vita Norberti archiepiscopi Magdeburgensis*, Acta Sanctorum, ed. Society of Bollandists, Junii 1 (Paris, 1867), 823. See Neel, "Philip of Harvengt and Anselm of Havelberg," 493 and n. 39.

disciples, both preacher and mystic, apostle and contemplative. Their life followed his, rising and swooping between mystical contemplation and earthly engagement with the eagle who figured the evangelist's experience, as Anselm wrote in his *Apologetic Letter*:

> John the apostle and evangelist, flying like an eagle in the heights and gazing directly upon the rays of the true sun, drank deeply from the fountain of the Lord's breast. Full of the spirit of wisdom and intellect, endowed with the special privilege of divine love, he penetrated the secrets of divinity and the hidden places of the heavens. Crossing into the active life he then taught in Ephesus and several other places, founded churches, ordained bishops and established priests. See how the living creatures of God burn and gleam like lightning![72]

The spirituality of the medieval Premonstratensians was then lived at no fixed location on a continuum between action and contemplation, but rather in their dynamic interaction. His identity as a white canon then became for Anselm a critical tool in his analysis of change and difference among communities and between communions in the three books of his *Anticimenon*.

Throughout these wide-flung discussions of doctrinal and ritual matters in Book 2 and 3 of his *Anticimenon*, Anselm of Havelberg shows himself a polished exegete with a special commitment to the historical level of interpretation—the material, political, even anthropological contexts of the biblical texts and figures he adduces—as well as a compelling apologist for Roman beliefs and, most especially, for the primacy of the Roman see. Throughout, he adduces Petrine authority as an ancillary argument, sometimes even a primary argument, for the superiority of Roman teaching and Roman worship.[73] But neither Anselm's intellectual and rhetorical prowess nor his loyalty to the Roman see is the salient feature of his work. Rather, his depiction of Nicetas as his own intellectual equal, his sympathetic portrayal of the theological tenets and ritual

---

[72] *Apologetic Letter*, trans. Antry and Neel, 55.

[73] Anselm first argues Peter's special status in *Anticimenon* 1.5, thereafter regularly recurring to its doctrinal consequences until the speaker Nicetas finally protests his Latin counterpart's monotony: *Anticimenon* 3.16.

traditions of the Greeks, and the overwhelmingly warm and affirmative tone of his work's second and third books strike many readers—particularly medievalists familiar with the multi-level twelfth-century conflict with the Byzantines—as extraordinary.[74] The conclusion of the debates recounted in the *Anticimenon*'s two later books emphasizes the author's generosity to his Greek opponent and the Greek-speaking audience gathered around them first in the Byzantine church of Holy Peace and, on the next day, in the great church of Holy Wisdom. At the end of Book 2 and again in Book 3 the interlocutor Anselm seems to have won over his opponent Nicetas with careful exegetical arguments on the procession of the Holy Spirit and sacramental practice. The two speakers nonetheless agree that the issues they have addressed should rather be decided by an ecumenical council in which the Roman pope should assume leadership but in which all the churches of Mediterranean and European Christianity should find full hearing such that all believers might be brought by reason and prayer—not by compulsion—to unity of belief and ritual.[75] Anselm is then the first author to have proposed an ecumenical council specifically for the reunification of the Roman and Greek communions.[76]

Anselm as Ecumenist

Anselm's apparent posture as bishop of Havelberg and papal legate in the crusade against the Wends, only a few years before his composition of *Anticimenon*, sheds suggestive light on his ecumenism toward the urbane Greeks, and further on his sense of

---

[74] Among scholarly notices of Anselm's generosity in representing the Greek perspective see esp. Morrison, "Play," 236–40; Lees, *Deeds into Words*, 45–46, 237–39.

[75] *Anticimenon* 3.22.

[76] Sieben, *Konzilsidee*, 153–57; Sigler, *Beiträge*, 42, 112. Notably, the standard English work on medieval conciliarism makes no mention of Anselm: Brian Tierney, *Foundations of the Conciliar Theory: The Contribution of the Medieval Canonists from Gratian to the Great Schism*, rev. ed., Studies in the History of Christian Thought 81 (Leiden: Brill, 1988). Tierney's focus is canon law texts, but that his discussion elides Anselm's early advocacy of an ecumenical council nonetheless emphasizes the anomaly of *Anticimenon*'s appeal for ecumenical engagement in the twelfth-century context.

his and his order's agency on the Holy Spirit's behalf. Bernard, the great Cistercian, had argued that the Eastern pagans must be converted or die. But Anselm of Havelberg, despite his admiration for the white monk, adopted a different tack. After a troubling incident in which the Slavs of Stettin claimed prior Christianity as defense against depopulation in the name of the cross, Anselm urged the secular princes gathered for the reduction of the Baltic coast and Wendish interior to cease their depredations—to leave the pagan Slavs to be converted by their now-Christian princes and by his Premonstratensian confrères through peaceful means.[77] Here Anselm recalled his mentor Norbert's consistent pattern of healing heresy, calming conflict, and advocating concord among secular and ecclesiastical lords.[78] Still more, Anselm here advanced a perspective outside of history, above the view of the faith from the ground east of the Elbe. By itself, Anselm's role in the Wendish Crusade is singular, most notable for its difference from Bernard's. Alongside his discourse with Nicetas of Nicomedia it seems to express his sense of his own membership in a church renewed with an eagle's youth.

Anselm of Havelberg's ecumenical dialogue, in turn, conforms to his ecclesiastical career and theory of history as an injunction to Roman Christians to "listen in charity" to the beliefs and practices of the Orthodox. The Holy Spirit might speak most clearly to those who took such care to hear others' truths, and this might be best accomplished in the context of an ecumenical council joining Eastern and Western churches. Most strikingly, the author of the *Anticimenon* presents both voices in his dialogue as acknowledging the power of custom and the affect associated with credal language and sacramental materiality as compelling, worthy of respect and response whatever the truth of doctrine. *Filioque* is repugnant to the Greeks; leavened host is dear. Roman orthodoxy and Roman primacy must acknowledge these realities of religious practice in order for the Holy Spirit to bring the body of Christ to appropriate

[77] Lees, *Deeds into Words*, 74–82; Sigler, *Beiträge*, 98–106.
[78] Lees stresses Anselm's reception of Norbert's example in peacemaking: *Deeds into Words*, 33.

wholeness.[79] Norbert's Premonstratensian followers, Anselm's work suggests, were impelled by imitation of their founder not only to be good servants of the church but to make peace, to do good, to act in the temporal world from the insights of their contemplative experience, most distinctively to see value in variety and novelty such as their new canonical foundations embodied. The historical experience of Anselm of Havelberg in a new religious order convinced that it authentically performed the will of the Holy Spirit led him to revalorize alterity—both difference from the Benedictines and difference across the Adriatic. Such embrace of the diversity of Christian experience was then no outlier to the twelfth-century reform, but instead mapped a region of its extent.

Anticimenon's Text and This Translation

This translation of Anselm's work is based on the Patrologia Latina text, itself reproduced from a seventeenth-century edition by Luc d'Achéry. Ideally, translation into English would have been based on a modern critical edition noting manuscript variants and choosing readings according to their appearance in better manuscript exemplars, but this particular work poses extraordinary editorial difficulties. In 1974, Johann Braun of the Monumenta Germaniae Historica published a definitive study of the thirteen known manuscripts of *Anticimenon*. His intention was to follow this outline of the manuscript tradition with a critical edition, but the project remains incomplete.[80] Braun's work, though, clarifies the path an eventual editorial effort should take. His essay on the *Anticimenon*'s manuscripts is a methodological *tour de force*, exemplary of the utility of statistical study of manuscript variants rather than traditional principles of textual criticism for determining which of available manuscripts are proximate to lost originals and for choosing among variant readings. As Braun establishes, all extant copies of *Anticimenon* are at least two generations removed from the archetype. The Berlin manuscript of *Anticimenon* (Berlin ms. theol.

---

[79] Anselm's speaker Nicetas expresses this emphasis on the emotional significance of familiar practice in *Anticimenon* 2.27 and 3.19.

[80] See Braun, "Studien," 133–34.

fol. 80) is the single best surviving copy; it contains a preponderance of better readings and itself represents collation with another family of copies, from which missing elements of its archetype have been replaced.[81] For this translation, problematic readings in Migne—as well as issues in the presentation and organization of the text's books, its various prologues and proems—have been resolved by collation with this primary Berlin manuscript. Even those readers of Anselm's text in translation with little interest in problems of textual scholarship or precision in editorial treatment of medieval Latin works should nonetheless be aware that the text of this important work calls for further careful study.

Meanwhile Braun's study is indispensable to all discussion of the text. It demonstrates that all extant copies are from the fifteenth century or later, yet the monastery of Cîteaux possessed two copies in the late Middle Ages. The relative poverty of Anselm's manuscript tradition and the late dates of all its representatives suggest that the work of the bishop of Havelberg met with only limited currency in centuries immediately following its composition, but received modest revival during the conciliar movement of the later Middle Ages, when schism, heresy, and doctrinal controversy were repeatedly addressed in intra-European councils.[82] Such interest makes obvious sense in the context of Anselm's advocacy of ecumenical councils, although it is ironic: Anselm was untroubled by variety in religious practice within Europe and concerned to resolve schism with the East. He would have been saddened to know how, as modernity approached, further disunity threatened Latin Christendom and distanced any realistic possibility of reunion with the Orthodox East.

Anselm of Havelberg's prose is lively and readable, without the rhetorical embellishment characteristic of many contemporaries, notably his Premonstratensian contemporary Philip of Harvengt.[83] In Book 1 he demonstrates himself opinionated and forthright, harsh in his assault on the critics of the reform orders and of

---

[81] Braun, "Studien," 173–76, 202–8; Valentin Rose, *Verzeichnis der lateinischen Handschriften der königlichen Bibliothek zu Berlin*, vol. 2 (Berlin: A. Asher and Co, 1901; repr. Hildesheim: Georg Olms, 1976), no. 376, pp. 207–8.

[82] Braun, "Studien," 136–39.

[83] On Philip's highly ornamented style, see Fulton, *From Judgment to Passion*, 364.

novelty within the church more generally. In the later books likewise he writes compactly, athletically, with clear intent to suggest
verisimilitude in his account of the debate between the speaker
Anselm and his Greek interlocutor, Nicetas. This author's theology
of history and his ecumenical dialogue are both, therefore—among
texts of interest for the Middle Ages' intellectual history and its
spiritual life—uncommonly exciting and engaging. The present
translation attempts to reflect Anselm's straightforward Latin style
and evocation of his readers' interest and investment. Occasional
notes explain technical or especially important usages, but for
the most part terms in translation have been chosen to reflect
contemporary American usage. Anselm's articulation of complex
theological arguments is sufficiently transparent that few readers
should experience difficulty in understanding his meaning.

Notes below introduce especially useful critical and historical
perspectives, and uncover those sources Anselm names as well as
many he—like most medieval authors—fails directly to acknowledge. Source references here are by no means exhaustive, but this
translation goes well beyond the PL edition and prior scholarship
in identifying Anselm's use of patristic texts and his reference to
the late-eleventh- and early-twelfth-century discourse about issues
in which he was interested. Like all medieval religious, Anselm
wrote in constant reference to the Vulgate Bible. Direct biblical
quotations are rendered here in italics with parenthetical verse
references, while more general allusions are identified in notes.
Quotations from biblical texts are adjusted to the Douay translation as the standard English version based on the Latin text Anselm
knew. Quotations from all other sources are fresh, befitting their
context in Anselm's work. Throughout, however, notes refer readers
to sources' outstanding English translations or, if none are available, those sources' best available editions, since these texts will
generally be most useful to a readership encountering the work in
translation. Wherever possible, however, standard textual divisions
(for instance, book and chapter numbers or letter numbers) are
included so that those to whom the Patrologia Latina or other such
resources are useful may find the relevant passages with facility.

References to scholarly literature are similarly aimed at English-
speaking readers potentially interested in following Anselm's dis-

cussion into its patristic sources, twelfth-century analogues, and general historical background. They emphasize English-speaking scholars' work on Anselm's period and on his two great interests, the theology of history and the rift between the Roman and Greek churches. References here nonetheless include foreign-language works where resources in English are unavailable or where German scholarship, in particular, makes essential contributions to understanding the work of this German bishop, courtier, diplomat, and apologist for twelfth-century religious revival. The bibliography gathered at the end of this volume likewise emphasizes sources in English translation, but includes primary works in the original Latin and scholarship in the European languages where these might be especially important to readers pursuing Anselm's concerns into the wider fabric of the medieval reformation, the history of ecumenism, and historical Christians' sense of the shape of time. This bibliography has, finally, been constructed specifically to assist readers to enrich their appreciation of Anselm's role as a Premonstratensian and to follow his work into the scholarly literature about the medieval white canons—their writings, their spirituality, and their sense of their place in the unfolding of providence.

Anticimenon: On the Unity of the Faith
and the Controversies with the Greeks

Prologue

Here begins the prologue of Anselm, bishop of Havelberg, in his book of Anticimenon, controversies, written as a dialogue and addressed to the venerable Pope Eugenius III in the year 1145, at the time of Saint Bernard.[1]

Anselm, poor man of Christ and unworthy bishop of Havelberg, proffers his absolute obedience in the Lord to that lord Eugenius who, as blessed pope of the holy Roman Church, compels our reverent embrace.[2]

When I was in Your Beatitude's presence last March, near the city of Tusculum, Your Holiness was pleased to discuss many things with me.[3] Among them you told me that a certain bishop had lately come to the apostolic see as an ambassador from the emperor at Constantinople, and that he brought with him a letter written

---

[1] This historical note was clearly added by a later copyist to Anselm's text. For discussion of the work's title, see the introduction above and, among scholarly studies, Jay T. Lees, *Anselm of Havelberg: Deeds into Words in the Twelfth* Century, Studies in the History of Christian Thought 79 (Leiden: Brill, 1998), 8. Although the title the annotator assigns indeed seems to have been Anselm's own, because he repeatedly so names his work later in the prologue, the date is inexact. Modern scholarship places composition of *Anticimenon* several years afterward, in 1149–50: see Lees, *Deeds into Words*, 85, 91, 164–65; Sebastian Sigler, *Anselm von Havelberg: Beiträge zum Lebensbild eines Politikers, Theologen und königlichen Gesandten im 12. Jahrhundert* (Aachen: Shaker, 2005), 266.

[2] See Ernst Werner, *Pauperes Christi: Studien zu sozial-religiösen Bewegungen im Zeitalter des Reformpapsttums* (Leipzig: Koehler and Amelang, 1956), 19. The Premonstratensians were among several twelfth-century reform groups with special attachment to self-description as *pauperes Christi*. Anselm had opened his epistolary apology for the regular canons with the same formula: Anselm, *Apologetic Letter*, in *Norbert and Early Norbertine Spirituality*, ed. and trans. Theodore J. Antry and Carol Neel (New York: Paulist Press, 2007), 38.

[3] Anselm had spent much of 1149 in Eugenius's court. See again Lees, *Deeds into Words*, 164–65; Sigler, *Beiträge*, 130, 334.

in Greek characters.[4] You also said that this bishop was deeply learned in Greek writings, that he was eloquent and confident in his speech, further that he spoke at length about the doctrine and ecclesiastical ritual of the Greeks. What he set forth accorded poorly with the teaching of the Roman Church, differing markedly from her ritual practice. The Greek bishop did violence to the authority of Scripture, twisting its meaning to fit his interpretation of sacred texts so that they seemed to support everything in which the Greeks differ from the Latins and prove incorrect those things in which the Latins differ from the Greeks. In sum the Greek bishop declared his own belief and practice entirely good because it was his own, not because it was rightly ordered. At the same time he altogether denounced our way because it was ours and not his own. As you told me, this legate disputed most vehemently about the procession of the Holy Spirit, whom the Greeks believe and declare proceeds only from the Father, while the Latins believe and declare that he proceeds truly from both the Father and the Son. The envoy also disputed contentiously about the ritual surrounding the sacrifice of the altar, which the Latins celebrate with unleavened but the Greeks with leavened bread, as well as certain other matters.

I had earlier been legate in Constantinople on behalf of the great Lothar, august emperor of the Romans. I had stayed there for a long time conducting many conversations and debates of this nature, sometimes private and sometimes public, about the doctrine and ritual respectively maintained by Latins and Greeks.[5] Therefore it pleased Your Holiness to direct me, after this recent encounter, to gather into one work what I had said in Constantinople and what I heard or understood others to say—that I write down a sort of *Anticimenon*, that is a book of controversies, in dialogue

---

[4] The specificity with which Anselm describes the circumstances of the pope's request, especially the letter carried by the Greek legate, confirms that the historical and biographical context he establishes for his work is more than a rhetorical device. The Greek embassy to which he refers probably took place only shortly before. See Lees, *Deeds into Words*, 85.

[5] Anselm refers to his own embassy to Constantinople some ten years before the composition of this work. See Lees, *Deeds into Words*, 42–44; Sigler, *Beiträge*, 35–39, 329.

form. You said that I should put forward for your consideration all that was said by or about those Greek people, or argued against them, so that you might consider these matters more freely in your judgment when they were better known to you. For some Latins are greatly deceived by the assertions of the Greeks when the former only listen to the topics the words of the latter address without understanding those words' exact meaning. So these Latins think they support what they do not or deny what they do not.

I have done as you commanded with that apostolic authority none should disobey. I have done so not only in devout humility but indeed for my eternal salvation. To the extent that my memory has served, I have maintained the tone of the dialogue I held with the learned and venerable archbishop of Nicomedia, Nicetas, in a public meeting in the city of Constantinople. I have made certain additions as essential to the faith and appropriate for this work.[6] This Archbishop Nicetas was the chief of twelve *didaskaloi*, those teachers who, according to the custom of the Greek sages, direct studies of both the liberal arts and the divine scriptures.[7] These twelve, preeminent in their learning, preside over the other Greek sages. The most difficult questions are directed to these sages and, when those questions are resolved, the answers of these men are immediately accepted and recorded without reconsideration, as established judgments.

I have set at the head of this dialogue, moreover, a book about the singularity of belief and the multiformity of life from the time

---

[6] The author acknowledges that this representation of his dialogue with Nicetas has been enriched by texts available to him during the present work's subsequent composition. Sigler argues that it was probably written in Magdeburg, where such a library was available: *Beiträge*, 154.

[7] Anselm refers to Nicetas with the Greek term here translated "sage." Throughout *Anticimenon* he includes Greek usages where he understands Latin to reflect their meaning inexactly, and also in deference to cultural difference. He thus reinforces his Latin readers' sense of how Greek intellectual and social life are constructed in a fashion they cannot assume mirrors the Western pattern.

On the role of the Greek sages, *didaskaloi*, with specific reference to Anselm's description here, see Michael Angold, *Church and Society in Byzantium under the Comneni, 1081–1261* (Cambridge: Cambridge University Press, 1995), 92–93. Anselm may have misunderstood the number and importance of this group of theologians.

of Abel the just until the last of the elect.[8] I had earlier been constrained to write this by the entreaties of certain brothers who declared that many ordinary folk, even wise men, are scandalized that—within one church holding one faith—so many new and varied forms of religious life arise in all times and places.[9]

Of course Your Beatitude's judgment, eminent above all others and rich in the priceless treasury of the Sacred Scriptures, is abundantly sufficient to respond to the Greeks, just as that Lamb slain from the beginning of the world opens the seal of divine Scripture.[10] Imitating the excellence of so great a teacher as you, other wise men among the Latins can indeed gather many arguments against the Greeks more decisive than mine. Nevertheless I hope that what I have written down as a dialogue in this *Anticimenon* may not be judged by those to be superfluous, since humble folk lacking the wit to reach quick conclusions might gladly read it to find out more precisely what the Greeks say. So these simple people may discover here how they too may respond. May whoever reads what I have written know that I did so not purporting to teach anyone or to vaunt what I have learned but to obey the holy mandate of your apostolic Beatitude. As I believe, not to obey would be a greater sin than obediently to write something of even little usefulness or merit. I have then done what I could, although it is less than I should have or wished to have done, and I have done what I should more laudably in my obedience than in my writing. To disobey a command is more serious a fault than obediently to write anything at all, so long as the correctness of the faith is intact. If a writer errs in ignorance, at least his humble fulfillment of obedience's command excuses his sin.[11]

---

[8] Gaston Salet (*Dialogues, Livre I: Renouveau dans l'église,* trans. Gaston Salet, Sources Chrétiennes 118 [Paris: Cerf, 1966], 40 n. 1) emphasizes the importance of the formulation of the history of the faith as proceeding from Abel until the last of the elect in patristic and liturgical traditions.

[9] Again Anselm notes that Book 1 is a preexisting text, now added as a preamble to his dialogues with the Greek Nicetas.

[10] See Rev 5:1-7.

[11] Anselm's depreciation of his abilities and his accomplishment in this work is conventional. In fact, he was the most experienced of all contemporary Latin ecclesiastics regarding the doctrine of the contemporary Greeks and in conversation with them—hence Eugenius's solicitation of his counsel.

Book 1

On the Unity of the Faith and the Many Forms of Life From Abel the Just to the Last of the Elect

Chapter 1
On how some are amazed at the varied forms of Christian religious life.[12]

Many people are amazed and skeptical at this, to the point of finding such variety scandalous and declaring it scandalous to others. They ask like cunning inquisitors, "Why does God's church present so many new things? Why do so many orders arise in her? Who could count the orders of clerics? Who is not astonished at the many kinds of monks? Who is not even scandalized by the number of them, disgusted by the great variety and disagreement among the many forms of religious life? Who can, still further, fail to scorn the Christian religious life when it is subjected to so much variety, changed by so many new practices, disrupted by so many new laws and customs, tossed about year after year by novel rules and customs?" As these people say, a practice at one moment advocated for the sake of the kingdom of heaven is thereafter forbidden by the same people who instituted it or by others, again for the sake of the kingdom of heaven, or a practice now banned as sacrilege is soon declared holy and salubrious.

Whenever critics of such novelty have the opportunity, they raise questions misdirecting the hearts of the simple. These skeptics assert that religious life in all its forms is the more to be scorned the more

---

[12] As Salet notes, for Anselm the term *religio*, in this passage translated "religious life," means variously regular life (that is, adherence to a religious rule such as the Rule of St. Benedict or the Rule of St. Augustine), the practice of Christian religion more generally, or—still more broadly—authentic, holy faith: *Dialogues*, 34 n. 1. Its translation below responds variously to its respective contexts.

47

it changes, for what could a wise man find to imitate in something so mutable and inconsistent? Surely religion reveals its loathsomeness in its variability. In our times, these same people say, we see in the church of God that folk appear who clothe themselves in strange habits on their own whim, choose for themselves a new form of life and—whether under the label of monastic profession or under the vow of canonical discipline—claim for themselves whatever they wish.[13] These innovators develop a new way of singing the psalms, establish a new kind of self-abnegation and fasting, and serve neither like monks in the soldiery of the rule of the blessed Benedict nor like canons who lead the apostolic life under the rule of the blessed Augustine, but do everything new, as their critics say, according to their fancy. They are their own law and their own authority. They gather together whomever they can into their communities under the pretext of new religious life. Apparently they believe that they appear more religious if they hold with none of the practice or discipline of those living under an established rule and if they seem a finger's breadth more distinctive than the others.

The skeptics say these things and the like. They disturb others with their many questions, slandering religious life not overtly but in secret, insidiously. They speak as if they loved and esteemed religion in saying "would that somewhere we might find something of certitude, a place where we could rest our heads confidently, in expectation of eternal salvation!" In fact, though, they are such irksome detractors that whenever they see anyone stray from the religious life to which he has committed himself, they are immediately inflamed against all such commitment. They ascribe the misdeed of one to all, scorning and rejecting everyone persevering in the fear of

---

[13] Anselm establishes monastic and canonical life as twin norms of religious commitment, so implying that such reform of regular clergy as his master Norbert promoted held importance commensurate with the long history and contemporaneous reform of monastic life. See the introduction above and, for an example of this sort of complaint targeting the followers of Norbert, Idung of Prüfening, *Cistercians and Cluniacs, The Case for Cîteaux: A Dialogue between the Monks, an Argument on Four Questions*, trans. Jeremiah F. O'Sullivan et al., Cistercian Fathers 33 (Kalamazoo, MI: Cistercian Publications, 1977), esp. 86. On the conservative Benedictine attitude toward the reform movements with specific reference to Norbert and Anselm see John Van Engen, *Rupert of Deutz* (Berkeley: University of California Press, 1983), 323–34.

God and in holy profession on account of one apostate, so ignoring the gospel text: *The kingdom of heaven is like to a net cast into the sea, and gathering together of all kind of fishes, which, when it was filled, they drew out, and sitting by the shore, they chose out the good into vessels, but the bad they cast forth* (Matt 13:47-48). And the parable of the cockle: *Suffer both to grow . . . lest perhaps gathering up the cockle, you root up the wheat also together with it* (Matt 13:29-30). In truth all those issues pointed out by men who dispute in this way about religious life, slandering it on account of its variety, might serve for their reform and improvement if they truly wished to be numbered among religious people.[14] As is written: *Much peace have they that love thy law, and to them there is no stumbling block* (Ps 118:165), and again, for the saints *all things work together unto good* (Rom 8:28).

Chapter 2
That the one body of the church is ruled and governed by one Holy Spirit, and manifests varied kinds of grace.

May the many such skeptics cease their amazement about variety within the church of God! May their irksome and importunate questions no longer find a place! Still more, may they—setting aside their duplicitous claim of scandal and recognizing the true way of the religious life—be misled about its variety no longer! And as for us who are truly religious, when we find others like us, may we recognize them inside, among us, rather than outside, against us! May we invite them to consider what we must hold and believe according to catholic faith and Sacred Scripture, how the church of God is one in herself and in her nature but multiform in respect to her children, whom she has shaped and will shape in diverse ways and by diverse laws and institutions from the time Abel's blood was shed until the last of the elect![15] For the voice of the Spouse

---

[14] See 2 Corinthians 10: 8.

[15] As the notoriety of Bernard's commentary on the Song of Songs has affirmed for modern readers, Solomon's poem was beloved of medieval spiritual authors, especially the major voices of the twelfth-century reform. The Premonstratensians shared the Cistercians' strong interest in this text. Anselm's contemporary, the Premonstratensian abbot Philip of Harvengt—also Norbert's immediate disciple— wrote one of the longest of extant Song commentaries and, as Rachel Fulton has

says: *One is my dove, my perfect one . . . the only one of her mother, the chosen of her that bore her* (Song 6:8). She is one—one in faith, one in charity, the only one without any stain of impious infidelity, without any blemish of perverse duplicity.[16] There is one generation of the just, of whom it is written: *The generation of the righteous shall be blessed* (Ps 111:2). So also there is one body of the church. It is brought to life, ruled, and governed by the Holy Spirit, the same Holy Spirit who is one in being, manifold, singular, mobile, eloquent, unpolluted, certain, sweet, loving of the good, sagacious, unhindered in his beneficence, humane, benign, stable, sure, having every virtue, foreseeing all, containing every spirit, intelligible, and beautiful in form.[17] In this Holy Spirit are, according to the Apostle, *diversities of graces, but the same Spirit* (1 Cor 12:4). And again: *And the manifestation of the Spirit is given to every man unto profit. To one indeed, by the Spirit, is given the word of wisdom; and to another, the word of knowledge, according to the same Spirit; to another, faith in the same Spirit; to another, the grace of healing in the one Spirit; to another the working of miracles; to another prophecy; to another the discerning of spirits; to another diverse kinds of tongues; to another, interpretation of speeches. But all these things one and the same Spirit worketh, dividing to every one according as he will* (1 Cor 12:7-11).

The one body of the church is thus clearly brought to life by the Holy Spirit, who is both singular in himself and manifold in the multiform distribution of his gifts. This true body of the church—so

---

argued, the most eroticizing: see Fulton's extensive discussion, *From Judgment to Passion: Devotion to Christ and the Virgin Mary, 800–1200* (New York: Columbia University Press, 2002), 295–350. Anselm's own representation of Premonstratensian spirituality tends less in Philip's affective direction, but it is nonetheless interesting that he here adduces the Spouse, generally identified with Christ, in a discussion centering on the Holy Spirit.

[16] See Ephesians 5:27.

[17] See Wisdom 1:22-23. Gregory of Nazianzus similarly lists the Spirit's attributes in his theological discourses: Gregory Nazianzen, *Faith Gives Fullness to Reasoning: The Five Theological Orations of Gregory Nazianzen* 31.29, trans. Lionel Wickham and Frederick Williams, Supplements to Vigiliae Christianae 13 (Leiden: Brill, 1991), 295–97. As Lees points out, the source of Anselm's Latin version of Gregory's work is mysterious, because it was virtually unknown in the West: *Deeds into Words*, 197 n. 109. See also Giles E. M. Gasper, *Anselm of Canterbury and His Theological Inheritance* (Aldershot: Ashgate, 2004), 25–26.

unified by the Holy Spirit, divided and articulated among different members in different times and ages—began with Abel, the first just man, and will be consummated with the last of the elect. It is always one in the singularity of its singular faith but expressed in multiple forms by the manifold variety of its ways of life.

Chapter 3
Concerning the differences among sacrificial rites by which the favor of the same and singular God was sought from Abel's time up to Christ's.[18]

So Abel, since he was a shepherd of sheep, faithfully made an offering to God from fat of the firstborn of his flock.[19] He was the first to do this in faith, without having received any special divine command or having been instructed by a written law, rather taught solely by the law of nature that a creature should honor its creator. God looked with approval upon this Abel and his gifts, although we read that as yet no sacrificial rite had been instituted for this or that manner of offering. The record shows clearly that God favored first Abel and then his gifts because, as we believe, God found Abel's justice—himself rather than his gifts—to be pleasing.[20]

Then Noah, in faith and in fearful obedience to the command he had received about what was to come, prepared an ark for the salvation of his household.[21] After he left the ark, he was the first to build an altar to the Lord. Choosing from among the flocks and the clean birds, he offered a holocaust upon this altar. Yet in the text the rite is not spelled out. We read that Noah made an offering of the clean birds and then of the firstborn of the flock, but not that the sacrificial rite is established.[22]

---

[18] In *Anticimenon* 1.3-4 Anselm suggests the periodization of history before Christ conventional among twelfth-century theologians of history, although respectively differently articulated. Here he is less concerned with the details of that periodization than with noting that the Old Testament documents doctrinal development.

[19] Genesis 4:2-4.

[20] Genesis 4:4.

[21] Compare Hebrews 11; Genesis 6 and 7.

[22] Genesis 8:20.

Abraham too faithfully made sacrifice to the Lord, counseled by a special divine vision but not yet instructed by written law. God spoke to him then, for the first time teaching the rite of sacrifices not by a written commandment but in his living voice. So Abraham realized that he alone in his time must do as God instructed, but not that he had to hand down this rite to posterity as a written precept: *Take me a cow of three years old, and a she goat of three years, and a ram of three years, a turtle also and a pigeon. And he took all these, and divided them in the midst, and laid the two pieces of each one against the other; but the birds he divided not. And the fowls came down upon the carcasses, and Abraham drove them away* (Gen 15:9-11). Abraham again faithfully offered up his only son Isaac at the Lord's command, as a test.[23] He trusted in God and was found just.[24] He was the first to receive the law of circumcision as a sign of his faith.[25]

Later Jacob, on his journey to Aran, when he awoke the next morning after the vision in which he saw the Lord leaning upon a ladder, faithfully set up as a memorial the rock on which his head had lain. He poured oil upon it, doing so without instruction by any law but in expression of faith alone.[26] Again in faith Jacob, as he was dying, blessed each of the sons of Joseph.[27]

Should we not consider that these and a great many others, confirmed in the testimony of faith, belonged to the unity of the church—they who worshiped the one God in one faith though in different patterns of life and by a diversity of sacrificial rites? From Adam until Noah lived many of the faithful whom we cannot name but who followed natural law and so worshiped God, knowing him to be the creator of all things, and who then did unto their neighbors those things they wished done to themselves.[28]

---

[23] Hebrews 11:17.
[24] Genesis 22.
[25] Genesis 17:10.
[26] Genesis 28:18.
[27] Genesis 48:15; compare Hebrews 11:21.
[28] Compare Luke 6:31. Here Anselm begins to introduce the detail of the periodization of biblical history according to six great ages: from Adam to Noah, from Noah to Abraham, from Abraham to Moses, from Moses to David, from David to Christ, after Christ. This schema was inherited by twelfth-century theologians from

And from Noah to Abraham we find many more of the faithful who followed natural law, serving God their creator rather than his creation, and refraining from any harm to their neighbors as much as they could, kindly offering instead whatever they wished for themselves.

Further, from Abraham to Moses we again find men who, similarly following the natural law and sometimes even receiving from the Lord the law of obedience, are accounted and indeed were part of the unity of the church. These men sometimes lay with maidservants whom their own wives offered to them in the hope of having children. They did so not because they were lustful but because they wished to leave a posterity in their children. They took those women as if they were their own wives out of obedience rather than in lust, for they firmly believed that in their descent, that is in Christ, all the peoples of the earth would be blessed.[29] During those times the rite of circumcision was made known, and the same men took up this sign of faith at the Lord's command.[30]

Afterward, from Moses' time to David's, when circumcision was already customary, the chosen people of God were set apart from the society of foreigners and gathered together into one church under the leadership of Moses, their faithful ruler.[31] The law he established was written by God's own hand, instituting a new rite and new sacrificial practice. So the law of the holocaust, the law

---

patristic sources, especially Augustine in the last chapter of *City of God* 22.30, and in *On the Trinity* 4.7. Among recent translations see Augustine, *City of God against the Pagans*, ed. and trans. R. W. Dyson (Cambridge: Catholic University Press, 1998), 1182; Augustine, *On the Trinity*, trans. Edmund Hill (Brooklyn, NY: New City Press, 1991), 158–61.

Anselm terms the six great ages *aetates*. Below (chap. 6 *et seq*), he designates each of the lesser divisions of the final, contemporary age *status*, in this translation "stage." See the introduction above for bibliography of various systems of periodization. On the uniqueness of Anselm's approach and for translations from the works of contemporary authors see Bernard McGinn, *Visions of the End: Apocalyptic Traditions in the Middle Ages* (New York: Columbia University Press, 1979), 94–116. McGinn translates passages central to Anselm's view of history and Revelation at pp. 114–16.

[29] Genesis 16:1-4; 30:1-13; 28:14.
[30] Genesis 17:9-14.
[31] Compare Numbers 19:20; 20:4; Deuteronomy 23:1-3; Judges 20:2.

of sacrifice, the law of votive offering took shape in great variety.[32] A new rule of life, new commandments, new precepts, and new prohibitions were drawn up for this church. Thus the people of God were set apart from the uncircumcised, from all other nations, in this variety of written law. They were governed and ruled by chosen judges.

We read that the famous Gentile Job lived at this time. He was outstanding in patience, clear in his faith in a future resurrection, courageous in resisting the shameful temptation of his own wife, prudent amid the burdensome consolation of his friends, powerful in faith under the great burden of every trial. God himself attested that this Job was unlike any other on earth.[33] Arising at dawn, he sanctified his children and offered holocausts for every one.[34] Yet I do not know by what rite pleasing to God he did so, whether he devised it himself or whether the religion of his people had chosen it to praise God, even whether God perhaps had instituted it through someone in those times for the Gentiles. Scripture itself hands down nothing to us about this matter.

Chapter 4
That we believe that the ancient fathers, although they did not fully know each article of the Christian faith, were nonetheless saved according to the future faith.

Afterward, from David's time to Christ's, since there were no longer judges leading that same church, kings were chosen and anointed, and scribes and Pharisees appointed. A glorious temple was constructed, in which the ark of the covenant was placed. Venerable prophets arose to speak and write various prophecies, proclaiming to the people various future goods or ills. New ceremonies and observances were added to the law previously recorded. Musicians were trained to sing psalms accompanied by the psaltery, tambourine, dance, organ, and every type of musical instrument.[35] The

---

[32] See, for instance, Leviticus 1–7.
[33] Job 1:8.
[34] Job 1:5.
[35] Compare, for instance, 1 Kings 18:6; 2 Samuel 6:5; 1 Chronicles 13:8.

Nazirites, who devoutly arranged fitting ornaments for the beauty of the house of God, came later. Thus the ancient fathers served the one God faithfully—in one faith but in many modes. They all served the faith that was to come and were saved in their future faith. Although many of them did not yet have such knowledge of that faith that they fully understood the sacraments of Christ and the church in their various aspects, and although they did not know the mysteries of the Incarnation, Nativity, Passion, Resurrection, and Ascension as fully revealed, nonetheless we must believe that they saw these things as if from a distance. Thus they hailed the Christ to come and awaited the grace of his hoped-for pledge that they too be joined in the unity of the catholic church and in *the holy city, the new Jerusalem, coming down out of heaven from God, prepared as a bride adorned for her husband* (Rev 21:2). We read about a great number of them: *This man began to call on the name of the Lord* (Gen 4:26); and again: *he called upon the name* of his God (Gen 13:4); and again: *he built an altar to the Lord* (Gen 12:7); and again: *he called upon the name* of the Lord (Gen 21:33). How exactly are we to understand this? Is it not in the sense that this man invoked the name of the Lord, believing that the name of the Lord was that Son of God who would come in the flesh? The prophet clearly implies thus when he speaks of the Incarnation of the Son of God as the Word of the Father, which is the name of the Lord: *Behold the name of the Lord cometh from afar* and his glory fills the earth (Isa 30:27). For just as someone makes himself known to another for the first time by his name, so God the Father reveals himself to the world by his own name, that is by his only Son, his Word.[36]

Chapter 5
That two transitions have taken place in religion as handed down to us—that is the Law and the Gospel—with earthquakes affirming their importance.

We must recognize that two great transitions have taken place in life and in religion as handed down to us—that is, the two testaments—

[36] See Daniel 3:45.

and that these events were marked with earthquakes on account of their great importance.[37] The former was the transition from idols to the Law, when there was thunder and lightning, with thick clouds, a trumpet blast, and a terrible din.[38] The second was the transition from the Law to the Gospel, when there was a great earthquake, the sun grew dark, rocks split, tombs opened, and the gates of hell were broken.[39] Yet a third earthquake is predicted for the future, when at the end of the world such things as will thereafter be changeless will again carry forward. In the prior two transitions or transformations divine wisdom acted gradually and in such different forms that, first removing the idols, she permitted sacrifices. Second, taking away the sacrifices, she allowed circumcision. Then, removing circumcision, she introduced baptism for salvation along with the institution and doctrine of the Gospel. So from Gentiles she created the Jews, and from Jews the Christians. Little by little—removing, transferring, and arranging almost as if in secret, as a teacher and a physician—she led humanity from the worship of idols to the Law. When that Law failed to attain the perfection of the Gospel, she finally set aside the entire prior dispensation and taught the Christian law as integral and complete.[40]

Chapter 6
That the Old Testament proclaimed God the Father clearly and God the Son in a hidden way—and that the New Testament taught God the Son clearly but at first hinted at the Holy Spirit, then taught him bit by bit more plainly.

What then? The Old Testament clearly announced the Father, but did not so clearly foretell the Son, rather did so subtly. The New Testament then revealed God the Son plainly, but offered only a

[37] See Gregory Nazianzen, *Faith Gives Fullness to Reasoning* 31.25-26, trans. Wickham and Williams, 292–94. As Salet notes (*Dialogues*, 58 n. 1), *Anticimenon* 2 is also heavily indebted to Gregory's third and fifth Theological Discourses. Anselm does not here cite Gregory by name, although he refers to other Fathers explicitly in the later books of *Anticimenon*.

[38] See Exodus 19:16.

[39] See Matthew 27:51-52.

[40] See Hebrews 7:19.

glimpse of the Holy Spirit, so implying his divinity.[41] Afterwards the Holy Spirit was announced, granting us still clearer evidence of his godhead.[42] It was not fitting that the Son be clearly announced before the divinity of the Father was made known, or that the divinity of the Holy Spirit be proclaimed to us when the divinity of the Son was still not acknowledged. Nor is it appropriate that human souls be overburdened by more nourishment than they can manage, for their minds to be overwhelmed, dulled as they are by life on earth and by the weight of their sins.[43] The transformation of things long held in veneration and affirmed in much custom was not easy. Therefore the health-bringing medicine of the Gospel was applied little by little to weak humankind—mixed with soothing elements, as if by a physician, with God's gentle skill.[44]

Yet the Holy Spirit himself is set beside the Son everywhere in the Gospel. When the Son is begotten, the Holy Spirit overshadows the Virgin in his conception. When the Son is baptized, the Holy Spirit is present in the form of a dove even as the Father is witness. When the Son is tempted, the Holy Spirit stays beside him and leads him back. When the Son works wonders, the Holy Spirit follows him everywhere, placing himself among the believers. When the Son ascends into heaven, the Holy Spirit comes in his stead to teach and to fulfill all truth.[45]

Thus faith in the Holy Trinity is measured out gradually according to the capacity of believers. It was offered, as it were, in part, then grew to wholeness and finally completion. In the period

[41] See again Gregory, *Faith Gives Fullness to Reasoning* 31.25-26, trans. Wickham and Williams, 292–94. Anselm imitates not only the content of Gregory's remarks but also their dismissiveness toward those unwilling to respond to the interpretive teaching of the Spirit. His discussion of the agency of the Spirit here looks forward to his treatment of the Spirit's procession in Book 2. Given that he has noted in his prologue to the entire *Anticimenon* that Book 1 was written before he conceived of composing the latter two books, this passage attests the integrity of his thought as articulated in the whole three-book work.

[42] Anselm points out below that the later period to which he here adverts saw the early ecumenical councils: *Anticimenon* 1.9.

[43] See Wisdom 9:15.

[44] Gregory, *Faith Gives Fullness to Reasoning* 31.26, trans. Wickham and Williams, 293–94.

[45] Compare Luke 1:5; Matthew 3:16; 4:1; Acts 10:38; John 14:26; 16:13.

called the sixth age, between the coming of Christ and the judgment day—the period in which the same singular church is renewed in the presence of God the Son—we find not one uniform
age but many different stages.[46] Christian religious life had one
aspect in the primitive church, when Jesus came up out of the
Jordan and was led by the Spirit into the desert, and when the
tempter left after testing him and Jesus crossed over Judah and
Galilee to choose his twelve apostles. The Lord shaped them by
a special teaching of the Christian faith to be poor in spirit and
so forth, as is written in the Sermon on the Mount addressed to
them. Jesus instructed them, preparing them to trample underfoot
this wicked time by teaching them many sound precepts of evangelical doctrine.[47] But after the passion, resurrection, and ascension of Christ and after the coming of the Holy Spirit, many who
saw the signs and prodigies worked by the hands of the apostles
joined themselves into their community. Then it happened that,
as Luke writes: *The multitude of believers had but one heart and one
soul, neither did anyone say that aught of the things which he possessed
was his own, but all things were common unto them . . . . Neither was
there anyone needy among them . . . . And distribution was made to
every one according as he had need . . . . But of the rest no man durst
join himself unto them, but the people magnified them* (Acts 4:32-35;
5:13).[48] So a new church of the faithful was assembled by the grace
of the Holy Spirit. It had been made anew first out of the Jews, then

[46] Here Anselm resumes discussion of the division of time according to the six
days of creation. In using the seven seals of Revelation as a figure for historical
change—an image heretofore explored but never developed with his focus and
optimism—Anselm makes an original contribution to the lively twelfth-century
discussion of the shape of time. See again the introduction above and McGinn,
Visions of the End, 109-10.

[47] Compare Matthew 5-7; Galatians 1:4.

[48] The centrality of this passage from Acts to the spirituality of the Premonstratensians—indeed, to many elements of the twelfth-century reform—is well
documented. Anselm highlights the establishment of the primitive church and its
lived *vita apostolica* as definitive of the sixth great age of doctrinal development.
For a survey of the place of the articulation of the apostolic life to which Anselm
here adverts in the medieval reformation, with special emphasis on the Premonstratensians and Anselm, see Ernest W. McDonnell, "The *Vita Apostolica*: Diversity
or Dissent," *Church History* 24 (1955): 15-31, esp. 19-21.

out of the Gentiles, little by little abandoning the ritual practice of the Jews as well as that of the Gentiles, while maintaining such characteristics from either natural or written law as neither were nor are contrary to the Christian faith, rather clearly beneficial to all who observe them in faith and devotion.

Integral faith in the Holy Trinity was first preached openly at that time, with the witness of the Old and New Testaments. That faith had heretofore been in shadow, then suggested as if step by step, but now was fully revealed. New sacraments, new rites, new commandments, and new institutions arose. Apostolic and canonical letters were written. The Christian law was established by teachings and by writings. The faith we call "catholic" was announced over the whole world.[49] The holy church, passing through various successive stages, has been so renewed up until our own times.[50] Like the eagle's youth, it will always be renewed.[51] Its foundation of faith in the Holy Trinity, beyond which no one might build, is maintained even when the multiplicity of different forms of religious life are constructed upon it. So we raise still higher this temple holy to the Lord.[52]

---

[49] Throughout this work the author and, in *Anticimenon* 2 and 3, the voices he records use the Latin term *catholica*, "catholic" or "universal," in various senses— sometimes to indicate the ideal of a singular body of Christianity and sometimes to describe the practice or belief that the author or speaker believes should be all Christians'. This term is translated below as "catholic" or "universal," as those English usages best accord with the respective contexts. Very occasionally "Catholic" has seemed the appropriate translation, although neither the author nor any of the speakers he represents has in mind a definitive split between Catholicism and Orthodoxy such as modernity has come to acknowledge.

[50] Here and throughout the present translation Anselm's term *status* is translated as "stage" rather than with its English cognate "state." The Latin *status* connotes many possibilities of the church's manifestation, implying succession and mutability more strongly than the English "age," which nonetheless usefully suggests temporal transition.

[51] See Psalm 102:5. Here Anselm first offers the psalmist's image of the eagle's flight as a figure for the church in time. He will later recur to this image, evocative of John the evangelist and reminiscent of the preaching of his master Norbert: *Anticimenon* 1.10. For attention to the use of this image by Norbert of Xanten and Philip of Harvegt as well as Anselm see Carol Neel, "Philip of Harvengt and Anselm of Havelberg: The Premonstratensian Vision of Time," *Church History* 52 (1993): 483–93.

[52] See 1 Corinthians 3:11.

Chapter 7
On the seven seals signifying the seven ages of the church, and that in the first stage, when the white horse goes forth, the early church grew in the newness of miracles and wonders.

The seven seals that John saw, as he explained himself in his Apocalypse, are evidently seven stages of the church from the coming of Christ until all things are consummated at the end and God is all in all.[53] For *when the Lamb had opened one of the seven seals . . . behold a white horse, and he who was sitting upon it had a bow and there was a crown given him, and he went forth conquering that he might conquer* (Rev 6:1-2). The white horse is the first stage of the church, shining and beautiful with the brilliance of miracles—an age in whose newness all were amazed and filled with praise. He who sat upon it armed with a bow is Christ governing the church, casting down and overthrowing the proud with the bow of apostolic teaching. *And there was given to him a crown,* since he went away into a distant land to assume his kingship. *And he went forth conquering, that he might conquer* (Rev 6:2).[54] So he said to his followers: *Have confidence, I have conquered the world* (John 16:33). Behold, in this first stage of the nascent church, the number of men and women believing in the Lord grew more and more, and daily the church of God shone forth in the power of miracles and in the number of believers.[55]

Chapter 8
That in the second stage of the church, when the red horse went forth, harsh persecution fell upon the saints.

And when he had opened the second seal . . . there went out another horse that was red, and to him that sat thereon, it was given that he

---

[53] Anselm now proceeds to overlay his description of seven stages of historical development since the coming of Christ on the patristic six-age schema for the unfolding of humanity's relationship with God. He continues to distinguish the six ages, *aetates,* from the seven stages, *statūs,* of the church.

[54] See Luke 19:12.

[55] See Acts 5:14:16.

should take peace from the earth, and that they should kill one another;
and a great sword was given to him (Rev 6:3-4). Behold, the second
stage of the church was revealed to that disciple whom Jesus loved,
for what else is that red horse issuing forth but the blood of the
martyrs poured out in witness of Christ, when peace was taken
away from the earth and the sword of persecution fell upon the
church? This age of persecution began with Stephen, the glorious
protomartyr whom the Jews stoned.[56] After his triumph the persecution was so harsh that soon the church could not remain in
the one region of Jerusalem.[57] The apostles spread out into every
land to preach the Gospel of Christ, and in their preaching of that
Gospel they consummated their lives in martyrdom. Then Peter
and Paul went to Rome, James to Jerusalem, Andrew to Greece,
Bartholomew to India, Matthew to Ethiopia, and the other apostles
too crowned their various regions in glorious martyrdom.

After them many others of the faithful endured mockery and
beating, even chains and imprisonment.[58] Suffering terrible, exqui-
site torments, they joyfully raised the banner of their Christian profession up to heaven, leaving us their memory as their blessing.[59]
Laws were written against the term "Christian," so that whoever
was found to keep this religion was handed over to punishment,
condemned without a hearing. But the church of God flourished
under persecution like a victory palm. Like a cedar of Lebanon,
the more it suffered the more it grew.[60]

Still, that ancient dragon-serpent who had stirred up such rage
against the church of God saw that the woman clothed with the
sun, standing on the moon with a crown of twelve stars on her
head, could not entirely absorb the river that he spewed forth. He
was angry with the woman, and again he decided to make war
with the rest of her offspring, who observed the commandments
and preserved the testimony of Jesus.[61]So when open persecution
ceased and the prohibition of the Christians was relaxed, a different

[56] See Acts 7:57.
[57] See Acts 8:1.
[58] See Hebrews 11:36.
[59] See Sirach 46:14.
[60] See Psalm 91:13.
[61] See Revelation 12.

law was promulgated to keep peace for the church. Kings hastened to baptism and princes of various provinces took up the faith of Christ. The whole world that had earlier reproached the term "Christian" now revered it humbly, and the cross of Christ previously met with scandal and mockery was held high in honor and veneration. Everywhere temples were constructed magnificently, and the bishops, priests, deacons, and clerics of other orders who had been expelled were called back from exile. Everywhere teachers of the faith were sought out. The holy order of bishops and clerics arose, sent throughout the world to proclaim the Gospel of God.[62]

Chapter 9
That in the third stage of the church, when the black horse went forth, the perils of heresy embroiled it.

And when he had opened the third seal . . . behold a black horse, and he who sat on him had a pair of scales in his hand (Rev 6:5-6).[63] Behold the third stage of the church, in which the black horse came forth. That black horse is the dark doctrine of those heretics whom the great dragon mentioned above stirred up against the church of God, so that by their wicked teaching he might disrupt her whom he had been unable to drown in the blood of the martyrs.

So heretics arose, carrying the mark of the beast imprinted on their hearts.[64] Judging according to their false scale, they promised impartiality in discussions about the faith, but they deceived the careless by the weight of even a small word, so drawing them into error. Among these heretics was the notorious priest Arius, foulest heresiarch of the church of God, along with his lackeys. They argued over the meaning of consubstantiality, thus separating themselves from the church. By false arguments they asserted several substances in the Trinity, so impiously asserting different

---

[62] This passage raises intriguing questions about Anselm's and the early Premonstratensians' historical reading as opposed to their theology of history. In Book 3 below Anselm reveals himself an avid researcher of chronicle texts, but the extent of his historical knowledge remains unclear. See esp. *Anticimenon* 3.14.

[63] See Proverbs 11:1; 20:23.

[64] See Revelation 19:20.

substances while we piously believe there to be different persons.[65] Sabellius correctly believed the Trinity to be one in substance but he also thought that we must believe Father, Son, and Holy Spirit to be only one in one person. The bishop Nestorius judged that there could not be a double nature without two persons; therefore, although he rightly acknowledged Christ's double nature, he incorrectly believed the Lord to have two persons, and so foolishly preached that one person was the Son of God and the other the Son of man. The abbot Eutyches the archimandrite thought that a double nature required two persons; although he did not believe that there were two persons in Christ, he judged that there must then be only one nature. Nestorius, on the other hand, correctly believed there to be two natures in Christ, that is the divine and the human, but sacrilegiously held that the Lord had two persons. Then Eutyches believed correctly that there is one person in Christ, but falsely asserted only one nature. In their disagreement all of these heretics were both deceivers and deceived. Like them were the bishops Macedonius, who asserted against the faith that the Holy Spirit was a creature and not God himself, and Donatus, who arrogantly taught that the Son is inferior to the Father and that the Holy Spirit is inferior to both. The bishop Photinus shamefully imputed Christ's conception by Mary to carnal union. And Manes of Persia, from whom the Manichees derive, obstinately taught the existence of two first principles, denying in his perverse doctrine that the only begotten Son of God is eternal.[66]

Many other heretics also framed various false doctrines in their respective times. Like enemies sowing a pestilential weed among the wheat of apostolic teaching, they cruelly plucked and mangled

[65] For a lucid summary of the Arian controversy and its conciliar resolution see Henry Chadwick, *The Early Church* (Grand Rapids: Eerdmans, 1968), 133–51. On Arius himself see Rowan Williams, *Arius: Heresy and Tradition*, rev. ed. (Grand Rapids: Eerdmans, 2001), 29–91. See also David Christie-Murray, *A History of Heresy* (Oxford: Oxford University Press, 1989), 45–61. Arianism was the central topic of the Council of Nicea, summoned by Constantine in 325 AD, but related heterodoxies appeared from the third to the fifth century, and Anselm meticulously lists these below.

[66] On these further christological heresies see Chadwick, *Early Church*, 169 and 192–212; Christie-Murray, *History of Heresy*, 62–77.

the dove of God—simple in her faith, holy and immaculate in her action.[67] Many famous councils were convened against them in various places and times. Their heretical depravity was condemned, their leaven of malice and worthlessness was cleansed, and mother church was fortified in the unleavened purity of sincerity and truth.[68] At the councils of Nicea, Antioch, Ephesus, Chalcedon, and Constantinople, and at many other synodal assemblies of the holy fathers in the various regions, the snakelike venom of the heretics was so expunged and voided that they dared not sprout or bubble up in any corner of the catholic church.[69] The orthodox faith was so strengthened, founded, and fortified after these attacks that from now on, by God's favor, it might always remain indestructible, unshaken, whole without accretions and inviolable without detractions. Thereafter the holy fathers rightly forbade that anyone dispute publicly about the faith, since it was now clear and unambiguous, for it is madness to seek artificial illumination in broad daylight. Anyone who investigates further when he has already found the truth only seeks a lie, so by his own fault wrapping himself in untruth.

After the catholic faith was thus rooted, various rules were added to shape its discipline. Because the holy fathers had approved them, these were fittingly called "canons." Among them are precepts, prohibitions, dispensations, rigor, necessary practices, indulgence, remission, things that should be feared, admonition, and so forth. Through these strictures the whole church grew throughout this stage in wondrous wisdom against the heretics,

---

[67] Compare Matthew 13:25, Song 5:2.

[68] 1 Corinthians 5:8. Here Anselm looks forward to Book 3's discussion of leavened and unleavened bread in the Eucharist, disposing his reader to appreciate leavening as negative.

[69] As Salet notes (*Dialogues*, 80 n. 4), Anselm frequently refers to fathers, *patres*, meaning the early ecclesiastical councils (as here below and in *Anticimenon* 2.23), not major patristic authors, whom he designates *doctores* (again see *Anticimenon* 2.23). On the various ecumenical councils and how they performed their work see Ramsay MacMullen, *Voting About God in Early Church Councils* (New Haven: Yale University Press, 2006). MacMullen lists the council to which Anselm refers here in the context of lesser such meetings at pp. 2–4. For the decrees of the councils of Nicea, Ephesus, Chalcedon, and Constantinople in the original languages with facing English translation see Norman P. Tanner, ed., *Decrees of the Ecumenical Councils 1: Nicaea I to Lateran V* (London: Sheed and Ward, 1990), 1–130.

just as in the previous stage it grew in triumphant suffering through the persecution of the martyrs. But behold *the roaring lion* does not rest, he does not sleep, but even now he *goeth about seeking whom he may devour* (1 Pet 5:8).

Chapter 10
That in the fourth stage of the church, as the pale horse comes forth, the church of God struggles beyond her strength against false brothers, and that in this stage many different forms of religious life have arisen.

And when he had opened the fourth seal . . . behold a pale horse, and he that sat upon him, his name was death, and hell followed him (Rev 6:7-8). This is the fourth stage of the church, in which grave, death-bearing danger arises among false brothers. Just as a pale color mixes together white and black without showing any pure white, but misleadingly presents both, so too innumerable false Christians or false brothers confess Christ publicly but deny him in their works.[70] They go to church and receive her sacraments, show due reverence to prelates, and treat each other with honor even as the apostle enjoins.[71] They build churches, adorning the altars gracefully as befits the house of God. They celebrate the solemnities and feasts of the saints with apparent great devotion. These false brothers acclaim long Masses and well-ordered processions of clergy. They impose fasts and food deprivation upon themselves, offering alms to the poor with their own hands. They warmly greet holy men when they encounter them, evincing internal joy and open respect, then treat these holy men politely as their guests and commend themselves to their prayers. The false brethren even visit that glorious sepulcher of the Lord in Jerusalem, the homes of the apostles, and other shrines of the saints. In every legal matter, their own or others', they aver that God is their authority. They claim that everything they say or do is in the name of the Lord.[72] In sum, they comport themselves fittingly in dress, speech, appearance,

[70] See Titus 1:16.
[71] See Romans 12:10.
[72] See Colossians 3:17.

gait—in every movement of the body—as religious, honorable
and disciplined, presenting themselves thus to the world. Among
them and with them this stage of the church seems peaceable, for
the sword of persecutors does not assail it outwardly, nor does the
deceitful insolence of heretics weary it.

But among these false Christians, false brothers assuming
the name and the practice of Christians, the church nonetheless
struggles such that he who sat upon the pale horse well deserves
the name death. Hellish, this death spares no mortal man, never
saying, "It is enough."[73] Death itself—murderer of souls, pale
with hypocrisy and pretense, with hell's gaping jaws eagerly following it—is in these false brothers. The Lord speaks about them
in the gospel under the names of scribes and Pharisees: *Woe to
you scribes and Pharisees, hypocrites, because you shut the kingdom of
heaven against men, for you yourselves do not enter in, and those that
are going in, you suffer not to enter. Woe to you scribes and Pharisees,
hypocrites, because you devour the houses of widows, praying long prayers.
For this you shall receive the greater judgment* (Matt 23:13-14). *Woe to
you scribes and Pharisees, hypocrites, because you tithe mint, and anise,
and cumin, and have left the weightier things of the law—judgment,
and mercy, and faith* (Matt 23:23). *Woe to you scribes and Pharisees,
hypocrites, because you make clean the outside of the cup and of the dish,
but within you are full of rapine and uncleanness* (Matt 23:27). *Woe
to you scribes and Pharisees, hypocrites, because you are like to whited
sepulchres, which outwardly appear to men beautiful, but within are full
of dead men's bones, and of all filthiness. So you also outwardly indeed
appear to men just; but inwardly you are full of hypocrisy and iniquity.
Woe to you scribes and Pharisees, hypocrites, that build the sepulchres of
the prophets, and adorn the monuments of the just, and say: If we had
been in the days of our fathers, we would not have been partakers with
them in the blood of the prophets. Wherefore you are witnesses against
yourselves, that you are the sons of them that killed the prophets. Fill ye
up then the measure of your fathers. You serpents, generation of vipers,
how will you flee from the judgment of hell?* (Matt 23:27-32).

Behold, beloved brothers, we have heard the terrible warnings
against such hypocrites. Let us fear the pale death of souls and the

[73] See Proverbs 30:15-16.

gaping hell that follows it. Let us flee detestable hypocrisy, cleaning and purifying ourselves within by sincere confession, washing ourselves with a frequent flood of tears. In public, moreover, let us never disagree with the standard discipline of the church, by which each of us is called into his respective way of life, lest we wish either to cause or to suffer scandal.

Invective against the Hypocrite[74]
Woe to you, wretched hypocrite, most wretched of men, you who pretend good but love evil, who are both God's enemy and your own, your own seducer, your own deceiver, self-swindler, flatterer, mocker, cheater, you who blame, condemn, betray and judge yourself! You are your own murderer when you purport truth but do falsehood, steal your own treasure, and persecute your own conscience. You are a perverse fox, a restless worm, a tortuous snake, a devouring cancer, a whitewashed wall, the most foolish of fools, a witness of the devil walking lifeless among the living while already dead and buried. Of all men you are the most lost, a worthless slave. You are bound up, shackled, pierced, imprisoned, concealed within yourself. You are filthy, stinking, disgraceful, unhappy, guilt-ridden, wicked, damned, cunning, pompous, vacuous, inconstant, wan, blind, gloomy, cowardly, suspicious, bombastic, demon-ridden, tainted in thought and action by the practice of magic. You are hopeless, a leaning wall, a crumbling border without foundation, on the point of ruin, dirty, muddy, filthy, foul, disordered, odious, insidious, a vendor of the holy oil whose own lamp is dark. You are lying, shut out and exiled from all good, already cast into hell, a deceiver destitute of all truth, in every way as detestable to God and the angels as to men.[75] Woe to you, wretched hypocrite! You have mounted the pale horse. Your name is death, and hell follows you, ready to devour you. Woe

---

[74] Although this invective is well-attested in *Anticimenon*'s manuscript exemplars and although its authenticity has been heretofore unchallenged, the invective against the hypocrite is notably discordant with both the tone and style of both this initial book and *Anticimenon*'s later dialogues, raising the possibility that it was added by a later hand. If this long paragraph is omitted, the text continues seamlessly with discussion of the developments of the church's fourth stage.
[75] Compare 2 Timothy 2:17, Acts 23:3, Matthew 18:32, Psalm 61:4.

to you, wretched hypocrite! Would that you convert in your heart and become a lover of truth trampling falsity under foot! Then you might really do those things that you have until now pretended. Would that you change not the nature of your good works but the wicked falsity of your perverse pretense! Then you might expect or hope for preferment from your good works, when before in your fakery you deserved to expect just punishment. For good or bad intention lends its character to action and calls for either preferment or punishment in just retribution.

In this stage of the church have nonetheless appeared holy men, lovers of the truth and restorers of religious life. Augustine, bishop of the church of Hippo and legate of the province of Numidia in Africa, decided to live the apostolic life by gathering to him true brethren. For them he prescribed a rule for common life.[76] This rule was subsequently spread and acclaimed through all the catholic church. It sought out and gathered together—and continues to this day to gather together—a great number into the holy association of common life in imitation of the apostles and of the example of so great a man. Following in Augustine's footsteps, a certain individual of great holiness appeared at Saint Ruf in Burgundy in the time of Pope Urban. After gathering together brothers of his own canonical profession, he first shed his light on that whole region, then bit by bit spread the canonical way of life into other places.[77]

Afterward, in the time of Pope Gelasius, appeared a holy priest of the same canonical profession in imitation of the apostolic

[76] George Lawless, *Augustine of Hippo and His Monastic Rule* (Oxford: Clarendon Press, 1987), presents the definitive text with English translation of the *Ordo monasterii* and *Praeceptum* to which Anselm refers: *Augustine*, 74–103. For discussion of these texts' history and usage see pp. 121–54, 165–71.

[77] Anselm apparently refers to Arbert of Saint-Ruf: see Ursula Vones-Liebenstein, "Der Verband Regular-Kanoniker von Saint-Ruf. Entstehung, Struktur und normative Grundlagen," in Gert Melville and Anne Müller, eds., *Regula Sancti Augustini: Normative Grundlage differenter Verbände im Mittelalter* (Paring: Augustinerchorherren-Verlag, 2002), 57–59. Anselm's mention of the Rufensians affirms the importance of their model of canonical community for Norbert's foundations. On the place of Saint-Ruf in canonical reform see C. H. Lawrence, *Medieval Monasticism: Forms of Religious Life in Western Europe in the Middle Ages* (London: Longman, 1984), 137–42.

life. His name was Norbert. On account of his religious fervor and because of the many irregularities and schisms then wracking the western church, he received the privilege of preaching from the same Roman pontiff.[78] The most illustrious and renowned man of his time in religious life, Norbert traveled through many regions as he preached. He gathered a great number of religious, established many communities, and formed them toward the perfection of apostolic life by his word and example.[79] This Norbert evinced much grace before God and among men, so that those who were able to join with him called themselves truly blessed. Afterwards he became archbishop of the church of Magdeburg. His holy and venerable body rests in the church of Blessed Mary in his archiepiscopal see, where he had established the brothers of his way of common life.[80] Religious life as renewed by Norbert grew

---

[78] Anselm conspicuously emphasizes preaching as Norbert's central response to the spiritual crisis of his day. For a summary of Norbert's career see *Norbert and Early Norbertine Spirituality*, ed. and trans. Theodore J. Antry and Carol Neel (New York: Paulist Press, 2007), 7–10. On the papal privilege of preaching see esp. *Life of Norbert: Version A* 5, trans. Antry and Neel, 131. For a useful introduction to the place of Norbert and his followers in the wider context of twelfth-century religious life see Christopher Brooke, *The Age of the Cloister: The Story of Monastic Life in the Middle Ages* (Mahwah NJ: HiddenSpring, 2003), 217–22. The indispensable scholarly introduction to Norbert remains the essay collection edited by Kaspar Elm, *Norbert von Xanten: Adliger, Ordensstifter, Kirchenfürst* (Cologne: Wienand, 1984).

[79] Caroline Walker Bynum has noted that teaching by word and example, *docere verbo et exemplo*, was the hallmark of twelfth-century canonical spirituality: Bynum, *Docere verbo et exemplo: An Aspect of Twelfth-Century Spirituality*, Harvard Theological Studies 31 (Missoula, MT: Scholars Press, 1979), esp. 50–55. See also Bynum, "The Spirituality of Regular Canons in the Twelfth Century," in her *Jesus as Mother: Studies in the Spirituality of the High Middle Ages* (Berkeley: University of California Press, 1982), esp. 36–40.

[80] Anselm here uses the term *ordo* to refer to Norbert's followers and to their way of life. This Latin word, whose English cognate "order" is laden with historical connotations, indeed by the end of the twelfth century became a conventional usage describing formally constituted religious groups such as the Premonstratensians and the Cistercians. Much scholarship, however, questions whether Norbert in fact intended to found an order in this specific ecclesiological sense. See the introduction above and Antry and Neel, *Norbert and Early Norbertine Spirituality*, 1–14; Stefan Weinfurter, "Norbert von Xanten als Reformkanoniker und Stifter des Prämonstratenserordens," in Elm, *Norbert von Xanten*, 165–75. Certainly in Norbert's or Anselm's time the term *ordo* was used broadly to describe different religious and even temporal paths. So Anselm refers above in *Anticimenon* 2.8 to various orders,

so widely over all the earth that hardly any province in the West lacked communities of his way of life: France, Germany, Burgundy, Aquitaine, northern Spain, Brittany, England, Denmark, Saxony, Leutitia,[81] Poland, Moravia, Bavaria, Suevia, Pannonia (also called Hungary), Lombardy, Liguria, and Etruria (also called Tuscany). All of these provinces, I point out, have communities of Norbert's religious affiliation, and those regions trust in such communities' continual prayer and example.[82] This same holy society even extends its branches in the East, for there is one community in Bethlehem and another there called St. Habacuc.[83]

---

ordines, of the clergy rather than varieties of regular religious. Literate medievals all used *ordo* still more generally to indicate the universal life-paths of those who worked, those who fought, and those who prayed: see Giles Constable, "The Ordes of Society," in idem, *Three Studies in Medieval Religious and Social Thought: The Interpretation of Mary and Martha, the Ideal of the Imitation of Christ, the Orders of Society* (Cambridge: Cambridge University Press, 1995), esp. 55–57. The present translation, in rendering Anselm's use of *ordo* as "way of common life" in this and similar contexts, acknowledges the looseness of the term within the discourse to which his text contributed. The Cistercians and Premonstratensians were the first "orders" to organize themselves through pan-European chapters in the course of the twelfth century, so developing a consciousness that they were mutually constituted in contrast to the relative disorganization of traditional Benedictinism.

[81] As Salet notes (*Dialogues*, 96 n. 1), *Leutitia* may be an orthographic variant referring to the lands of a tribe of Wends, the Liutices. It may, however, be a scribal error for Lusatia, a region of Saxony more comparable in importance to the other large geographical areas Anselm lists here. The Premonstratensians were nonetheless important in the conversion of the Wends: see Franz Winter, *Die Prämonstratenser des zwölften Jahrhunderts und ihre Bedeutung für das nordöstliche Deutschland: Ein Beitrag zur Geschichte der Christianisierung und Germanisierung des Wendenlandes* (Berlin, 1865; repr. Aalen: Scientia, 1966), esp. 97.

[82] Here Anselm emphasizes the Premonstratensians' "prayer and example," rather than—in the more frequently encountered formula—"word and example," in which "word" connotes preaching. He thus suggests the importance of the contemplation his *Apologetic Letter* on behalf of the regular canons has presented as integral to the canons' spirituality: see Antry and Neel, *Norbert and Early Norbertine Spirituality*, esp. 55–57.

[83] St. Habacuc was founded in Jerusalem in 1137/8, probably near Joppa. Premonstratensians were given a former Cistercian house, St. Samuel in Jerusalem, in 1141, but Anselm seems to have been mistaken in thinking there was ever a community of white canons in Bethlehem. See Norbert Backmund, *Monasticon Praemonstratense*, vol. 1, part 2 (Berlin: Walter de Gruyter, 1983), 508–9.

Anselm's extensive description of the Augustinian canonical reform, with its emphasis on the role of Norbert of Xanten, effectively privileges the regular canons

In the monastic way of life also appeared the blessed Benedict, who followed after many fathers of the monks living in Egypt. He was a worthy man of God, filled with the Holy Spirit. Drawn away from the solitude of Nursia, where he had lived in quiet, he became abbot of the monks at Monte Cassino in Campania. This Benedict, fervent in the practice of religious life, prescribed for his monks a rule dictated by the Holy Spirit. He renewed and strengthened a monastic path previously in decay. Both by his own action and afterward through his rule Benedict founded many new monasteries of monks.[84] Then in recent times in Tuscany, in a place called Camaldoli, appeared a holy man named John. Under the banner of the monastic profession, vesting himself and his brother monks with new fervor as well as a new habit, he found many disciples eager to follow his model. Not long after, in another place near the Perusino Mountains called Vallombrosa arose a new, intensely pious congregation of monks. These differed from the other monks in their new way of life and a new habit, and many followed their model.[85]

Then in Burgundy, in a place called Cîteaux, arose almost in our own times yet another new monastic congregation differing in pattern of life and in dress from all those who are called and indeed are monks. Because they seem to stand out, excelling others in the strength of their patient suffering, their humility of dress, their

---

in relation to contemporary monastic reform, for which he nonetheless shows due respect in the succeeding passage. Augustine indeed lived more than a century before Benedict, but Anselm's inclusion of the attribution of the twelfth-century Augustinians, including the followers of Norbert, in the African father's context here points out the chronological priority of regular life for clergy to monasticism in its widespread Western form. In addressing his work to Eugenius III, a Cistercian, hence a reformed Benedictine, as well as because of his master Norbert's clear admiration for the Cistercians, Anselm evidently honored their role in the ongoing reformation of religious life. But in the order of his presentation here he subtly claims the canons' greater antiquity and, hence, prestige. He had argued the canons' legitimacy more aggressively in his *Apologetic Letter*, trans. Antry and Neel, 42–48.

[84] The definitive edition of Benedict's *Rule* offers a facing translation and many supporting materials: *Rule of St. Benedict*, ed. Timothy Fry (Collegeville, MN: Liturgical Press, 1981). On the rule and spread of Benedictinism see Brooke, *Age of the Cloister*, 44–85; Lawrence, *Medieval Monasticism*, 20–35, 76–124.

[85] On the background and character of Camaldoli and Vallombrosa see Brooke, *Age of the Cloister*, 87–90; Lawrence, *Medieval Monasticism*, 125–28.

diligence in observance of the rule as in their love of holy poverty
and ardent piety, these monks' form of religious life has innumerable
imitators.[86] Among them in our own time, in the place called Clairvaux, appeared a certain abbot named Bernard, a man of the highest
piety, distinguished by the power of miracles and hugely famous for
his sanctity from west to east. The venerable Pope Eugenius, at one
time a monk of Bernard's monastery, frequently honored the latter
with great reverence in councils of many bishops.[87]

Likewise, not long ago a new institute of religious began in Jerusalem, the city of God. Laymen, pious men who called themselves
the Knights of the Temple, have gathered in that place, abandoning
their property, and living and fighting in obedience to one master.
They have renounced excess and extravagant dress and are prepared
to defend the glorious tomb of the Lord against the assaults of the
Saracens. Peaceable at home, abroad they are vigorous warriors;
obedient to the discipline of their rule at home, abroad they follow
military discipline; trained in holy silence at home, abroad they
are undaunted by the din and force of war. In short, they fulfill
everything they are ordered in absolute obedience whether they
are at home or in the outside world. Pope Urban first confirmed
their life and intention at the advice of many bishops whom he
had convened in a council. He ordained that each man whom they
had gathered in their society in the hope of eternal life and who

---

[86] Among the vast literature on the Cistercians, two major recent works are of
particular interest from the perspective of their relationship to the Premonstratensians: Constance Hoffman Berman, *The Cistercian Evolution: The Invention of a
Religious Order in Twelfth-Century Europe* (Philadelphia: University of Pennsylvania
Press, 2000); and Martha G. Newman, *The Boundaries of Charity: Cistercian Culture
and Ecclesiastical Reform, 1098–1180* (Stanford: Stanford University Press, 1996).
Berman's challenge to the historiographical assumption that the reform orders
were so formally constituted from the second quarter of the twelfth century is
important for reconsideration of the Premonstratensians' early decades: see esp.
221–36. Newman's synoptic assessment of the white monks' sense of their place
in the monastic and ecclesiastical cultures calls for similarly attentive treatment of
the followers of Norbert, who were always—as Anselm's description of the Cistercians' success here emphasizes—acutely aware of comparison with them: see esp.
141–70, on clerical reform.

[87] Anselm had himself encountered Bernard in Eugenius's presence in 1136,
some fifteen years before he dedicated *Anticimenon* to the same pope: see his *Apologetic* Letter, trans. Antry and Neel, 48–49.

persevered in it faithfully might obtain the remission of all his sins. Urban asserted that their merit was no less than that either of the monks or of the canons of the common life.[88]

In the Eastern church as well—among the Greeks, Armenians, and Syrians—are various types of religious persons. They are in harmony in the one catholic faith but differ greatly from one another in customs, pattern of life, dress, food, and practice of psalmody. When I was in Constantinople as the legate of Lothar the Great, most Christian emperor of the Romans, to Kalojohn, emperor of that royal city, I was an avid observer and zealous investigator of different kinds of religious life.[89] There I saw many forms of Christian religious practice. I saw nearly seven hundred monks serving under the rule of blessed Antony in the monastery called *Pantocrator*, that is the Almighty. I saw no fewer than five hundred monks serving under the rule of blessed Pachomius in the monastery called *Philanthropos*, or the Lover of Men. I also saw many communities under the rule of blessed Basil the Great. They are learned men, serving faithfully.[90]

[88] The Templars were chartered in 1139 by a papal privilege of Innocent II: see *Omne datum optimum* in Malcom Barber and Keith Bate, eds., *The Templars: Selected Sources* (Manchester: Manchester University Press, 2002), 59–64. Anselm probably errs in attributing their foundation to Urban II because the earlier pope had preached the First Crusade in 1095. The Templars had been approved by the Council of Troyes ten years before Innocent issued his bull on their behalf: see Malcom Barber, *The Templars: A History of the Order of the Temple* (Cambridge: Cambridge University Press, 1994), 8–15.

Anselm's specific assertion that "Urban" declared the Templars equal in dignity to monks and canons fits his overall point about the value of diversity in the church but is unsupported in extant sources about the military orders' foundation. Perhaps he refers generally to Bernard's famous laudation of the Templars: *In Praise of the New Knighthood*, in Barber and Bate, eds., *Sources*, 215–27.

[89] Anselm's embassy to Constantinople had been in 1136: see again Lees, *Deeds into Words*, 42–44; Sigler, *Beiträge*, 35–39, 329. The emperor then was John II Comnenus (1118–1143). Anselm uses the familiar designation of this emperor, which seems to refer more to his benevolent manner than his beautiful appearance. Here Anselm emphasizes his longstanding interest in varieties of religious life.

[90] On the Antonine, Pachomian, and Basilian traditions see Brooke, *Age of the Cloister*, 28–35; Lawrence, *Medieval Monasticism*, 5–10. On the role of Orthodox monasticism in Anselm's time see Angold, *Church and Society*, 265–382. On Anselm's interest in Eastern monasticism see Georg Schreiber, "Anselm von Havelberg und die Ostkirche," *Zeitschrift für Kirchengeschichte* 60 (1941): 354–411, at 375–406.

One and the same Spirit worketh all these divine, holy, and excellent things at different times and in different ways of life, *dividing to every one according as he will* (1 Cor 12:11). That Holy Spirit who governs the whole body of the church from the beginning, now and always, has recognized how to renew the sluggish souls of men, of faithful people cloyed by a long-familiar religious life, by the beginning of a new form of religion. The Spirit sees that, when such folk see others ascend to a higher form of religious life they are the more inspired by new models. Leaving behind that sluggishness and love of the world in which they are held back, they then quickly and fearlessly grasp perfection, for all wonder more at the novel and the unaccustomed than at the commonplace and the ordinary. So by God's wondrous design, since from generation to generation new forms of religious life always arise, the youth of the church renews itself like the eagle's, so that it may fly the higher in contemplation, with the strength to gaze directly, unblinded, at the rays of the true sun.[91]

But do you think that in such a great crowd of good men it might be possible that false brothers arouse no scandal? Would that it were so! Truly, would that it might be so! But I am afraid that I doubt it. For when I hear the Lord saying in the gospel, *Have not I chosen you twelve; and one of you is a devil?* (John 6:70), yes, when I hear this, I fear greatly. If the devil was present in the company of the apostles, those few chosen by the Lord himself, how could one think that in such a great crowd of just men there would not be false brethren, limbs of the devil? There have indeed been false prophets and false apostles, so no wonder that there are false brothers with us, even among us. But let us bear them in charity and prayerfully wait for them to lay aside their pretense and become true brothers.[92] Now we are together in one net, but when we reach shore, we will not all be gathered in the baskets of the saints. Now we grow together in one field, but at harvest time

[91] See. Psalm 102:5. Anselm's use of the figure of the eagle for the history of the church is at the center of much scholarly discussion of his optimistic vision of time, distinctive among the twelfth-century theologians of history: see again Neel, "Philip of Harvengt," 483–93.

[92] Compare 1 Peter 2:1; 2 Peter 2:1.

we will not be gathered together in one barn.[93] For they mingle
with us and we with them, although in different paths and with
different intention, until this fourth stage of the church ends, and
the saints follow the Lamb *whithersoever He goeth* (Rev 14:4), while
those who carry the pale sign of death will be buried in hell.

Chapter 11
**That in the fifth stage of the church the souls of the saints
under the altar of God cry out, how long, O Lord, holy and
true, dost thou not revenge our blood on them that dwell on
earth? and so forth.**

*And when he had opened the fifth seal, I saw under the altar the souls
of them that were slain for the word of God, and for the testimony which
they held. And they cried with a loud voice, saying, how long, O Lord,
holy and true, dost thou not . . . revenge our blood on them that dwell
on the earth? And white robes were given to every one of them one, and
it was said to them that they should rest for a little time till their fellow
servants and their brethren who are to be slain even as they should be
filled up* (Rev 6:9-11). This is the fifth stage of the church. Heretofore
it struggled in persecution and grew in suffering. It struggled in the
subtle deceit of the heretics and grew in wisdom. It suffered among
the false brethren and hypocrites and grew in endurance. But now
the souls of the saints beneath the altar, that is Christ, deserve to
rest because of their outpouring of blood, but seeing the boundless
miseries of the suffering church, they cry out for her in great voice
of compassion, *how long, O lord, dost thou not revenge our blood.* The
rest of this text pertains to the fifth stage of the church.

Chapter 12
**That in the sixth age of the church, after a great earthquake at
the time of the Antichrist, will begin a terrible persecution.**

And when he had opened the sixth seal . . . there was a great earthquake
(Rev 6:12). This is the sixth stage of the church, in which will be a
great earthquake, that is, a terrible persecution in the time of the

---

[93] See Matthew 13:30.

Antichrist—a great persecution indeed, for the Lord says, *in those days shall be such tribulation* as never since the nations began.[94] For in other times of persecutions, even if many torments were arrayed against the very name "Christian," the faith was still preserved as correct and certain. But in this case the torments are put forth and, further, a false faith argued in the name of Christ. For it is said, *Lo, here is Christ, there is Christ* (Matt 24:23), and *there shall be . . . tribulation such as hath not been* (Matt 24:21), not only because of the magnitude of the persecution but also because of such subversion of the faith that men do not know what they should believe or hold true. *The sun became black as sackcloth of hair* (Rev 6:12) because Christ, the sun of justice, and the name "Christian" will then be cast down, in thick and shameful darkness. Like Christ himself, so too will Christians be held worthless and abject in the eyes of the Antichrist and his men—as though they were a sackcloth of hair, the vilest of clothing. *The whole moon became as blood* (Rev 6:12) because in the entire world bloody persecution will devastate the church, as the moon symbolizes when it waxes, then wanes. *And the stars fell from heaven upon the earth* (Rev 6:13). The stars of heaven, that is the saints who shone as doctors in the firmament of the church, then will fall to earth, disappearing from the faith under this terrible persecution because they cleave to earthly pleasures. In their earthly love they will collapse into iniquity, as the text then says, *As the fig tree casteth its green figs when it is shaken by a great wind* (Rev 6:13). Although in the Gospel the fig tree sometimes represents the synagogue, in this case it signifies the entire church, from which those who have been empty of good works will fall. For green fruit is unripe, blown down before it reaches maturity. So too are those men who have not yet reached the maturity of good works. They are empty, shaken by the wind of the last persecution. They fall to the earth, into earthly pleasures. This wind is called great because, as was said above, persecution will fall even on the elect. *And the heaven departed as a book folded up* (Rev 6:14). Heaven here signifies the church, in which the ecclesiastical sacraments are kept wrapped and preserved, so that they disappear from the use of Christians, hidden away from solemn

[94] See Mark 13:19.

public ritual. *Men are withering away for fear* of the Antichrist and in *expectation of what shall come upon the whole world* (Luke 21:26). *And who shall be able to stand?* (Rev 6:17) The rest of this text also concerns things found in this sixth stage of the church.

Chapter 13
That in the seventh stage of the church, after many trials, will come a great silence and a time of infinite blessedness. And so the church of God—one in faith, one in hope, one in charity—is multiform in the variety of her different stages.

And when he had opened the seventh seal, there was silence in heaven, as it were for half an hour (Rev 8:1). The seventh seal is the seventh stage of the church, in which silence will fall. After the trials of the church as she gave birth to the sons of God in great sorrow, and after the judgment at the coming of the Son of God, the silence of divine contemplation will fall *in a moment, in the twinkling of an eye* (1 Cor 15:52), when all has come to an end. The year of jubilee will be inaugurated.[95] The eighth day of infinite beatitude will be celebrated; the Holy of Holies will be opened to the faithful when the veil of the law has been lifted. The song of songs will be sung with infinite joy before the throne of God and of the Lamb.[96] It will be called *a solemn day . . . even to the horn of the altar*, that is, even to the highest summit of contemplation, *among the branches* (Ps 117:27), that is, among all the throngs. The truth of all the figures and mysteries of all time since the beginning will then be revealed, and all things will be consummated by and in this silence. But because the silence is said to last for half an hour, I think this is really what is meant: that although all the elect will contemplate God in his glory, no creature may be understood to comprehend—to know as if actually seeing it—the fullness of the divine substance as it exists.[97] For God himself is incomprehensible, dwelling in light

---

[95] See Leviticus 25:10.

[96] Compare Numbers 29:35; Revelation 5:8-9.

[97] Unusually for Anselm, he here uses the first person singular—*puto*, "I think"—to emphasize his own agency in this reading of the Apocalypse, especially in the notion that all allegorical figures will be clarified in the end time.

inaccessible to every rational creature, whether man or angel.[98] Therefore the text mentions a half hour and not an entire hour, because that time suffices for beatitude even if none may attain such full knowledge of God himself as may fully comprehend his immense divinity.

Let no one then be amazed or protest if the church of God differs from that God who never changes in the variety of its laws and observances before the law, under the law, and under grace.[99] It was necessary that the signs of the spiritual graces grow in the succession of time. Those signs might thus proclaim the truth more and more fully, so that the knowledge of truth might be increased in time to effect salvation. So first came forth good things, then better, and finally the most excellent. This variety reflects not mutability in God, for he is *always the selfsame . . . whose years shall not fail* (Ps 102:28), but the fragility of the human race and the changing of times from generation to generation.[100]

[98] See 1 Timothy 6:16.

[99] Here Anselm adverts to the alternative, not incompatible, tripartite division of time whose great patristic source is, again, Augustine: see esp. *On the Trinity* 4.7, where Augustine reconciles the division of time into on the one hand six and on the other three great ages. The tripartite scheme was favored by Rupert of Deutz, whom he probably knew even before he encountered Norbert. Like Anselm, but writing a quarter of a century earlier, Rupert in his great work on the Trinity moved easily among different images and systems of numbering for epochs of historical and doctrinal development: see Rupert of Deutz, *De Trinitate et operibus suis* 3.36, PL 167, esp. cols. 324–26.

John Van Engen's discussion of Rupert's theology of history provides rich background for Anselm's *Anticimenon*. Although no direct textual correspondence links Anselm's work with Rupert's, the proximity of their ideas is marked, especially with regard to the agency of the Holy Spirit, in which Van Engen points out Rupert's innovative posture: *Rupert of Deutz*, 89–94. Nonetheless, Anselm's integration of a trinitarian plan for history with his use of the seven seals as a means for interpreting historical and future time departs from Rupert's model. Although Rupert wrote an extensive commentary on Revelation he did not view the seven seals historically: Rupert of Deutz, *Commentaria in Apocalypsim*, PL 169, esp. cols. 1007–09.

[100] Here, even more overtly than in his recurrent image of the eagle's youth, Anselm affirms that doctrinal and ecclesiastical development proceeds to the very apocalypse. So, by implication, his own times see the truth proclaimed "more and more fully" than not only the five prior great ages, *aetates*, of the church before Christ but also the three earlier stages, *status*, since the Incarnation—this despite the plague of hypocrisy in his own century's fourth stage.

Yet the church of the elect is one and subject to one God. She is one in the faith in which she steadfastly holds to those things we must believe about both past and future. She is one in the hope in which she patiently looks toward the things for which the faithful must hope. And she is one in the charity in which she loves God and her neighbor in God, and whose embrace she extends even to her enemies for God's sake.[101] The glory of that daughter of the king, that is of the church, is therefore within, in the beauty of the faith and in the testimony of a pure conscience, but she is clothed in golden threads, that is in the variety of forms of religious life and works.[102] She is *the chariot of God . . . attended by ten thousands, thousands of them that rejoice* (Ps 67:18).

Therefore from now on may none of the faithful suspect any scandal if the faith of the church remains the same even if her form of life changes. For the time being let this suffice to have answered those who slander so much variety in the holy church. Although those skeptics think wrongly, I hope that, if they may accept these honest responses to their questions, no scandal may otherwise offend them so that they despise any form of religious life or turn away from some religious community—if they are willing and if God, who draws all things to himself, presents it to them.

Here ends the first book.

[101] See 1 Corinthians 13:13.
[102] Psalm 44:14.

Prologue to the Remaining Books

Here begins the prologue of the second book of Anticimenon, or controversies.[1]

I thought that I had responded sufficiently in what I have written so far to those who complain of so much variety in the holy church—so many forms of religious life, so many changes, innovations, forms of profession. Now it seems that, although what I said to those skeptics evidently prevents them from assailing me further on that question, they have moved on to others, continually disturbing me. What they seemed before to do out of malicious zeal, though, they now seem to ask as men changed for the better, in an upright and humble spirit. I shall answer them willingly, as I have been commanded from above, because they ask humbly.[2] For *God, who resisteth the proud, but to the humble gives grace* (1 Pet 5:5), wishes us to be humble, so that he not resist us because of the arrogance of our questions and answers, rather give us grace and offer us understanding us because of our true humility. These same questioners say that I have responded sufficiently to the question they posed and that I was able to do this easily, further that they could easily agree after considering my many arguments and authorities. Moreover they acknowledge that nothing forbids different customs in the one faith, so long as the rite of the ecclesiastical sacraments is unchanged and the institutions of the

---

[1] This sentence is unlikely to be Anselm's own. The following passage clearly belongs with the second book, but its order in the text as well as its content suggest that it was written after *Anticimenon* 2 properly speaking. It is therefore represented here, as in the PL edition, as interstitial: Anselm, *Dialogi,* cols. 1159-62.

[2] Anselm reminds his reader of the papal commission to write about the Greeks he had mentioned in *Anticimenon* 1, Prologue.

ecclesiastical order are universal. Neither of these may be changed by anyone, else he is insane.

Yet why is it, these skeptics ask, that some in the church appear to disagree in regard to faith in the Holy Trinity and the rite of the sacraments, as the Greeks do from the Latins? Now if they should be different in everything else, so long as the unity of faith is preserved and the rite of the sacraments is one, such difference could be tolerated with little scandal or danger. But since the Greeks seem to hold different opinions about the faith—which cannot please God—and they practice the rite of the sacraments differently, you must respond to us on what our opinion should be, or what we should believe.

Indeed we admit that we are greatly scandalized when we hear that the wisest Greeks, learned in scriptures, neither believe nor aver that the Holy Spirit proceeds from the Son just as he also proceeds from the Father.[3] If this is the case, it is indeed the occasion for very grave scandal. Yet many thousands of Greek names are found in the catalogue of saints.[4] Their bodies were either buried in peace in Christ or sometimes they handed over their own bodies to punishment for God's sake, so washing their robes in the blood of the Lamb that they were awarded eternal crowns.[5] Many churches have been built and dedicated in these saints' honor, and their feasts are celebrated solemnly, far and wide among the churches, every year.

Moreover, in the holy Roman Church many pontiffs of Greek birth have sat upon the chair of the blessed Peter, prince of the

[3] On the deep origins of this difference between Eastern and Western churches through the patristic period see Henry Chadwick's lucid summary in *East and West: The Making of a Rift in the Church from Apostolic Times until the Council of Florence* (Oxford: Oxford University Press, 2003), 12–39.

[4] Anselm's own brief treatise on the litany of the saints, composed close to the time in which he was writing *Anticimenon*, emphasizes the essential unity of Greek and Roman faiths: Franz Winter, ed., *De ordine pronuntiandae letaniae ad Fridericum Magdeburgensem archiepiscopum*, in Winter, "Zur Geschichte des Bischofs Anselm von Havelberg," *Zeitschrift für Kirchengeschichte* 5 (1882): 144–55, at 145. Anselm further includes many Greek saints in his version of the litany: Winter, *De ordine*, 151–55.

[5] See Revelation 7:14.

apostles.[6] In his stead they have steered the church, the bark of Peter, with the rudder of correct faith and the oars of sound doctrine, so that they too are rightly counted among the number of the saints. This very same holy Roman Church, mother of all churches, received this privilege from the Lord—that she especially is so founded upon firm rock that no wind of heretical depravity may shake her. So it is astonishing, since the Greeks are counted among the number of the saints and Roman pontiffs have been chosen from them, that they have so erred in the faith in the Holy Trinity that they state and believe that the Holy Spirit proceeds only from the Father and not at all from the Son. This error is indeed astounding unless perhaps someone would dare say that it might be in accordance with the Christian faith or the salvation of believers for it to be insignificant what anyone said, even for someone not to hold any belief about this matter, as if that article of faith by which the Holy Spirit is held to proceed or not proceed from the Son were unnecessary for a Christian person. Then how, they ask, could it be that any Greek-born Roman pontiff might believe as do the Greeks that the Holy Spirit does not proceed from the Son, but might preach in the Roman Church as do the Latins that the same Spirit does proceed from the Son?[7] For these pontiffs to have believed in one way and preached in another is an abomination. But even if they believed one thing and preached otherwise, then how did the Roman Church listen to them without complaint, when she neither did then nor does now approve their doctrine concerning the procession of the Holy Spirit as only from the Father and not from the Son?

My questioners often raise these and similar issues in our meetings, sometimes in private and at other times openly before our brothers, urging me to respond even when I wish to remain silent.[8] Now at last, won over by their vehemence and numerous

---

[6] Below, Anselm names them: *Anticimenon* 3.13.

[7] Anselm is aware that between the second and the eighth century there were fourteen popes of Greek origin. For discussion of Greek presence and influence in Rome throughout this period see Bernard Schimmelpfennig, *The Papacy*, trans. James Sievert (New York: Columbia University Press, 1992), 62–64.

[8] Anselm here makes it clear that his own religious community has actively discussed these doctrinal variations. Although he has claimed papal assignment

entreaties, I am compelled to respond. Their relentlessness has made me set down my foot where before, in reading the divine scripture, I only passed over because its sense was clear.[9] Although I do not think myself able to resolve so important a question entirely—lest I seem to be altogether silent, giving no answer to the questioners and so offending the charity of my confrères, and since I may please them by speaking—I prefer to say something even if it must be amended later rather than offend, by maintaining silence, the generosity of those to whom I owe response. Moreover, the command of the Lord and of the blessed Pope Eugenius compels me to make this reply.[10] Just as I should deny nothing to the just and faithful demands of my brethren, still less do I dare disobey such commands. For me to write down my debate with Nicetas, archbishop of Nicomedia, in the royal city of Constantinople, recording it in dialogue form, will surely constitute a response to this question. Then it will be clear to the reader what the Greek on the one hand or the Latin on the other believes with regard to the procession of the Holy Spirit. The archbishop Nicetas was prominent among the Greeks as a model of religious life. He was keen in mind, deeply learned in the study of Greek letters, eloquent in his speech, and careful in interchange, never failing to mention anything supportive of his position or defeating ours. Moreover he was at that time the most eminent among the twelve chosen sages customarily presiding over the studies of the Greeks.[11] Therefore this Nicetas was selected from all those arguing against me to participate in our debate.

---

to the task he now assumes, his emphasis and his rhetorical posture here respond more directly to longstanding discussion with his confrères.

   [9] The author implies that the procession of the Holy Spirit is so plainly expressed in Scripture as through the Son as well as the Father that it would call for no special discussion if the Greeks had not challenged it.

   [10] Anselm's term here for fraternal affection is *caritas*, "charity," but in the sense of brotherly love rather than the narrower sense frequently accorded the English term in contemporary usage.

   [11] See again Michael Angold, *Church and Society in Byzantium under the Comneni, 1081–1261* (Cambridge: Cambridge University Press, 1995), 92–93.

BOOK 2

On The Procession of the Holy Spirit, Whether He Proceeds, as the Greeks Hold, Only from the Father Or, as the Latins Hold, from the Father and at the Same Time from the Son[12]

Chapter 1
How a dialogue was held in the city of Constantinople on the procession of the Holy Spirit by Anselm, bishop of Havelberg and Nicetas, archbishop of Nicomedia, and how translation of the interlocutors' words was done.

Since I was resident in the royal city and often exchanged questions on various matters with the Greeks, the devout emperor Kalojohn and N., a religious leader of the patriarchal city, decided to hold a public assembly, setting a day when the view of this side and of that might be set forth so that all might hear.[13] Many wise men convened in the Pisan district at the church of Hagia Irene, called Holy Peace in Latin, on the tenth day of April, if memory serves me.[14] The members of the imperial court took their places according to custom. Arbiters were appointed and notaries seated to take down faithfully in writing everything said

---

[12] For discussion of the historical development of this controversy, with emphasis on its long-term role in East-West schism, see Chadwick, *East and West*, 27–32, 89–94, 202–3, 211–18, 219–27.

[13] Norman Russell notes that the debates likely were heard by the patriarch Leo Stypes as well as John II Comnenus: Russell, "Anselm of Havelberg and the Union of Churches," *Sobornost* 1 (1979): 19–41; 2 (1980): 29–41, at 1:24.

[14] On the circumstances of this dialogue see again Anselm's references to his embassy to Constantinople in *Anticimenon* 1. Prologue and 10. See also Chadwick, *East and West*, 228–29; Jay T. Lees, *Anselm of Havelberg: Deeds into Words in the Twelfth Century* (Leiden: Brill, 1998), 42–45.

on either side. Then the whole multitude of listeners fell silent. Many Latins were also present, among them three wise men fluent in both languages and learned in letters. One, a Venetian by origin, was named James and another, a Pisan by nationality, was named Burgundio. A third, one Moses, was eminent even beyond the others, for he was the most illustrious of either people in the teaching of both Greek and Latin letters. He was an Italian by origin, from the city of Bergamo, and was chosen from all the rest to be the faithful interpreter for both sides.[15] Then when all was ready, the seats arranged by the hearers' respective regions of origin, silence fell and everyone waited eagerly to listen.

Anselm, bishop of Havelberg, spoke first: "Reverend fathers, I did not come here seeking conflict, for the apostle says, *not in contention and envy* (Rom 13:13). Again he says, *if any man seem to be contentious, we have no such custom* (1 Cor 11:16). Rather I have come to inquire concerning and come to know better the faith we share—and above all I have come because you have so wished."

Nicetas, archbishop of Nicomedia responded: "What you say is pleasing, and your humility pleases us as well, for truth emerges more quickly in humble conversation than in any arrogant disputation aimed at victory."[16]

Anselm, bishop of Havelberg, rejoined: "We should remember what is written in the Gospel when Jesus joined *two disciples going* from Jerusalem to the village *of Emmaus and they talked together* about him. He went with them.[17] *And . . . they knew him in the breaking of the bread* (Luke 24:35). So if we also wish to travel together speaking about the truth without disputing, then that very Truth will draw near us. We will recognize this truth in the breaking of bread, the opening up of divine scriptures. Therefore let us walk together in the path of charity, not contending in prideful argument but following the path of truth together, searching it out humbly."

---

[15] On the translators see Lees, *Deeds into Words*, 44 n. 23; 46 n. 28.

[16] Both interlocutors immediately set a tone of mutual rapport and openness.

[17] Compare Luke 24:13-15. Anselm's concern here about the accuracy of translation—not only its content but also its tone—bespeaks his lengthy experience of negotiation with the Byzantines, in which he must have seen many conversations go awry because of inaccurate translation.

Nicetas, archbishop of Nicomedia, then said: "It seems to me that the appointed interpreter should translate what we are about to say word for word, because in this way we can better understand each other, and he can easily do this."

Anselm, bishop of Havelberg, replied: "But I do not speak in this way and such translation is suspect, in my view, because I can be misunderstood word by word if the translation is inexact, and we should not quibble over words. Rather the translation between us should gather and then set forth our respective speech as it develops, in its full meaning. In this way of speaking and translating we shall examine thoughts rather than be fixed on their expression."[18]

Nicetas, archbishop of Nicomedia, then said: "Let it be as you say, for this pleases me if it pleases you."

Anselm, bishop of Havelberg, responded: "I wish to suggest something further. We propose to address a difficult question, but I was called suddenly to this conference and have reflected on none of this before, even yesterday or the day before yesterday. Therefore I beg the consideration of all sitting and standing here that, if some word offensive to the ears of some of you escapes me, as sometimes happens in such situations, you not immediately clap your hands against me but wait patiently with your accustomed courtesy, remembering that I am a guest among you.[19] Because I was fearful of just such quick offense in word-for-word translation, I asked that our conversation not be so treated. So let no battle of words arise between us, but let us carefully discern the truth of each other's thoughts."

Nicetas, bishop of Nicomedia, responded: "You have spoken well. I too request this very thing."

The whole crowd then affirmed: "This is good, an honorable way to proceed—so be it, so be it!"

---

[18] The interlocutor Anselm's concern about the accuracy of translation bespeaks his belief, expressed below and throughout, that isolated terms have needlessly become obstacles to the unity of the faith.

[19] Cultural difference is evidently maintained here, such that the Latin interlocutor is dismayed by the Greek custom of applauding as a negative comment on the course of discussion.

Anselm, bishop of Havelberg, then said: "Following holy and apostolic teaching we believe and teach that the Father, Son, and Holy Spirit are one God in substance, three in their persons. We also believe that the Father is begotten of no other, that the Son is begotten by the Father, and that the Holy Spirit proceeds from both, that is from both the Father and the Son. We believe and we teach this."[20]

Nicetas, archbishop of Nicomedia, replied: "You say that these things are catholic teachings and that we must accept them, but you say that the Holy Spirit proceeds from the Son just as from the Father. With this we do not agree nor do we accept it, for no rational argument nor authority of canonical scriptures—finally no general council—says or teaches this very thing."[21]

Anselm, bishop of Havelberg, answered: "You have posited three supports for your position: reason, the authority of the canonical scriptures, and general councils. You posited reason first. Therefore I should like first to know by what reasoning you are prevented from believing or stating that the Holy Spirit proceeds from the Son just as from the Father."

Nicetas, archbishop of Nicomedia, replied: "In all learning, but especially in lofty theology, we must fear *polyarchia*, that is, multiplicity of principles.[22] The wisest of the Greeks have indeed

[20] Here and below, Anselm refers generally to the elements of the Nicene Creed as established by the First Council of Nicaea in 325 and affirmed by subsequent ecumenical councils. See Norman P. Tanner, ed., *Decrees of the Ecumenical Councils 1: Nicaea I to Lateran V*, vol. 1 (London: Sheed and Ward, 1990), 4–5. See also Jaroslav Pelikan and Valerie Hotchkiss, eds., *Creeds and Confessions of Faith in the Christian Tradition*, vol. 1 (New Haven: Yale University Press, 2003), 158–67.

[21] Beginning here, Nicetas's extended explanation of Greek resistance to the *filioque* looks back to a response to the Western position by Photios I, ninth-century patriarch of Constantinople: Photios, *On the Mystagogy of the Holy Spirit*, trans. Holy Transfiguration Monastery (Astoria, NY: Studion, 1983), 70–123. For an introduction to Photios's position see Chadwick, *East and West*, 153–63. Although the central elements in Nicetas's argument mirror Photios's, the Greek spokesman of *Anticimenon* is clearly indebted to centuries of intervening discussion. His tone is markedly more irenic.

[22] Anselm's term *principium*—principle, origin, or beginning—is here generally translated as "principle" according to the widely accepted philosophical usage. Occasionally, however, when the context implies physicality or temporality, it is rendered as "origin."

avoided it thus far, as indeed they also have avoided *anarchia*, that is, the absence of principle. On the other hand, those same sages have carefully identified *monarchia*, that is, singularity of principle, teaching us to accept this reverently. Thence they have refused to accept that God be of plural principles, *polyarchos*, for this would only impute conflict to him, as they have said. But neither have they wished to acknowledge that God might be *anarchos*, without principle, because, as they have said, anything without principle is disordered. So the Greek sages, appropriately avoiding the latter two positions, have thoughtfully turned to reverent acceptance of *monarchia*. So we, too, reverently accept and embrace this notion. All orthodoxy must accept it.[23]

"Further, if there were two principles, either the two would by themselves be respectively insufficient or the second would be superfluous, for if something were lacking to the prior of the two, that first principle would not be supremely perfect. At the same time, if nothing were lacking to the first, given the presence of the second, and if everything were present in the first, then the second would be superfluous. So we believe that the Father, Son, and Holy Spirit are one God—the Father begotten by no other, the Son truly begotten of the Father, and the Holy Spirit proceeding only from the Father and not from the Son. If we were to say that the Holy Spirit proceeds from both the Father and the Son, such that the Father were the principle of the Holy Spirit and likewise

---

[23] Here and below, as the two interlocutors carry forward an extensive discussion of the problem of principle among the persons of the Trinity, neither names specific patristic or more recent sources. As Russell points out, however, their discussion here owes much to Gregory Nazianzen, *Oratio* 29.2. Russell suggests that this Greek Father's relevant texts may have been the direct object of Nicetas's and Anselm's discussions: "Anselm of Havelberg," *Sobornost* 1:26 n. 29. Gregory's thought suffuses much of *Anticimenon*'s second book: see also Giles E. M. Gasper, *Anselm of Canterbury and His Theological Inheritance* (Aldershot: Ashgate, 2004), 25–26. Yet the course of the conversation here, despite this indebtedness, seems to be substantially original, only loosely founded on the long theological exchange about this issue among Gregory, Augustine, and many other authors, both Latin and Greek. In general both speakers ground their arguments in logic and Scripture without appeal to intermediate authorities. In *Anticimenon* 2.7 below, however, Anselm begins to name patristic sources. For a précis of Anselm's and Nicetas's arguments see Chadwick, *East and West*, 229–30.

the Son the principle of the Spirit, then we would be imputing two principles to the Spirit, and we would err in attributing *polyarchia*, that is, plurality of principles, to that Spirit. But this is contrary to all reason. Therefore we believe and teach that the Father is the principle of the Son whom he begot and the same Father is the principle of the Holy Spirit who proceeded from him alone. Thus we affirm that the Father is the principle of both not in time but in cause, for both are from the Father as if from one principle, the one by begetting and the other by procession—not temporally but causally."

Chapter 2
That in the Lord there is not *anarchia*, absence of principle, nor is there *polyarchia*, plurality of principle, but rather *monarchia*, singularity of principle.

Anselm, bishop of Havelberg, then said: "With you I deny plurality of principles in God, that he might be *polyarchon*, as you say, since that is contrary to all reason. A certain heresiarch called Manes, a Persian by nationality, from whom arose the Manichaeans who polluted nearly all of Africa, was rightly condemned by the catholic church for arguing the existence of two principles and for teaching several other things contrary to the Christian faith.[24] I utterly reject, as you do, that God might be what you term *anarchos*, that is, that there be in God an absence of principle or no principle because God, unless he were himself the highest of principles, would then exist without himself, and if he were to exist without himself then certainly he would not exist at all. Therefore we must say neither that God has multiple principles, else he would be in conflict with himself, nor that he has no principle, else he would lack order. Each of those alternatives threatens his dissolution and destruction. For if we say that God has multiple principles, then much conflict must follow, or if we say that God has no principle, no order would maintain. Either case, I repeat, is entirely absurd, since again either predicates God's dissolution and destruction, in

---

[24] Anselm had described the Manichean heresy in the same language of principles, *principia*, in *Anticimenon* 1.6.

the first instance because of conflict and in the second because of disorder. Therefore with you I maintain that God has one principle, as you say that he is *monarchos*, since he is himself the highest and complete principle, and he is himself patently his own principle. What might be beyond him and outside him would be without principle, but nothing of this sort exists. So God has no multiplicity of principles, nor is he without principle, rather he is his own unique principle in himself, alone possessing absolute and exclusive monarchical power. Just as he is his own life by which he lives, so too is he his own principle by which he is governed.[25]

"But you say that if the Holy Spirit proceeds from the Father and from the Son, two principles then exist. I judge, though, that your argument should by no means be accepted with such hastily constructed proof. In fact, your false inference does not follow from your premise. It is true that the Holy Spirit proceeds from the Father and from the Son but false that there are therefore two principles, so your argument falls apart.[26] Pay attention, then, in all charity. We say, for our part, that the Holy Spirit proceeds from the Father and from the Son, but we do not concede that God therefore has two principles, because the Father and the Son together are one principle just as they are one God. In the same way we say that God comes from God, yet not that there are two gods. Again similarly we say in figurative terms that light comes from light, yet we do not mean two lights of different substance. We say too that wisdom comes from wisdom, yet not that two wisdoms exist. So too we say rightly that a principle comes from a principle, yet not that there are two principles. When the Lord was asked in the Gospel: *Who art thou?* he responded: *the beginning who also speak unto you* (John 8:25). So he revealed himself to be one and the

---

[25] Anselm's wordplay, responding to Nicetas's turnings on variants of Greek *archia*, supports his meaning, but is lost in English. Here he states of God: *ipse est sibi principium quo principatur.* The Latin *principium* is etymologically close to a verb for ruling, *principare.*

[26] Ironically, given the interlocutors' respective roles and cultures, Anselm controverts Nicetas's argument on the basis of a logical flaw, not revealed truth. Anselm says below that the Greeks typically fall into theological error in their fascination with philosophy: *Anticimenon* 2.21.

same principle as the Father in unity with that Father's substance, but from that principle in his person as Son.

"Certainly we must consider what is said in the Gospel—about what it was said, for what reason, and in what way.[27] For since the Lord says: *the beginning who also speak unto you*, and since he does not say, 'the beginning and I am speaking to you,' he clearly meant that he is one with the Father in common substance but not one with the Father in the distinction of his person. For the Son is the same principle as the Father himself in his substance, but not the same as the Father in his person. We can also understand this in another way in his saying: *the beginning who also speak unto you*, that is, that he also wishes to reveal himself to be the creator, the principle of creation, just as the Father is the principle of creation because all things are from him. Thus in the book of Genesis: *In the beginning God created heaven and earth* (Gen 1:2). So hear the evangelist John, saying that Christ himself is the principle in the beginning and with the beginning: *In the beginning was the Word, and the Word was with God . . . . All things were made by him, and without him was made nothing that was made. In him was life* (John 1:1-4). And in the Psalms: *With thee is the principality in the day of thy strength* (Ps 109:3). Consequently we call the Father, in relation to creation, the principle from which all things exist. We also call the Son, in relation to creation, the principle through whom all things exist. And we further call the Holy Spirit, in relation to creation, the principle in whom all things exist. Yet these are not three principles. They are not three creators, since the works of the Trinity are inseparable. Therefore God as one, not as two or three, is called the principle in relation to creation.

"Just as these principles relate mutually within the Trinity, the one who begets is the principle of the one begotten, that is, the Father is the principle of the Son because he begets him. Whether the Father is rightly called the principle of the Holy Spirit because

---

[27] Throughout this book Anselm has in mind Augustine's discussion of the Holy Spirit in *On the Trinity*, especially its final book, 15. Here, however, he seems to advert to Augustine's opening discussion of exegetical and theological principles in *On the Trinity* 1.28 (*The Trinity*, ed. John E. Rotelle, trans. Edmund Hill [Brooklyn, NY: New City Press, 1991], 86).

the Spirit proceeds from him, and whether the Son is rightly called the principle of the Holy Spirit because the Spirit also proceeds from him, is doubtful to some. But if the one given, the Holy Spirit, has as his principle that very other by whom he is given, and if indeed he takes his principle from no other source than him whence he proceeds, then we must acknowledge that the Father and the Son together are the principle of the Holy Spirit. Yet Father and Son are not therefore two principles because, just as the Father and the Son are one God, so too in relation to the Holy Spirit they are one principle. Clearly, then, the Holy Spirit is given and proceeds from nowhere other than the Father and the Son together as one principle. The Father is the principle and the Son is the same principle, for if the Son were other than the Father then he would not be the same principle as the Father. He would already exist in this other thing and would cease being a principle. Therefore let us attribute to the Son whatever we have attributed to the Father. If the Father is in the Son and the Son is in the Father, and if everything of the Father is also of the Son, while everything of the Son is also of the Father, then the Father's principle is the Son's principle, that is, the principle that is the Father is the principle that is the Son. So the Holy Spirit, proceeding from both, namely from Father and Son, has a singular principle in his procession, not two principles. We then describe the principle in the Father as in three modes: in substance in regard to himself; in relation in regard to the other persons of the Trinity, as Father to Son; and again in relation as Creator in regard to creation."

Chapter 3
That that which is eternal is not therefore without a principle, for the Son is coeternal with the Father but he is not without a principle because he is from the Father.

"Perhaps you wonder that coeternal beings are not called *synarcha*, mutual principles or co-beginnings. There we must note that whatever has no principle is eternal, but what is eternal is not on that account without principle. To be sure, the Father, Son, and Holy Spirit are three persons entirely mutually coeternal and coequal, but they are not at the same time entirely without principle, for the

Father is indeed *anarchos*, without principle, yet he is the coequal principle of his coeternal and consubstantial Son. So he is the principle with respect to cause, source, and eternal light. Although the Son is coeternal and consubstantial with the Father, nevertheless he is in no way *anarchos*, without principle, since he has the Father as his principle and cause, and the Father himself is the principle of the universe. Rather, when I say "principle" you should not infer any intervention of time or interpose anything between him who begets and him who is begotten. Nor should you think to divide their nature by some ill-conceived and ill-established separation between persons always coeternal. If time were older than the Son, then the Father would be the first cause of time rather than of the Son.[28] The Son would then not have been the maker of temporal succession but would have existed in time. Nor would the Son have been the Lord of all by nature but rather assumed into the power of the Father by grace—or not even have been Lord at all. In sum, the Son would be cast out from deity as not coeternal with the Father but constituted under time.

"Therefore the Father is the principle of the Son in respect to cause and the Father is, with the Son, the principle of the Holy Spirit in respect to cause. But a cause is clearly not prior in time to those things it causes any more than the sun is older than its own light. Thus evidently all three persons are mutually coeternal and coequal but the three are not alike in lacking a causal principle. The Father is, as you say, *anarchos*, that is, without temporal or causal principle, because he exists of himself, not from anywhere outside himself. But the Son is not *anarchos*, for he has the Father

---

[28] Here Anselm refers in Aristotelian terms to the first of four causes, *prima causa*, the efficient cause. Anselm is concerned that the categories of causation support his argument that the Son is cocreator. For an introduction to this usage see Etienne Gilson, *The Spirit of Medieval Philosophy*, trans. A. H. C. Downes (New York: Scribner, 1940), 84–107. On the Aristotelian tradition of God as efficient cause see, more recently, John Marenbon, *Medieval Philosophy: An Historical and Philosophical Introduction* (London: Routledge, 2007), esp. 183–84. As *Anticimenon* 2.23ff. below testifies, Anselm was familiar with such discussion from Abelard's theological works. Here see Peter King, "Chapter 3: Metaphysics," in *Cambridge Companion to Abelard*, ed. Jeffrey E. Brower and Kevin Guilfoy (Cambridge: Cambridge University Press, 2004), 103–5. Here, as well, Anselm seems to respond again to Gregory of Nazianzus: see *Oratio* 29.3.

not as his temporal but as his causal principle, if you understand his principle as outside of time in the sense that the Son is also *anarchos* and the Holy Spirit too is *anarchos*, without a principle in time. The Trinity, the maker of temporal succession, did not indeed begin with time or under time. All the Trinity—Father, Son, and Holy Spirit together—is one God. So too it embraces one and the same principle, as you call it *monarchos*, *pantokratoun*, that is, one in principle, one authority governing all things, in his substance. The Trinity expresses no duality of principle—in your terms, then, is not *diarchos* or *triarchos*.[29]

"So we read in the Athanasian creed honored throughout the church that the Father is eternal, the Son eternal, and the Holy Spirit eternal, yet there are not three eternal beings but one.[30] The Father is beyond measure, the Son beyond measure, and the Holy Spirit beyond measure, and yet there are not three immeasurable entities but one. And the Father is God, the Son is God, and the Holy Spirit is God, yet there are not three gods but one God. The Father is Lord, the Son is Lord, and the Holy Spirit is Lord, yet there are not three lords but one Lord. So too the Father is the principle, the Son is the principle, and the Holy Spirit is the principle, yet there are not three principles but one. All together and at the same time are one principle, but each is in himself a complete and perfect principle. But although we rightly call the three persons consubstantial, yet we do not properly say that they are consubstances, so perhaps we rightly say that the three persons are principles together, yet we do not rightly call them three mutual principles—as the Greeks say that they are *synarcha*, for which notion the Latins have no term.

"Now perhaps someone wishing only to argue, or someone led astray by a false opinion, thinks then that two principles might be said to exist because when a principle is said to lack its own principle, or again if a principle is said to be from another principle,

[29] See Gregory Nazianzen, *Oratio* 29.3.

[30] Anselm refers to the creed attributed to the fourth-century anti-Arian Athanasius, bishop of Alexandria, but probably first written in Latin and witnessed in sixth-century Western sources: see Pelikan and Hotchkiss, eds., *Creeds and Confessions*, vol. 1, 673–77.

there seem then to be two principles. But such an argument omits to note that we rightly say that God is not from God as Father but as Son, yet there are not on this account two gods. Again we rightly say that light is not from light and yet is indeed from light, but there are not two lights. Then if we said that the principle that is the Father is not the principle that is the Son, and that the principle that is the Son is not the principle that is the Father, and from this we wished to infer two principles, then we would be altogether mistaken, since we may not call the principle that is the Father the principle that is the Son, and when we say that the principle that is the Son is not the principle that is the Father we understand or state nothing else than that the Father is not the Son and the Son is not the Father, even as we always distinguish their persons.

"So according to the distinction of persons we rightly state this negatively: that the principle that is the Father is not the principle that is the Son, and the principle that is the Son is not the principle that is the Father. But according to the identity of their shared essence we rightly state positively that the Father is the same principle as the Son and the Son is the same principle as the Father. Although the one is not the other, nevertheless that one is what the other is. Although the one is not the same as the other, nevertheless it is the same as what that other is. And although the other is not the same, it is that which he is. Nor is the one himself the other, but they are both the very same thing—always one God, always one principle. Never are there two gods, never two majesties, never two principles.

"Then if the Holy Spirit does not proceed from the Son, as you consider is the case, show if you can how he might truly proceed from the Father! For if as you say we must believe that the Spirit does not proceed from the Son, we must also believe—although you deny this—that he does not proceed from the Father, since the Father and the Son are one, as Christ himself says: *I and the Father are one* (John 10:30). Again he says: I am in the Father, and the Father is in me.[31] Therefore he who says that the Holy Spirit proceeds from the Father who is in the Son must also say that the same Holy Spirit proceeds from the Son who is in the Father. Or

[31] See John 10:38.

if he denies that the Spirit proceeds from the Son, he is also forced to deny that the same Holy Spirit proceeds from the Father who is in the Son, for the Father and the Son are one. When we say in turn that the Son is in the Father, then we understand that the one is in the other not as different in substance but as one and the same in substance. Thus the Lord answered Philip's demand, *Lord, show us the Father and it is enough for us,* by saying: *Philip, he that seeth me seeth the Father also . . .* because *I am in the Father and the Father is in me* (John 14:8-9). On this account we speak of the unity of the Son's substance with the Father's. And when the text says, *I and the Father are one,* 'one' refers to the unity of their substance. This point is against Arius.[32]

"And 'are' refers to the plurality of their persons. This latter point is against Sabellius.[33] It is as if the Son said, I and the Father are one, that is, I am what he is according to substance. So in this way we seem to have concluded that—while you wish to persuade me not to believe that the Holy Spirit proceeds from the Son, so that I do not fall into the error of asserting two principles—you are therefore compelled to deny what you first believed, that the Holy Spirit proceeds only from the Father. In this you have fallen into such a snare that, although you set out to deny procession from the Son and affirm something else, procession from the Father, now either you dare confess neither according to your prior position or, to affirm rightly as I do, according to the catholic faith and the argument we have set forth."

Nicetas, archbishop of Nicomedia, then responded: "Your reasoning about this matter of principle is compelling. But while you say that the Holy Spirit proceeds from the Father and the Son, you do not admit two principles, and you demonstrate this through the unity of Father and Son. By the same reasoning we might prove that the same Holy Spirit proceeds from himself as from the Father and the Son, since Father, Son, and Holy Spirit are one divine essence. Thus if he proceeds from those others with whom he is one in substance, we must also say that he proceeds from himself as one in substance with the other persons."

---

[32] Anselm had treated Arius in *Anticimenon* 1.9.
[33] Again see above, *Anticimenon* 1.9.

Chapter 4
That just as the Father begot, but did not beget himself, and just as the Son was begotten, but not by himself, so too the Holy Spirit proceeds, but not from himself.

Anselm, bishop of Havelberg, then said: "The Father is God, the Son is God, and the Holy Spirit is God, yet there are not three gods but one. And although we say rightly that God the Father begot God the Son, since there is one God, nevertheless we cannot rightly say about God the Father, 'God the Father begot himself,' nor can we rightly say of God the Son, 'God the Son was begotten by himself.' So too, although the Father, Son, and Holy Spirit are one God and we rightly believe that the Holy Spirit proceeds from the Father and the Son, nevertheless we cannot therefore correctly say that he proceeds from himself. Although the Spirit is one in substance with the Father and the Son, he is by no means the same as the Father or the Son such that he might proceed from himself as he proceeds from them. Therefore just as the Father begot but did not beget himself, and just as the Son was begotten but not by himself, so too the Holy Spirit proceeds but not from himself. The Gospel of John reveals this in the text about the Holy Spirit: *For he shall not speak of himself, but what things soever he shall hear he shall speak* (John 16:13). This speech will not come from the Spirit because he is not of himself, and because he is not of himself neither does he—whose essence is the same as that which proceeds—proceed from himself. Therefore whence he exists, thence he proceeds, and whence he proceeds, thence he exists. His being consists in his procession. Just as the role proper to the Father is to beget the Son, and just as the role proper to the Son is for the Father to beget him, so too the role proper to the Holy Spirit is to proceed from both as if from one principle."

Nicetas, archbishop of Nicomedia, answered: "We intended to treat of the procession of the Holy Spirit, but in order to prove your opinion you have adduced your thought on the Father as begetting and the Son as begotten. You have done so appropriately, for I acknowledge that your arguments are satisfying. But respond now to this question: what is the procession of the Holy Spirit of which we speak, or how does it occur? Does it seem true to you that we must say that the Holy Spirit proceeds according to the substance common to the other persons or according to his discrete and proper person?"

Chapter 5
That just as we do not understand how the Father is begotten by no other or the Son is begotten, so too we do not understand how the Holy Spirit eternally proceeds.

Anselm, bishop of Havelberg, then said: "Tell me how the Father is begotten by no other and how the Son is begotten, and I shall then tell you how the Holy Spirit proceeds! But we should both be foolish to pry so into divine mysteries, wishing to find rational explanation for these things we know to be ineffable, beyond all the comprehension of any rational creature. They surpass all human, even all angelic understanding in their profundity and sublimity. But if you press me and if you wish to be irksome over this question, then suffice it to hear what it suffices for me to believe: the Father is begotten by no other, the Son is begotten, and the Holy Spirit proceeds. This is enough for my belief. As I see it, how the Father is begotten by no other, how the Son is begotten, or how the third person proceeds should be honored in reverent silence. Our role is so to believe these great matters as not to investigate how they are so with our intellectual curiosity, for to understand how is granted not even to the angels, much less to us.[34] But the Father who begot, the Son who was begotten, and the Holy Spirit who proceeded from both all understand the Son's divine, eternal generation and the Holy Spirit's divine, eternal procession in that conscious rationality only they eternally possess. So they know the manner and character of the Spirit's generation and procession, but these matters are inaccessible to the dark cloud of human lowliness in which vanity sometimes works against truth. Yet I think that we say appropriately that the Father always was and is begotten by no other, that the Son always was and is as begotten, and that the

---

[34] The speaker implies that Nicetas's urgency in inquiry verges on the sacrilegious. As Russell suggests ("Anselm of Havelberg," *Sobornost* 1:29–30), he seems again to refer to Gregory of Nazianzus: *Faith Gives Fullness* 31.8, trans. Wickham and Williams, 282–83.

Holy Spirit always was and is as proceeding. The Father's begetting accords with that Father's essence, the Son's being begotten at the same time accords with his essence, and the Holy Spirit's procession accords correspondingly with that very Spirit's essence. Neither one nor the other is before or after with respect to time."

Chapter 6
That being is one thing in the highest Trinity and another thing in Father, Son, and Holy Spirit.

"Nevertheless in that highest Trinity the act of begetting does not constitute being, nor does being begotten, nor does procession. For the Father does not exist for that reason, nor does the Son, nor the Holy Spirit. Yet therefore their substance is one in the Trinity. But in respect to the Father's begetting, the Son's being begotten, and the Holy Spirit's coming forth in procession, their persons are not one but three. In substance, rather in that essence in which they are three, they are also one, yet in the personality by which the three are distinguished they are again three. As I have said, in the Trinity there is no being who is the Father, nor is there the Son, nor the Holy Spirit who proceeds, rather that being who is God—great, good, and wise. And the three persons are proper to each respectively even as each alone and all together are one in substance."

Chapter 7
Why the Holy Spirit alone is so called, and why he is the third person of the Trinity— that this is not a level of dignity but an order of enumeration and the designation of a distinct person.

"Certainly the Father is a spirit and he is holy, but he is not the Holy Spirit, the third person of the Trinity. The Son too is a spirit and holy, but neither is he the Holy Spirit, the third person of the Trinity. Likewise the Holy Spirit is a spirit and holy, but he alone is rightly called the Holy Spirit and the third person of the Trinity. Perhaps for this reason the Holy Spirit alone is properly called the Holy Spirit: that he alone by the breath of deity joins himself and the other two together in one essence, ineffably distinguishing and wondrously conjoining their unity in Trinity and their trinity in unity. Therefore let us believe that their highest unity and trinity embraces both distinct persons and persons conjoined distinctly—a paradox completely beyond all human understanding, inconceivable to it. So the Holy Spirit is the coeternal bond between the other two persons, the communion of those two and their concord, charity, sweetness, and sanctity.[35] For what sort of being is God the Father if not holy? And what is the Son of God if not holy? If you take away this holiness from God the Father or from God the Son, in removing it you also remove their divinity. For how might divinity not be holy? Would it not be imperfect if it were not holy? Would that divinity not rather be nothing at all if it were not holy? Therefore because the Holy Spirit, as I have said, is the coeternal holiness of the other two, we rightly say that this Holy Spirit is one with the Father and the Son in their common holiness, fulfilling the Trinity in the character of his person. Further, the unity of the substance the spirit shares with them is undivided, simple and one in him. It remains so eternally undivided, simple, and one in him since no number is ever withdrawn from him. This for us is the one God.

"The plurality of divine persons originates in unity eternally and causally, not temporally. It is moved—as I have thus said—toward duality but is coeternal in its procession, so remaining eternally in the coeternal Trinity and embracing the number of the Holy Trinity outside all time. This Trinity is for us the Father, Son, and Holy Spirit. They are one although they are three in number, since one person is the Father's, another the Son's, and another the Holy Spirit's, and although only one person is the Father's, two persons are the Father's and the Son's, and three persons are the Father's, Son's, and Holy Spirit's. But still no difference in dignity can be discerned in this same coeternal Trinity. Nowhere in any writings of those who treat of the Holy Trinity, as I believe, do we find—as if in order of dignity—first the person of the Father and second the person of the Son. We sometimes find the person of the Holy Spirit as the third person in the Trinity, but we say this not according to his level of dignity but in distinction or designation

[35] See Augustine, *On the Trinity* 15.37, (Rotelle, ed., *Trinity*, 424).

of his discrete and singular person. For the Trinity is not ordered successively in dignity, rather is contained by number and equal in dignity, so that indeed it embraces three persons continually and at once. The first, second, and third persons are not so called in rank, that is, in their respective degrees of discrete and ordered dignity. Rather the very number three indicates in its plurality not degrees of respective dignity but the plurality of the Trinity. Further, when the Holy Spirit is called the third person in the Trinity, he is not called third with respect to the first or second person as if he were lesser in dignity, but he is called third—that is, one among three—by the particular designation of his person.

"Augustine, that bishop of the city of Hippo and outstanding doctor, spoke thus when he wrote to Orosius: 'And the Spirit of the Lord, the third person in the Trinity, was borne over the waters.'[36] Again he wrote in the book of *Questions on the Old and New Testament*, in Chapter 113: 'Why should the Son of God be sent, and not another? The devil wished to be called god after God the Father. He strives after that even now, although that can never happen because the Son of God is second after God the Father, not in nature but in order.'[37] Likewise Augustine said in the same book, in Chapter 195, writing against Eusebius: 'The Holy Spirit is third in order, not in nature, nor in rank, nor in divinity, nor in person, nor in ignorance. Just as the Son of God is second to the Father but not lesser in divinity, so too the Holy Spirit follows after the Son, not as unequal but as equal in the divinity of his substance.'[38] So Hilary, bishop of Poitiers, a famous and eloquent defender of the universal faith in ancient times, said in *On Trinity*, Book 12: 'The Son is the true God from you, O God the Father. We must thus confess him after you and with you as begotten by you, because you are the eternal author of his eternal origin, for because he is

---

[36] Here and immediately below Anselm makes use of later works wrongly attributed to Augustine by medieval authors: see Pseudo-Augustine, *Dialogus quaestionum 65 Orosii percontantis et Augustini respondentis*, PL 40, cols. 733-52.

[37] Pseudo-Augustine, *Quaestiones veteris et novi testamenti 127*, 113.5, ed. Alexander Souter, Corpus scriptorum ecclesiasticorum latinorum 50 (Vienna: F. Tempsky, 1908), 301.

[38] *Quaestiones veteris et novi testamenti*, in fact 125.22, CSEL 50, ed. Souter, 391–92.

from you, he is second to you.'[39] He is second, I say, in his mode of existence, not in the degree of his dignity. Indeed, the Son sits next to God the Father as if in the first place, while the Holy Spirit sits as in the second place from the Father but next to the Son.

"Hence the priest Jerome—learned in Latin, Greek, and Hebrew letters—also calls the Father the principal spirit in the Son, saying this in his work on the three virtues: 'David assumes three spirits in the psalm, saying, *Strengthen me with a perfect spirit* (Ps 50:14). *Renew a right spirit within my bowels* (Ps 50:12). *Take not thy holy spirit from me* (Ps 50:13).' Who are these three spirits? The perfect spirit is the Father, the right spirit is the Son, the holy spirit is the Holy Spirit himself.[40] And so the Holy Spirit is second from the Father but first after Christ according to the order in which we speak of him, naming him so in an orderly and proper mode, that is, according to the way of being and pattern of numbering inhering in their persons, not according to any difference in their dignity. Certainly the Father is from no one, the Son is from the Father alone, and the Holy Spirit draws his being from them both. Therefore you should imagine, as I have said, no lesser degree of nature or of dignity, rather an order in mode of being and in order of speaking.

"Likewise Augustine says in his book of *Questions on the Old and New Testament*, Chapter 22, regarding their origin: 'The Son

---

[39] Hilary of Poitiers, *Trinity* 12.54, trans. Stephen McKenna (New York: Fathers of the Church, 1954), 541.

[40] Anselm may have found this patristic quotation in Abelard's *Christian Theology*, to which he makes further unacknowledged reference below, in *Anticimenon* 2.23ff. Abelard had brought together the same references to Hilary (in Anselm's prior paragraph) and an author he named as Jerome: see Abelard, *Theologia Christiana* 1.67, in his *Opera Theologica*, vol. 2: *Theologia Christiana*, ed. Eligius M. Buytaert (Turnhout: Brepols, 1969), 99–100. Neither medieval author realized that the work on virtues he cited was falsely attributed: Pseudo-Jerome, *Epistolae* 8, PL 30, col. 117. Compare Jerome's translation of Origen in *Homiliae Origenis in Jeremiam et Ezechialem*, PL 25, col. 626. Gillian Evans notes the general proximity of *Anticimenon's* discussion here to Abelard's but argues for no direct dependence: Gillian R. Evans, "Anselm of Canterbury and Anselm of Havelberg: The Controversy with the Greeks," *Analecta Praemonstratensia* 53 (1977): 158–75, at 164–66. On the proximity of Abelard's various works and Anselm's text, see also Russell, "Anselm of Havelberg," *Sobornost* 1:37 n. 72; Hermann Josef Sieben, *Die Konzilsidee des lateinischen Mittelalters (847–1378)* (Paderborn: Schöningh, 1984), 157 and n. 17, 161.

differs in no way from the Father—certainly he does not differ at all in substance—because he is the true Son. Yet he differs in cause or in order because all potency from the Father is in the Son. So even if in substance the Son is not lesser, nevertheless in authority the Father is greater, as the Lord himself gives witness when he says: *If you loved me, you would indeed be glad because I go to the Father, for the Father is greater than I* (John 14:28). The apostle Paul shares this interpretation: *There is but one God, the Father, of whom are all things, and we unto him, and one Lord Jesus . . . by whom are all things, and we by him* (1 Cor 8:6). Thus the first in order is that of which all things are, the second is that by which all things are, the third is that in which all things are. None of them is lesser, but all are indicated in the unity of God, as the Apostle says: *For of him and by him and in him are all things. To him be the glory forever, amen* (Rom 11:36).'[41] So reason demands and catholic faith teaches that in our designation of the Trinity such proper order of verbal expression be observed—that is, Father, Son, and Holy Spirit. Although equal in dignity, they cannot be named in speech at one and the same time, and although they share the unity of self-same majesty, they also maintain the Trinity as discrete in personality but with no distinction of dignity, yet admitting of order in oral expression. The Son of God himself, who knew all, plainly taught this order in the Trinity when he spoke thus to the disciples: *Going therefore, teach ye all the nations, baptizing them in the name of the Father, and of the Son, and of the Holy Spirit* (Matt 28:19)."

Chapter 8
That the names of the Trinity may be transposed.

"Some, though, are accustomed to judge the Holy Spirit to be lesser because he is third in order, even though divine scriptures present such transparent simplicity that sometimes we find the third placed first because he is at issue in a given passage. It then does no injury to any of the persons since their divinity is one. So we read in Isaiah that the Lord says: *I am the first, and I am the last.*

[41] Again, Anselm believes he refers to Augustine: Pseudo-Augustine, *Quaestiones veteris et novi testamenti* 122.26-27, CSEL 50, ed. Souter, 373–74.

My hand also hath founded the earth, and my right hand hath mea-sured the heavens (Isa 48:12-13). And below: *I, even I have spoken and called him. I have brought him, and his way is made prosperous. Come ye near unto me, and hear this: I have not spoken in secret from the beginning. From the time before it was done, I was there, and now the Lord God hath sent me and his spirit* (Isa 48:15-16). Whom do we think founded the earth? It is he who says, *I am the first,* and it is he who says that he was sent. Do we think that this is the Father because he says, *I am the first?* Far from it! For what follows, *and now the Lord God hath sent me and his spirit,* clearly shows that he is the Son saying that he was sent by God and with the Holy Spirit. Yet he says, *I am the first.* Behold these equalities between the Son and the Holy Spirit!

"Just as we read that the Holy Spirit was sent by the Father and the Son, so too Christ was sent by God and the Holy Spirit. Only the Father is not said to have been sent. Let us also note the words of the Apostle, who expresses the Trinity in another order, for he says among other things in the second letter to the Thessalonians: *May the Lord direct your hearts into the charity of God and the patience of Christ* (2 Thess 3:5). Whom do you think he calls Lord here but the Holy Spirit, who directs our hearts into the love of God, that Father who sent his Son, and into the patience of that Christ who was obedient to his Father even unto death? And in the first letter to the Corinthians, departing from the order traditional in the faith, the apostle begins with the Holy Spirit in mentioning the ministry and actions of grace, then adds the Lord Jesus, and places God third, whom he says works in the Holy Spirit and in the Lord. So the Lord himself says: *The Father who abideth, he doth the works* (John 14:10). Because of this, because the Holy Spirit and Christ are from God the Father, their action is the work of God. Further the apostle speaks of the Holy Spirit and the Lord as the same Lord and God, and he does so on account of the unity of their nature. Therefore, after the apostle says here that the same God works all things in all, he concludes thus: *But all these things one and the same Spirit worketh, dividing to everyone according as he will* (1 Cor 12:11).

"So we say in transposing the order of personal names in the Trinity that the three are one in action, because when one acts, three are also properly said to act. Why? Because the persons are one in divinity, their names may be positioned in any order at all. In the fiftieth psalm David prays, invoking God as Spirit, and transposes the names of the three persons in simple faith, believing that the three persons of the divinity have the same nature: *Create a clean heart in me, O God, and renew a right Spirit within my bowels* (Ps 50:12). Here the psalmist called Christ the right spirit. And again: *Cast me not away from thy face, and take not thy holy Spirit from me* (Ps 50:13). He called the Holy Spirit himself this holy spirit. Below: *Restore unto me the joy of thy salvation, and strengthen me with a perfect spirit* (Ps 50:14). There he called the Father the perfect spirit—that Father who is his own principle and first cause, indeed the causal principle of the Son and the Holy Spirit. And John says in the Apocalypse: *'I am the Alpha and the Omega, the beginning and the end,' saith the Lord God, who is and who was and who is to come, the Almighty'* (Rev 1:8). And below: *I am the first and the last . . . was dead, and behold I am living* (Rev 1:17-18). Likewise below: *Thus says the first and the last, who was dead and is alive* (Rev 2:8). Behold we see the simplicity of scripture, how it transposes the names of the Trinity, at one time placing the Father either before or after, at another time the Son, at another the Holy Spirit! This in no way opposes that universal faith confessing the three to be of the same nature."

Chapter 9
That Father, Son, and Holy Spirit are not deficient, rather sufficient as names, signifying no lessening or diminution of substance.

"We must also know that Father, Son, and Holy Spirit are by no means deficient as names, implying that the Father is deficient because he is not the Son or the Holy Spirit, or because the Son is not the Father or the Holy Spirit he himself is deficient, or because the Holy Spirit is not the Father or the Son he either is deficient in this sense. They are, rather, full and sufficient names, signifying no lessening or diminution of substance. Moreover, we call one the Father, another the Son, and another the Holy Spirit, so that the three hypostases, that is the three persons, may be described without confusion as one in nature and their dignity as deity. And although when three persons are mentioned—Father, Son, and Holy Spirit—a plurality of persons occurs to the understanding as these linguistic expressions are apprehended, the unity of their same essence should never recede from the faith and understanding of believers. When the phrase 'one God' is spoken—although the unity of the divine essence presents itself to a human understanding that is by itself incomplete—according to the proper meaning of this linguistic expression nevertheless the plurality of divine persons should rightly remain in the faith and understanding of believers. Just as we believe in our hearts, so too let us confess with our mouths the unity of the divine substance, nevertheless preserving their trinity of persons, and let us confess their trinity of persons while preserving the unity of divine essence.[42] So our usage of 'one' is not Sabellian but Christian, nor does it consist in a confused unity of persons but in the true and simple unity of the same substance.

"In the same way our usage of 'three' is not Arian but Catholic, nor does it consist in a plurality of substances but in the correct distinction of persons. Let us not, dashing against the promontory of either Arian or Sabellian impiety, drown in that morass! Many have ventured there and, navigating carelessly, have suffered the shipwreck of heretical damnation. Such persons dispute often and greatly about the faith but never attain to its truth. Meanwhile they are ignorant of the things of which they speak and declare. If only the poverty of human speech could devise a single name appropriately and sufficiently signifying the unity of God's substance as well as the Trinity of his persons to the point of full and sufficient understanding! Surely then the church of God—which has labored so often to explain the many words and names for God faithfully, in many ways—would labor less in both its language and belief. Yet the Christian faith does not consist in the confession of mere names and words, but in the pure truth of trinity and unity. True and healthful confession arises from the very truth that the true God is one, and that truly he is the true Trinity in his persons. Therefore, when the Father is called God, the Son is called God, and the Holy

---

[42] See Psalm 19:14.

Spirit is also called God, no one thinks that there is *tritheia*, that is three deities or a triple deity. Rather, since the three are of the same nature, their divinity and honor are rightly understood to be as one, as I believe the Greeks term it, *homotimia*. Neither is it fitting for Christians to be said to be *tritheitai*, that is, worshipers of three gods, but rather *monotheitai*, that is, worshipers of one God."

Chapter 10
That we say that the Holy Spirit proceeds not according to the substance he has in common with the other persons, nor according to his own person—that is, in himself—rather in his relation to the other persons.

"As for the question you asked, whether we say the Holy Spirit proceeds according to his substance as in common with the other persons or according to his distinct and proper person, I respond thus. The Holy Spirit is consubstantial with the Father and the Son. No different substance comes from a same substance, so his substance is common to all three persons as one and the same God. So too is it common to them as one and the same substance. Yet we say that the Father is begotten by no other, the Son is begotten, and the Holy Spirit proceeds neither according to their common substance nor according to person. For if we say that the Father is begotten of no other, the Son begotten, and the Holy Spirit proceeds according to that substance in which they are one, then according to that common substance we might say that the Father is both begotten of no other and begotten, and also that he proceeds. Thence would arise a kind of new and confused mixture of the one who is begotten of no other, the one begotten, and the one proceeding, for whatever we say about the divine substance according to substance must be common to all three. Therefore if we say that according to their substance the Father is begotten of no other, that the Son is begotten, and that the Holy Spirit proceeds, then each attribute must be common to all three, such that we say that the Father is at once begotten of no other, begotten, and proceeding. Likewise we term the Son begotten of no other, begotten, and proceeding, and also call the Holy Spirit begotten of no other, begotten, and proceeding. In this great confusion neither the clear trinity of their persons nor complete identity of their substance would remain.

"On the other hand, if we say that the one who is begotten of no other, the one begotten, and the one who proceeds exist respectively in substance, then he who is begotten of no other can neither be the one begotten nor the one proceeding. Neither is the one begotten also begotten of no other nor he who proceeds. And neither is the one proceeding either he who is begotten of no other or the one begotten, for then they would not exist in unity of substance, rather in three different substances, according to which we would say the one begotten of no other, the one begotten, and the one proceeding were different from each other. So the Trinity would not be *homoousion*, of the same substance, but *heterousion*, of diverse substance. In this understanding the confusion and commingling of persons would on the one hand throw us into the pit of Sabellian heresy and, on the other, the plurality of substances would tumble us into the depths of Arianism. Therefore we do not say the Holy Spirit proceeds according to his substance, although his procession is in his substance.

"Further, if we say the Holy Spirit proceeds according to his person, we raise the same absurdity. For we speak of his name and person in the lofty, ineffable, and incomprehensible Trinity as in relation to himself, and whatever we say of him is according to his substance. Thus we properly speak of his person in his substance, for clearly that person is subject to his nature and we cannot speak of him except in his nature. So in the case of the Trinity, when we speak of the person of the Father, we also mean the substance of the Father. When we speak of the person of the Son, we also mean the substance of the Son. And when we speak of the person of the Holy Spirit, we mean too the substance of the Holy Spirit. Although in each case we mention only one substance, the three persons always exist and we refer also to them. Therefore because we speak of each person in respect to his substance in relation to himself, we say that the Holy Spirit proceeds, but no more according to his person than to his substance. Finally we must say that just as we call the Father 'Father' in relation to the Son and 'begotten of no other' in relation to the one begotten, and just as we call the Son 'the Son' and 'the one begotten'—and he is also called Word, image, seal, character, and splendor in relation to the Father—so too we call the Holy Spirit in relation to the others 'him who proceeds.' He is sent by each who sends him, as a gift from each giving him, as love from each in his love.

"Here we must note about what, according to what, and on account of what we speak, since we speak of things in relation to themselves as according to substance. But as for things of which we speak otherwise than in relation to themselves, these we treat in relation to the distinction of their persons, since the very term 'person' was invented because of the poverty of words by which the ancients might express the meaning of the Trinity. We use it not in relation to itself, rather in reference to itself, that is, regarding its substance or essence. Indeed we employ, among the other usages of the Latin language, singular terms for singular beings such as Father, Son, and Holy Spirit, not using them collectively but rather in reference to each respectively. At the same time we use those terms referring to common character, such as substance, God, omnipotent, and the other terms of this sort, not only in respective but also in collective reference. For just as the Father alone is called Father, and the Son alone is called Son, and the Holy Spirit alone is called the Holy Spirit—all terms referring specifically to singular persons—so too we rightly call all three both collectively and respectively God, substance, omnipotent, and other names of this sort. These terms are just as appropriate respectively as they are to all three persons collectively. In this way, just as we speak of things differing in number and person as different in number, so too we term those alike in number and substance as alike again in substance."

Chapter 11
Whether we rightly say that the Son, like the Father, sends forth the Holy Spirit—as the Greeks say, that the Son is *proboleus*.[43]

Nicetas, archbishop of Nicomedia, then replied: "What you have said is fair enough, but I ask now whether you concede that the

---

[43] As Russell suggests ("Anselm of Havelberg," *Sobornost* 1:32), the author seems to return to discussion of Gregory of Nazianzus' terminology: see *Oratio* 29.2.

Father sends forth the Holy Spirit as it proceeds, and is then *proboleus*, as the Greeks say?"

Anselm, bishop of Havelberg, answered: "I do not know what *proboleus* may mean, since I am not Greek, but rather a Latin.[44] But I gladly concede that the Father sends forth the Holy Spirit and that the Holy Spirit is then truly sent. I also say, however, that the Son likewise sends forth the Spirit. For the Gospel clearly says this of both Father and Son. About the Father it says: *The Paraclete, the Holy Ghost, whom the Father will send in my name* (John 14:26). And about the Son: *When the Paraclete cometh, whom I will send you* (John 15:26). The Gospel says further: *But if I go, I will send him to you* (John 16:7). Thus the Father sends forth the Holy Spirit, and also the Son does. The Holy Spirit is sent by both, yet promised by the one, that is, by the Son."

Nicetas, archbishop of Nicomedia, said: "If the Father and the Son both send forth the Holy Spirit, then there are two who send him, two who give him. Thus there seem to be two principles of the Holy Spirit."

Anselm, bishop of Havelberg, responded: "As I see it you wish cunningly to bring up the problem of two principles against me. Moreover you raise again what we decided above when we treated the matter of principle, but now as if in a casual question, as though you had forgotten what we already said.[45] Still, nowhere in scripture do I find two principles. Your concern is whether we can rightly say that two send the Spirit forth or two give him—that there might be two of him whom the Greeks name *proboleus*—and whom we call, as you say, him who sends forth. But since the exact meaning of this Greek term is unclear to me, I do not for now wish to define it precisely. Rather I wish that you listen to me patiently.

"You say that the Holy Spirit does not proceed from the Son. When you say this, you do great wrong to both Son and Holy Spirit. Since the Father and the Son are in respect to each other he who begets and he who is begotten, and likewise the Father and the

---

[44] Anselm surely intends this remark ironically, because he has just effectively explained to a native speaker the correct meaning and usage of a variety of terms central to Greek discussion of the nature of the Trinity.

[45] Nicetas indeed conceded this point to Anselm above in *Anticimenon* 2.3.

Holy Spirit are in respect to each other he who sends forth and he
who is sent, as the giver and the one given—since this is so I beg
that you tell me whether you do not greatly wrong both Son and
Holy Spirit when you attribute to them no mutual relation, or
worse, when you disjoin them from shared procession, as I have
said. Why is it that the Son bears the Holy Spirit only some neu-
tral relation, or the Holy Spirit is thus in respect to the Son, if you
take away the procession of the one from the other from between
the two? They clearly are, as I have said, Father and Son in mutual
respect by generation, or as I again have said the Father and the
Holy Spirit are in mutual respect by procession. But in your view
the Son and the Holy Spirit then remain without any mutuality or
relationship in which to regard one another. And what is this but
to some extent to dissolve the supreme and venerable Trinity?"

Chapter 12
**That the Holy Spirit is the *symponia*, that is, the concord, and
the *synneusis*, that is, the mutual relation, of the other two
persons.**

"Truly the Holy Spirit is *symponia*, that is, the concord, and *synneusis*, that is, the mutual relation of the others. He partakes in
the holiness proper and natural to the Father and the Son in their
common substance but is distinct in person, so completing and
encompassing, as I have said, the threeness in the Trinity but articulating its oneness in the context of threeness. So consider closely
what you are saying and see what you think. Be careful to offend
neither Son nor Holy Spirit, lest you alienate both along with the
Father. For he who sins against the Son also offends the Father,
as the Son himself said: *He that despiseth me, despiseth him that
sent me* (Luke 10:16). And again: *He who honoureth not the Son,
honoureth not the Father who hath sent him* (John 5:23). Surely he
who would deny the Son this honor, that the Holy Spirit proceeds
from him just as from the Father, does him none. Surely that man
blasphemes greatly against the Holy Spirit when in his incorrect
belief he separates the Spirit from communion with the Son in
taking away the Son's role in the Spirit's procession. Therefore such
a man offends both—the Son, in judging him unworthy that the

Holy Spirit should come from him, and the Spirit in judging him too unworthy to proceed from the Son. Thus, sinning grievously against both Son and Spirit and also against the Father, such a man blasphemes the entire Trinity. What greater blasphemy against the Holy Spirit is there than to believe and to teach that the Holy Spirit does not proceed from the Son? Indeed, it is written: *Whosoever shall speak . . . against the Father, or against the Son . . . it shall be forgiven him, but he that shall speak against the Holy Ghost, it shall not be forgiven him, neither in this world nor in the world to come* (Matt 12:32). Not only does such a blasphemy seem to pertain to the Macedonian heresy, which said that the Holy Spirit is a creature and not God, but also we find it clearly written that such blasphemy against the Holy Spirit is in itself a sin. The man who commits this sin of blasphemy, infidelity, or impatience—unless he recovers his senses—will be forgiven neither in this age nor in the age to come, although that passage of scripture can also be expounded in many other ways."

Chapter 13
That no one should silently or patiently endure being called a blasphemer, for the Lord did not when it was said to him: You have a demon. And that the Holy Spirit is given different names in his different actions.

Nicetas, archbishop of Nicomedia, then said: "You have constructed the question you propose with great thoughtfulness, but then you have added that we who deny that the Holy Spirit proceeds from the Son do injury to both Spirit and Son, rather that we offend the whole Trinity in this—further that, as you claim, we commit blasphemy. To this neither could nor should we listen with equanimity. Even though every sort of reproof calls for patience, this is another matter altogether. For who would patiently bear being called a blasphemer? The Lord, the model of complete patience, listened patiently to every hateful word addressed to him by the Jews when they called him a glutton and a drunkard and the son of a carpenter and many other such things. But when they finally said to him, thou *hast a devil* (John 8:48) and by Beelzebub *the prince of devils he casts out devils* (Matt 9:34), he responded, *I have not a devil* (John 8:49). Thus he clearly taught that we should patiently endure every reproach against us, but that no one should let pass in silence that he be thought not a catholic but a heretic, so a stranger to the Holy Spirit and the friend of devils.[46] Therefore I shall respond to what you have said as the Lord instructs me: in no way do we offend the holy and undivided Trinity, but like good catholics we truly venerate it in the unity of its substance with the honor due its divinity. Nor do we divide it, cutting apart its divine substance as does Arius, or confuse its persons as does Sabellius, or separate the Holy Spirit from the deity by calling him a creature as does Macedonius. Nor do we blaspheme by attacking the Holy Spirit like the Pneumatomachi.[47] Indeed, we adore God the Father, God the Son, and God the Holy Spirit, three persons, one deity undivided in glory, honor, power, and substance.

"Consider, then, whether we blaspheme the Holy Spirit: we believe that the Holy Spirit is to be adored with the Father and the Son, one God who through baptism deifies and brings to life the spirit of God, the spirit of Christ, the intellect of Christ, the spirit of the Lord, the Lord in himself, the spirit of filiation—of the Son of God himself as of our adoptive filiation—the spirit of truth, of liberation, of wisdom and understanding, of counsel and fortitude, of knowledge and piety, of fear of the Lord. For indeed God the Holy Spirit effects all these things, filling all with substance, containing all things, replenishing the world in its substance, incomprehensible to the world in his power—good, righteous, and an origin. He sanctifies rather than is sanctified, vivifies rather than is brought to life, measures rather than is measured, offers participation rather than takes part, fills up rather than is filled, contains rather than is contained. He is our inheritance from Christ by the apostles. That Spirit brings clarity and glorifies. He is numbered in the Trinity of divine persons. He is the finger of God, fire of God, love, charity, the spirit who knows all, teaches, who breathes where

[46] The speaker Nicetas finally responds with outrage to Anselm's characterization of his belief as blasphemy. Here again the author develops depth in his characters and drama in their interaction—as well as sympathy for Nicetas among his readership. This sympathy is reinforced when Nicetas now begins a passionate eulogy of the Spirit.

[47] The speaker here refers to the Macedonian heretics.

and how much he wills. He guides, speaks, was tempted in the desert, provoked when Jesus expelled the merchants and traders from the temple, and aroused in the resurrection of Lazarus. He is the illuminator, vivifier, but still more light and life in himself. He creates a temple, deifies, accomplishes through faith his anticipation of baptism, seeks out baptism in the laying on of hands. He is God effecting whatsoever he effects, dividing through grace in tongues of fire, portioning out his charisms and creating apostles, prophets, evangelists, pastors, and doctors. He is intellectual, manifest, great, immense, accessible, undefiled. He is coequal in his influence, wise and manifold in actions, manifesting all things, under his own power, unalterable, omnipotent, and *pantepiscopos*, overseeing all things. He is the spirit surpassing all intellectual, pure, subtle, and angelic virtues as well as the prophetic and apostolic virtues—even other virtues otherwise elsewhere appropriately defined, in which he manifests his boundlessness. But whatever we humbly say of the Spirit—that he is given, sent, shared, a charism, a gift, a breath, a promise, a mediation, or any other such description—we must refer all to their first cause, so that we may demonstrate something from that.[48] Since we hold and teach such things about the Holy Spirit, we are confident that we are not guilty of any unforgivable blasphemy. But do not be surprised if we have difficulty believing that he proceeds from the Son. However much argument you supply, we cannot accept it hastily because no authority of the Gospel or of canonical scriptures, or even of the holy councils persuades or teaches us so to believe."

Chapter 14
That no one should align the meaning of that scripture we rightly call divine to his own understanding, but rather should accommodate his own understanding to the meaning of scripture.

Anselm, bishop of Havelberg, then said: "If you demand authorities to persuade you of what I have set forth, would that when

---

[48] Anselm here expands upon his laudation of the Holy Spirit based on Gregory of Nazianzus in *Anticimenon* 1.2: see Gregory, *Oratio* 31.29.

you hear them, you accept them with right understanding! But
I am afraid that this common proverb applies to you: a wolf was
sat down to learn his letters but, not paying attention to what
the teacher said, he kept repeating over and over again what he
bore in his heart, "Lamb, lamb, lamb."[49] If you have hardened
your heart and barred your obstinate mind such that you will
not acquiesce no matter what is said, then what point is there in
my speaking? It is better to keep humble silence than to speak
uselessly, beating the air with idle words, for there is a time to
speak and a time to keep silence.[50] But if you wish to struggle
to twist around any authorities I set forth to your own interpretation rather than troubling yourself to accommodate your
understanding to divine scripture, I am afraid that perhaps in this
too you may resist the Holy Spirit. You will be unembarrassed
to twist to your reading even those texts dictated by the Holy
Spirit, rashly distorting the Spirit's intent.[51] Yet we have come
together not to best one another in argument but to search out
what is true. As Truth himself says: *The words that I have spoken
to you are spirit and life* (John 6:64). And elsewhere: *The spirit of
life* (Ezek 10:17) who was in you, that is to say the spirit of the
holy scriptures."

Nicetas, archbishop of Nicomedia, responded: "How wicked
it would be to bend the meaning of that scripture we rightly call
divine to fit one's own interpretation by a distorted exposition!
Rather we should humbly surrender, accommodating our own
understanding entirely to the meaning of divine scripture. This
should be clear to anyone who is accustomed to devote time to
sacred reading, so your warning is well taken. But now you too
ought to do what you have cautioned me.[52] If you wish to adduce
sacred authorities, you should then expound them so that you
seem not to force your interpretation to supporting your own
opinion because it is yours, not because it is true. For it is written:

[49] Anselm's image of the wolf rings of a folk saying, but it is unrepresented in
the PL or collections of Latin proverbs.
[50] Compare Ecclesiastes 3:7.
[51] Anselm responds with feeling commensurate with Nicetas's.
[52] The interlocutors nonetheless quickly find common ground.

He that strongly squeezeth the paps to bring out milk, straineth out butter: and he that violently bloweth his nose, bringeth out blood (Prov 30:33). But now say what authorities support your views in the question before us."

Anselm, bishop of Havelberg, then spoke: "Thus far it has been appropriate for each of us to press our opinions in our own words. But now that we begin to treat directly of holy texts we should speak without contention, supporting one another with due respect and giving honor to the Holy Spirit as the author of divine scripture who reveals to us what he wishes us to investigate in humility, without contention. Some men prefer to continue to argue on even when they are defeated—to struggle against the truth with contentious words rather than to confess their own errors. Such men never discover what they should accept because they do not know how to keep humbly quiet."

Nicetas, archbishop of Nicomedia, said: "Well said, but this is not a matter to be passed over in silence, so that if one of us disagrees with the other in expounding scripture, his view should immediately be called wrong. He might sometimes disagree in good faith. One passage of scripture often elicits different and equally valid interpretations. By no means should these be spurned, even though they have small relevance to the present question."

Anselm, bishop of Havelberg, then answered: "Excellently put.[53] Now may you yourself remain obliging in this way, and be generous and quick to trust. May you not seek, as it is commonly said, a knot in a bulrush, for just as *wisdom will not enter into a malicious soul* (Wis 1:4), so too divine wisdom will fill a well-disposed soul to overflowing."[54]

Nicetas, archbishop of Nicomedia, replied: "Be so assured, for I believe freely what we must if I have been well persuaded. Now go on."

---

[53] Anselm and Nicetas agree that disagreement over particulars of exegesis is acceptable—an important step toward their mutual attentiveness in doctrinal issues.

[54] Jerome had repeatedly talked about finding knots in bulrushes: see, for instance, Jerome, *Dialogus adversus Pelagianos* 2.30, PL 23, col. 568.

Chapter 15

That the Lord breathed the Holy Spirit upon the apostles, yet that physical breath was not itself the Holy Spirit but the sign of his procession, and how one should understand: Receive the Holy Ghost.

Anselm, bishop of Havelberg, said: "After the resurrection, when the Lord Jesus showed himself to his disciples, *he breathed on them and he said to them, 'Receive ye the Holy Ghost'"* (John 20:22). What else, I ask, did that breath signify but that the Holy Spirit proceeds, and from the Lord himself? For that breath was not the very substance of the Holy Spirit but the manifestation that the Holy Spirit proceeds also from the Son."

Nicetas, archbishop of Nicomedia, responded: "I aver that the bodily breath was not the substance of the Holy Spirit, but I do not agree that this breathing was the signification of his procession from the Son."

Anselm, bishop of Havelberg, answered: "If when Christ breathed out and said, 'Receive the Holy Spirit,' the apostles received the Holy Spirit, then how could this breath not be held to be the signification of the Spirit's procession? And if the Holy Spirit was given to the disciples in the Son's breath when he said, 'Receive the Holy Spirit,' tell me, I ask, how the Spirit came forth from the Son who gave him to the disciples who received him except by proceeding from him who always is, and by coming forth to them for whom he was then given as a gift? For in order for the apostles to receive the Holy Spirit, the Lord had to give him, so that the Holy Spirit might proceed from the one giving into those receiving. For his procession is eternal and in his substance. The Spirit who proceeds is no less eternal because those who received him were not. Even if he was not then precisely said to have been given, he can still be called 'a gift' or 'able to be given' because he can be given or even if he was not in fact given, even if we do not say he was given unless in fact he were. Indeed, the Holy Spirit, in the natural essence proper to him, in which he is of the Father and the Son, is able to proceed or is given only by procession, nor is he given except by procession, nor is he received except by procession, nor does he effect anything except by procession. So when he is said to be sent or to be given by either Father or Son, the Spirit is not said to be given any other way than by procession, for their giving or sending him is his procession. Now the Holy Spirit proceeds from the Father and the Son in two modes. The first is his eternal procession according to affect, the love the Father bears the Son and the Son bears the Father, and the second is his procession in time according to the effect of his gifts for men."

Nicetas, archbishop of Nicomedia, then said: "Since the Holy Spirit is everywhere in his essence and is thus everywhere present, what do you think Christ gave those apostles by breathing upon them, or what did the apostles receive when it was said to them: 'Receive the Holy Spirit?' For if we say that they received the Holy Spirit, the third person in the Trinity who is everywhere and was already in their hearts, how can we properly say that they then received him whom they already possessed as present already in their hearts?"

Anselm, bishop of Havelberg, then responded: "The Holy Spirit who proceeds from the Father and the Son and is the third person in the Trinity, the complete and perfect God, everywhere and never absent in his divine being, was himself already present in his divinity in the hearts of the apostles. Afterwards, however, he was also given to them, humble and elect as they were, through indwelling grace. For he says about himself: *But to whom shall I have respect, but to him who is poor and little, and of a contrite spirit, and that trembleth at my words?* (Isa 66:2). And again: *God resisteth the proud, and giveth grace to the humble* (Jas 4:6). So they received the Holy Spirit as bearing fruit through his indwelling grace, that is, they received him who previously had been among them but without bearing fruit, though everywhere in his divine essence. This was as if the Lord said: 'Receive in grace that Holy Spirit who was with you before only in essence. Receive as a gift him who was with you before as a stranger. Receive for your use and favor him who was with you before without your accepting his favor. Receive in the effect of his spiritual grace him who was with you until now only in his presence. Receive for your sanctification him who was with you before, without the manifestation of his strength.' So we might say to someone whose eyes were apparently clear but lacked sight: 'Receive eyes that you might see, when before you could not.' Or as

if this were said to someone with ears, but deaf: 'Receive now for
hearing those ears, which you had before without that power.' Or
to a mute with a tongue: 'Receive a tongue with which to speak,
when before you were dumb.' Or to a man with withered hands:
'Receive hands for working, which before yours could not do.' Or
to a cripple whose feet appear whole: 'Receive feet for walking,
which before yours could not.' Or as if this were said to someone
holding the money of another in trust: 'Receive this money, and
take for your own use what you possessed but not for your own
needs or benefit.' In this way the Lord seems to say: 'Receive that
Holy Spirit, he who was with you before in the immensity of his
divinity, for your own use, as a gift of spiritual grace.'

"Before the Lord's solemn and manifest gift of the Holy Spirit,
the apostles were inexperienced in spiritual grace. Therefore the
Lord said to Peter when the apostle confessed Christ to be the Son
of God: *Blessed art thou, Simon Bar-Jona: because flesh and blood hath
not revealed it to thee, but my Father who is in heaven* (Matt 16:17).
This is as if he had said: 'You have received this through a heavenly
and divine inspiration, not by a human revelation in flesh and
blood.' To be sure, the other apostles also had divinely inspired
faith before the gift of the Holy Spirit, but not enough to be saved
by faith. But what they had had in a lesser degree was now made
complete through the solemn and manifest gift of the Holy Spirit.
Is this not right? Is this not the case for Peter, prince of the apostles,
who when he was with Christ said that he was ready to go both to
prison and to death, but immediately denied him at the sound of
the portress's voice?[55] The same Peter nevertheless was clothed in
virtue from on high after the gift of the Holy Spirit. He responded
confidently to the chief priests when they threatened him: *We ought
to obey God rather than men* (Acts 5:29). Indeed, this gift of the Holy
Spirit happened first on earth through the Lord's breath for the
sake of love of neighbor, and afterwards it occurred from heaven
in the many tongues, for the sake of love of God.[56] That the Holy
Spirit was given twice instructs us that we should believe him to
proceed from two persons at the same time, and not in two pro-

[55] See Matthew 26:70-74.
[56] See again Matthew 16:17; Acts 2:4.

cessions but in one. He was given from heaven as from the Father who is in heaven and on earth as from the Son who dwelled with men on earth in his humanity, although when the Son gave the Spirit, he was not then on earth as a mortal amongst mortals. For after his resurrection and before his ascension he was pleased to reveal himself to the apostles and then to grant the Holy Spirit to them abundantly."

Nicetas, archbishop of Nicomedia, responded: "Since we speak of the loftiest theology, comparisons to bodily things should have no place, for we should not compare higher to lower things. The enduring nature of what does not change cannot be fully known from the instability of what does. Indeed, what is comparing spiritual things to the corporeal or adapting the divine to the human other than looking for the living among the dead?"[57]

Chapter 16
That spiritual things are sometimes compared to the corporeal, and sometimes corporeal to spiritual.

Anselm, bishop of Havelberg, then spoke: "I acknowledge what you say, for no metaphor fully expresses the exact, precise truth of the thing it figures. An image is never a whole, but only a part, otherwise it would be the thing itself rather than its image. Nor is any image entirely like what it represents, even among corporeal things when they are compared to one another figuratively. Thus we interpret images of this sort as if they were theatrical, certainly not as expressing the pure truth of what they represent, but as raising the mind of the viewer to a better understanding. So we often come to know through this kind of instruction something we did not heretofore understand because of its lofty nature, as the mind rises through the familiar things it knows to the unfamiliar things it does not yet recognize. *For the invisible things of him . . . are clearly seen, being understood through the things that are made* (Rom 1:20). Many other passages make this point. And just as spiritual things are often understood through images of corporeal things, so too sometimes corporeal things are learned through spiritual

[57] See Luke 24:5.

things. As God said to Moses: *Look and make . . . it according to the pattern that was shewn thee in the mount* (Exod 25:40). There God clearly commanded that Moses physically arrange everything for the construction of the tabernacle according to the image of those things he had seen in a spiritual vision on the mountain. Then we ought never scorn the theoretical aspects of corporeal things or the physical images of incorporeal things, even if these images are unable to express the truth of their referents to perfection.[58]

"Most of the time words are inwardly formed invisibly, through visible things known to the intellect, in the invisible soul of one whose understanding is incomplete. In a similar manner visible strokes of letters are formed visibly on a visible sheet of parchment, then speak by being silent and are silent even as they speak. Yet through those same visible strokes the soul of a reader frames an invisible understanding. He retrieves the words when he looks back at the same letters after forgetfulness has removed them from the understanding in which they were first written. So visible letters and new, invisible understandings come about in the image of spoken words, even if those visible and invisible things connote not each other but divine nature. The Lord himself spoke through images in parables, now comparing the corporeal to the spiritual, now the spiritual to the corporeal. But I do not think we can find any utterly clear likeness of creature to creator."[59]

Nicetas, archbishop of Nicomedia, responded: "I concur in what you have said about these matters. But now if you have any authoritative texts on the procession of the Holy Spirit from the Son, set them forth."

[58] For a survey of the patristic exegetical principles on which Anselm's discussion here is based see Henri de Lubac, *Medieval Exegesis*, vol. 1: *The Four Senses of Scripture*, trans. Mark Sebanc (Grand Rapids: Eerdmans, 1998), especially, on the Augustinian model central to Anselm's spirituality and hermeneutics, 123–32. Although Anselm effectively patronizes Nicetas, whom he has heretofore described humbly but probably accurately as the more learned, the Greek's response below is markedly tolerant of the Latin interlocutor's condescension.

[59] See Morrison's discussion of this passage as central to Anselm's distinctive theory of language: Karl F. Morrison, "Anselm of Havelberg: Play and the Dilemma of Historical Progress," in Thomas F. X. Noble and John J. Contreni, eds., *Religion, Culture and Society in the Early Middle Ages: Studies in Honor of Richard E. Sullivan* (Kalamazoo, MI: Medieval Institute Publications, 1987), 221.

Chapter 17
That when the woman touched the hem of the Lord's garment, power went forth from him, and we call that power the Holy Spirit who proceeds from him.

Anselm, bishop of Havelberg, answered: "Hear and attend to what the Son said about the woman who suffered from a hemorrhage and who was healed upon touching the hem of his garment: *Somebody hath touched me, for I know that virtue has gone forth from me* (Luke 8:46).[60] We call this virtue or power the Holy Spirit, as we know from that passage where the angel instructs Mary, saying to her: *The Holy Ghost shall come upon thee and the power of the Most High shall overshadow thee* (Luke 1:35). For when the angel had fittingly announced, *The Holy Ghost shall come upon thee*, he added, *and the power of the Most High shall overshadow thee.* He did so to show that the Holy Spirit is the same as the power of the Most High. So the Lord himself promised the Spirit to the disciples, saying: *But stay you in the city till you be endued with power from on high* (Luke 24:49). And again he said: *You shall receive the power of the Holy Ghost coming upon you, and you shall be witnesses unto me* (Acts 1:8). As we believe, the evangelist says of this power: *virtue went forth from him and healed all* (Luke 6:19). Therefore the Holy Spirit evidently proceeds also from the Son—unless you wish to close your eyes in order not to see what is clearer in the light, and not to hear scripture crying out, forcing itself upon you although you try to be deaf to it."

Nicetas, archbishop of Nicomedia, then replied: "If the Holy Spirit, as you assert, therefore proceeds from the Father and the Son, why did the Son speak of the Spirit *who proceedeth from the Father* (John 15:26) but say nothing regarding the Spirit's procession from himself?"

Anselm, bishop of Havelberg, countered: "Why indeed, except that he often refers what is his to the Father, from whom he himself also is? Thus the Son also says: *My doctrine is not mine, but his that sent me* (John 7:16). If we thus understand his teaching to be, as he says, not his own but his Father's, should we not still

---

[60] Luke 8:46.

more understand the Holy Spirit to proceed from him, in the passage where he says: *He proceedeth from the Father?* Then the Son would not say, 'He does not proceed from me', for he knows from the Father that he is God, for he is God from God, and the Holy Spirit certainly knows from the Father that he proceeds from him. Through the same Father the Holy Spirit knows too that he also proceeds from the Son just as he knows from the Father himself that he proceeds from the Father. These things are clearly implied in the Gospel when the Lord says: *Whom I will send you from the Father* (John 15:26), showing that the Holy Spirit is of both the Father and the Son. When the Son said, *whom the Father will send,* he added *in my name* (John 14:26). Yet he did not say, 'whom the Father will send from me', but w*hom I will send you from the Father.* He was clearly showing that the Father, the author of both generation and procession, is the origin of all divinity, or perhaps it would be better to say of all deity. Therefore we rightly refer him who proceeds from the Father and the Son to him of whom the Son was born. So the Holy Spirit is the power of the Most High, that is the Father, and he is also the power of the Son, who is himself the Most High. Since the Spirit is the power of both, we correctly believe him also to proceed from both, for just as their communion is not of one but of both, so too his procession is not from one but from both."

Nicetas, archbishop of Nicomedia, then said: "We believe that the Holy Spirit is of both Father and Son, for indeed we recognize that the Lord himself said: *For it is not you that speak, but the Spirit of your Father that speaketh in you* (Matt 10:20). We also know that the Apostle says: *If the Spirit of him that raised up Jesus from the dead dwell in you* (Rom 8:11). Here he surely means the Spirit of the Father. Again the Apostle says: *God has sent the Spirit of his Son into your hearts crying: 'Abba, Father'* (Gal 4:6). And in another place: *Now if any man have not the Spirit of Christ, he is none of his* (Rom 8:9). And so on account of these and many other such testimonies in which we have been instructed, we well believe, as I have said, that the Holy Spirit, the third person in the Trinity, is of the Father and of the Son. Yet we are not so bold as to confess that he proceeds from both, because perhaps it is one thing to have being of the Father and another to proceed from Him."

Chapter 18
That just as being for the Holy Spirit comes from the Father in his procession from the Father, so too his being comes from the Son in his procession from the Son.

Anselm, bishop of Havelberg, then said: "The Holy Spirit, who is of the Father and who proceeds from the Father, either is of the Father in his procession from the Father or is not of the Father in his procession from the Father. For if he proceeds from the Father in being of the Father, why does he not similarly proceed from the Son in being of the Son? He is of the Father as he is also of the Son, and he is of the Son as he is also of the Father. And so his being is of both Father and Son, unless perhaps we venture to say that he has one being from the Father and another from the Son, which is utter madness. He does not have one being from the Father and another from the Son, nor does he have one procession from the Father and another from the Son. Rather he has one and the same being and one and the same procession as much from the Father as from the Son. He neither exists nor proceeds twice. Nor is he two, nor does he have two processions, nor even—as would be impious to say—do two Holy Spirits proceed. Just as it is certain that the Spirit's being of the Father is nothing other than his procession from the Father, so too undoubtedly his being of the Son is nothing other than his procession from the Son, for his procession is in substance.

"But if you posit that it is one thing for the Spirit to be of the Father and another for him to proceed from the Father, then you at once make him different from himself, whose existence of the Father is nothing other than his procession from the Father. The Spirit then exists by procession from the Father and he proceeds from the Father by existing in procession in substance—and in a substance that can and does proceed. Then show, if you can, that the Holy Spirit has being otherwise, from the Son. And show, if you can, that his being from the Father and the Son is one thing and his procession another. If then you have thus rendered him different from himself, then you have rashly voided sound faith about the Holy Spirit.

"Again, if it is the same thing for the Spirit to exist of the Father as for him to proceed from the Father, and if he has the same being of the Father and of the Son, then he proceeds from the Son just as from the Father. But if he does not proceed from the Son, then his being of the Son is not the same as his being of the Father. And if his being of the Son is not the same as his being of the Father, then either he has other being of the Son or no being whatsoever of the Son. Yet either of these possibilities rings false. If the Spirit is not of the Son, neither is he of the Father, for the Father and the Son are one. If he is not of the Father, neither does he proceed from the Father. Again, because the Spirit is able to proceed from the Father, he does indeed proceed from that Father. For the same reason, because he is able to proceed from the Son, the Spirit proceeds also from the Son. For it is as great or rather the same for the Holy Spirit to be of the Father and of the Son as to proceed from the Father and from the Son. Thus is written about the Spirit: *For he shall not speak of himself, but what things soever he shall hear he shall speak* (John 16:13). Whence he will hear, thence he will speak, and whence he will speak, thence he proceeds. Whence his being, then, thence his hearing; whence his hearing, thence his knowledge; whence his knowledge, thence his procession. So too, since the Spirit's being is of both Father and Son, his procession in existing, hearing, and knowing is from both as well. Therefore we speak of the Son's being of the Father as birth from the Father and the Holy Spirit's being of the Father and the Son not as birth but as procession.

"The difference between being by birth and being by procession is difficult to discern, yet we say that also the Son himself proceeds from the Father, as where scripture says: *I came forth from the Father and am come into the world* (John 16:13). And again: *From God I proceeded* (John 8:42). Nevertheless, the procession of the Son is a different procession from that of the Holy Spirit. For the Son is sent with his own mission and procession in his birth, and in birth he proceeds from the Father, while the Holy Spirit proceeds with his own mission and procession in his very procession. In the Spirit's procession he is sent as much from the Son as from the Father. Therefore attend to what you say, being careful not to deny the Holy Spirit's procession from the Son so that you also be convinced to deny to the Spirit the being he has from the Son. Since the Holy Spirit's existence and procession are the same, whoever denies that he proceeds from the Son also denies that he exists of the Son. And whoever denies that he exists of the Son also denies that he exists of the Father, for they are surely one. Further, whoever denies that the Spirit exists or that he proceeds as much from the Son as from the Father denies that the Holy Spirit exists. Consequently, to say either of these things is to dissolve the entire Trinity. See how perverse and impious that would be!"

Nicetas, archbishop of Nicomedia, then said: "I must respond first, I think, that in substance the Son and the Holy Spirit are the same as the Father, but for the Son to be begotten or for the Holy Spirit to proceed is not the same as for the Father to beget. Just as you said a little while ago, however, to define either how the Father begets or how the Son is begotten—or how the Holy Spirit proceeds—is neither easy to investigate nor possible to state. Nevertheless, we can say advisedly that the one begets in one way, the other is begotten in another way, and the third proceeds in still another way, yet by no means should we impute to them any activity or passivity in these matters. Although the being of the Father is the same in substance as that of the Son and the Holy Spirit, nevertheless one being alone is the Father in his person, not the Son or the Holy Spirit. Another being alone is the Son in his person, not the Father or the Holy Spirit. And the third being alone is the Holy Spirit in his person, not the Father or the Son. For the former usage, being in substance, denotes the identity of the same substance in the three, but the latter, being in person, indicates the distinction of persons among the same three.

"Consequently, when you investigate by logical argument whether the Holy Spirit has the same being from both the Father and the Son, and again when you inquire whether his existence and procession are the same—thus striving to prove that his existence from both is the same as his procession from both—when you do this, as I assert, you should undoubtedly pay careful attention. Although the Holy Spirit may pertain to both and be of both, still he does not seem to exist and proceed equally from both. Certainly he is of the Father as of that Father who is himself of nothing else. The Father who is himself of nothing else nonetheless has that Holy Spirit who takes his being from the same Father. But at the same time the Spirit is of the Son as of one who is himself of the

Father, who has from the Father that the Holy Spirit is also his own and takes his being from him as Son. So it seems that the Holy Spirit truly is of both and from both, but that Spirit does not seem to be equally of both or proceed equally from both."

Chapter 19
Whether the Holy Spirit proceeds equally from Father and Son, given that the Father has his being from no other, but the Son has his being from the Father; and a figurative interpretation of the first-made man, Adam, the separation of the first-made woman, Eve, and their progeny, Abel.

Anselm, bishop of Havelberg, then spoke: "That Father who is of no other has nothing from the Son or from the Holy Spirit. Neither does the Son who is from the Father have anything from the Holy Spirit. But the Son has everything—even his very being as God—from the Father, for he is God from God. The Son has as well from the Father that the Holy Spirit proceeds also from him. Further, the Holy Spirit has from the same Father that he proceeds from the Son just as he proceeds from the Father. Thus anything that is the Son, or anything the Son has, and anything that is the Holy Spirit—all of these—take their beginning from the Father himself. He is the Father, author and origin of generation and procession from no other. He has nothing from any other. Perhaps thence we might think that the Holy Spirit does not belong equally to both Father and Son or proceed equally from both. But what then? We undertook this discussion not about how the Holy Spirit might proceed from both, but about whether he proceeds from both. As soon as we have established that, then if it is agreeable we may examine the question of how he proceeds.

"But I wish you to turn briefly to the latter question, how he proceeds, if you will. For I say that by no means does equality of existence and of procession from both detract from the Holy Spirit, because the very Father from whom he exists and proceeds is himself from no other, and indeed the other from whom the Spirit likewise exists and proceeds, namely the Son, is himself of the Father. For the Spirit exists or proceeds neither earlier nor later, neither more nor less on account of one or the other. He proceeds

eternally at the same time, once and for all, from both—not in unequal measure but equally, that is, in that equality we acknowledge.
Nevertheless, some might say that he exists and proceeds more
properly from the Father, as from a first cause, than from the Son
whose cause the Father is. Yet although we say that the Father is of
no other and the Son is of the Father, we should by no means understand priority or succession in this, nor greater stature in one and
lesser in the other person, but rather equality of majesty in the two.
Even though the Father has no cause and the Son has the Father as
his cause, the same power and glory inhere in the one caused and
the one with no cause, as I have said, that is, for the one having a
cause and the one not having a cause. How could they who are of
the same eternity, majesty, power, capacity, will, and equality send
forth that Holy Spirit as proceeding from them unequally rather
than equally? The procession of the Holy Spirit is in his substance
just as the begetting of the Son is in his substance.

"We can understand this through a figurative reading. Adam
was the creature of God alone, without any other generative cause.
Eve was then created from Adam, divided off from him as her preceding cause, and Abel descended from them both neither by a new
creation nor by dividing off from a creature, but by the effluence
of natural human generation. Adam was human, Eve was human,
Abel was human, and so they were *homoousion*, that is, alike in
substance or of the same nature. But the one who was Adam was
neither Eve nor Abel, the one who was Eve was neither Adam nor
Abel, and the one who was Abel was neither Adam nor Eve. Or
do you not think that Abel was begotten as much from his father
Adam, who was his cause, since nothing else begot him or divided
him off, as from his mother Eve, who was brought into being not
by being begotten but by separation from Adam himself as her
cause? Just as Adam and Eve together generated Abel, so too Abel
himself was truly begotten equally from them both. Although we
discern difference between those begetting him, that is, between a
creature and one divided off from that creature, still Abel is not different from his parents, rather like them, having been so begotten.
Nor is Adam prior to the mother Eve in being Abel's father, but the
two are father and mother at the same moment, and Abel is again
at once their son, descending from each by the equal effluence of

their generation of him. Eve's existence by separation from Adam does not prevent Abel from being the son of one as much as the other, the son neither more nor less of the one than of the other. Indeed, Eve's role is to be from Adam by separation, and Abel's role as son of Adam is also to be the son of Eve in her giving birth to him. Eve takes her motherhood of Abel, whom she bore, from Adam, who is himself the father of Abel whom he begot.[61]

"We should look upon this figure I have set forth as if it were a dramatic scene. So no one would say that the Holy Spirit exists in one way in proceeding from the Father and another way in proceeding from the Son, even though the Father from whom he takes his being and from whom that Spirit proceeds is the very Father who is of no other, while the Son from whom the Spirit similarly takes his being and proceeds is of the Father. Just as we argued before, the Holy Spirit takes the same being from each, and that same being is to proceed just as truly and as ineffably from each. To believe this is both necessary to the faith and essential for salvation."

Nicetas, archbishop of Nicomedia, responded: "As you have constructed your argument, that the Holy Spirit has the same being of the Father and of the Son does not seem absurd, but you have not demonstrated whether he proceeds equally or unequally from each of the two."

Anselm, bishop of Havelberg, then said: "Since you concede that the Spirit's being is the same from each of the other persons, you must also admit that that Spirit's being proceeds from each, for we clearly demonstrated already that for him to have the same being from each is to proceed from each, and to have the same procession from each is to take his being from each. Consequently, just as the Spirit is of the Father, so is he of the Son, nor is he of the Father in one way and of the Son in another. Now the Spirit is of the Father by proceeding from him, and meanwhile he takes his being as much from the Son as from the Father—and the Spirit's

---

[61] Although the interlocutor Anselm makes a theological point through his use of this figure, the author Anselm here buttresses the unity of the three books of *Anticimenon* with attention to this image. The descent of the church from Abel marks the beginning of Christian history as expounded by Anselm and many of his patristic and medieval antecedents: see *Anticimenon* 1. Prologue.

being is nothing other than his procession from each. But now listen closely. You concede that the Holy Spirit is sent by the Son, and I know you concede this because we clearly read this in the Gospel—unless some impiety has stricken it from your copies of scripture, as I doubt—that, as the Son says, *whom I will send you* (John 15:26). You also concede that the Spirit receives and announces what is from the same Son, whose being he shares. For this is also in the Gospel, unless, as I have said, it is erased in the copies of the Greeks: *He shall receive of mine*, it says, *and show it to you* (John 16:15), *for he shall not speak of himself, but what things soever he shall hear, he shall speak* (John 15:13)."[62]

Nicetas, archbishop of Nicomedia, then said: "I indeed concede all these things, that the Spirit is of the Son, that he is sent from the Son, that he receives and announces what is of the Son, that the Spirit hears from the Son and that he speaks on the Son's authority. All this that the Gospel teaches I concede. But I neither teach nor presume to teach that the Spirit proceeds from the Son, for the Gospel does not teach it."

Anselm, bishop of Havelberg, replied: "I marvel at your scrupulousness, that you should so abhor this word 'proceed' regarding the Holy Spirit in relation to the Son, when the Gospel presents an equivalent term and this exact meaning, and you are confident in agreeing with the Gospel. For what else is the Spirit's being sent forth from the Son, or what else could it be, than his procession from the Son? If indeed the Son sends the Spirit forth, then it follows that the Spirit so sent proceeds from the Son who sends him. Nevertheless the Spirit as sent is not then absent from the Son who sent him, nor is he separated from the Son, rather the Spirit is always present to the Son, who is in turn always present to the Spirit. Again, the Spirit is of the Son who also takes all his being from the Father, so that Spirit is of the Son and likewise has from the Father what he has from the Son. How could we imagine that Spirit not to proceed from the Son when, as we have said again and again, his procession is nothing other than his being and his

---

[62] The speaker's sarcasm about defects of Greek manuscript transmission suggests his agitation at this point in the discussion. He begins to abandon his posture of cool rationality and civility.

being is nothing other than his procession, while his hearing and his speaking are nothing other than his being and his procession—and all of this not of himself? For the Spirit exists in his procession and proceeds by being, for his being is in being able to proceed. We therefore conclude without doubt from all that we have said that the Holy Spirit is of the Father. He is also of the Son. He is from the Father and he is from the Son. He is sent by the Father and he is sent by the Son. And he proceeds from the Son just as he proceeds from the Father."

Nicetas, archbishop of Nicomedia, replied: "I cannot deny that you seem to have demonstrated what you proposed by careful arguments and appropriate authorities. As for me, I would not wish to oppose the Holy Spirit. But still I want you to hear what utterly confounds and terrifies about this word 'procession.' Our Lord Jesus Christ—Savior of the human race, founder of the faith, author of the Gospel, lover of our salvation—taught the apostles a faith sufficient for their salvation. He would not suffice as Savior unless he had sufficed as teacher.[63] But never did the Lord Jesus speak about the Holy Spirit's procession from the Son as he did about the Spirit's procession from the Father. Hence it seems to me wildly rash to presume to add or subtract anything from that Christian faith already fully established and sufficient for salvation—especially regarding faith in Holy Trinity. And it seems to me that, in offering due reverence to the Gospel, we should use the word 'procession' precisely as it is ascribed to the Holy Spirit in his procession from the Father. By no means should we say that procession from the Son is ascribed to the Holy Spirit. Thus we may walk safely in faith, adding nothing, subtracting nothing, but simply holding what we have been taught from the Gospel. Just as it is unsafe to subtract anything, so too it is dangerous to add anything to that faith."[64]

[63] Here the speaker Nicetas plays elegantly in Latin on the terms *doctor* (teacher or physician) and *salvator* (savior or healer). These terms' doubled spiritual and physical meanings enhance the persuasiveness of the author's account of Nicetas's reluctance to affirm the procession of the Holy Spirit from Christ.

[64] The author here allows Nicetas a simple, emotionally evocative and highly sympathetic expression of the Greek position. Although his Latin interlocutor will

Chapter 20
That, while we do not find in the Gospel that the Holy Spirit proceeds from the Son, we do not find that the Spirit does not proceed from the Son, nor that he proceeds from the Father alone.

Anselm, bishop of Havelberg, then said: "You have spoken as befits the maturity and the prudence of so great a man as you. Nevertheless, we should not fear when there is no cause for alarm. Now stay and listen carefully to what I say. If you are afraid to say that the Holy Spirit proceeds from the Son because the phrase 'proceeds from the Son' is not written anywhere in the Gospel, tell me, I ask, what boldness or foolishness leads you not to fear to say the opposite regarding his procession, that he 'does not proceed from the Son,' when we also find that written nowhere in scripture, even in the Gospel?[65] Why are you not silent where, as you think, the Gospel is silent? Where do you get that 'not,' that negation, that the Gospel does not teach you? Who could ever persuade you to say 'he does not proceed from the Son' when the Gospel does not say this, yet the Gospel could not persuade you to say 'he proceeds from the Son' when it neither denies nor prohibits this assertion? You respect the Gospel so much that you would not dare to say 'he proceeds from the Son,' and yet you do not respect the Gospel enough that you would not say 'he does not proceed from the Son.' You are afraid where we should not fear and you are not afraid where we should be. I admit to you that the expression 'proceeds from the Son' cannot be found anywhere in scripture so simply put. And you must also admit that the expression 'does not proceed from the Son' is nowhere found there either. What then? Shall we argue about terms that mean one thing here and another thing there? Should we wrangle over letters or syllables or expressions and leave behind the truth of the matter?

---

now refute it, here as elsewhere the author demonstrates respect for the Orthodox view and willingness to represent it authentically.

[65] Anselm's logic, as Nicetas fails to point out, is weak. If scriptural texts were open to interpretation regarding everything they do not directly deny, they might be seen to support all manner of absurdities.

"Let us rather leave games of grammar and dialectic to children, instead delving into the meaning inhering in the words.[66] You say, then, that the Holy Spirit proceeds either from the Father alone or not from him alone. If you were to say the Spirit proceeds from the Father alone, then you certainly did not get this from the Gospel. But if you might choose to say the Spirit does not proceed from the Father alone, then you would be saying that he proceeds from the Son even as from the Father, else you would acknowledge that you do not know whence he proceeds. But perhaps you would dare choose neither, since neither is found articulated in that Gospel to which you suppose absolutely nothing must be added. Therefore we may say in clear faith, contradicting neither the Gospel nor yourself, that the Holy Spirit proceeds from the Father and from the Son. For since the Gospel says that the Spirit proceeds from the Father and not from the Father alone, it clearly allows us to say that he proceeds not only from the Father but also from the Son."

Nicetas, archbishop of Nicomedia, replied: "In saying that the Spirit proceeds from the Son and that he proceeds not only from the Father, you force me to say that he proceeds from the Father alone. Then you force me to deny rashly what the Gospel does not say, but you yourself seem to assert similarly rashly something outside it. These words pertain to the one speaking no more than to the one so forced to speak."

Chapter 21
That nothing should be asserted rashly or refuted angrily.

Anselm, bishop of Havelberg, responded: "This was the Platonic way of teaching in the schools of the Academics: to assert without rashness and to refute without anger.[67] Reason is sometimes deceptive, for it sometimes is deceived by the likeness of truth, but honest reason embraces truth with certain knowledge. When

[66] Anselm refers back to his prior discussion of the disparity between words and meaning: *Anticimenon* 2.13.

[67] With some humor and more rhetorical effect, Anselm turns Greek against Greek.

reason misleads, we rightly refute it without anger. So too when it is honest, we defend it without proud rashness, with modest assertion and praiseworthy humility. You should then reprove your own rashness, not mine, because I hold this procession of the Holy Spirit from the Son of which we have treated as demonstrated by many witnesses of the Gospel and of other scriptures. I neither add it rashly nor with misleading argument to the faith. I believe it faithfully. But you know of nothing, nor could you, to the contrary in the Gospel and the other scriptures, so you should reprove your own rashness in denying what neither the Gospel nor any other scripture denies. You rashly seek to disprove what we must demonstrate and ignore what we must disprove. But my faith, as I assert and know it, is blameless. I argue for this faith without rashness, in the testimony of the scriptures and with the assistance of the Holy Spirit. Therefore I am not rash in adding what is certain, rather I believe it faithfully, and I truthfully demonstrate what we must believe. But likewise you must refute what seems dubious to you without anger. Therefore confess with me that the Holy Spirit proceeds also from the Son.

"If you do not yet dare to do so, perhaps because you are too weak-spirited, you are anxious when there is nothing to fear. So at least do this: keep your silence as I confess it. Do not deny what leaves you uncertain, what I affirm with solid certainty, with the impudent monosyllable of negation 'not.' But if you want to respond, respond thus: that you are entirely ignorant as to whether the Spirit does or does not proceed from the Son. Then you will have responded rightly, that is by confessing your ignorance and meanwhile not denying my faith. For how can anyone properly judge what he does not know? And you cannot deny your ignorance about this. Stop judging this matter, presuming to deny what you heretofore held only to be uncertain, and what you rashly then denied even though you were ignorant in the matter. Indeed it is not fitting for one who wanders off the path without knowing he is lost to try to correct another wisely following the correct way. Likewise it is incongruous for one whose faith is clear to imply doubt, unless perhaps that false opinion of the Academics still remains with you or with some of your fellows, by which they considered the highest wisdom to be endlessly-argued ignorance of all things.[68] For that reason they are called masters of ignorance, since they responded to every question with: what if you are mistaken? Aristotle, one of their sages, therefore says: to doubt everything will be useful."[69]

Nicetas, archbishop of Nicomedia, then said: "The Greek sages never said that opinion should be taken for truth. Rather they chose humbly to express doubt concerning ambiguities about faith rather than rashly to frame definitions, since we must hand over to the fire of the Holy Spirit matters of which scripture says only little, or when the human intellect fails to comprehend them. We are men, and our human temptation is to understand something otherwise than as it is. To perform the sacrilege of breaking communion, to begin a schism, or to partake of heresy for love of one's own opinion or for envy of one's betters—this is diabolical presumption.[70] But it is angelic perfection to understand in nothing something other than what it is. Therefore since we are men, so often deceived and mistaken, let us beware of diabolical presumption until we reach the perfection of angelic thought. For this reason, then, our fathers humbly shunned affirmation of this procession with the phrase 'he proceeds from the Son,' because they did not know the truth of the matter and guarded against rash expression. Nor did they ever adopt the negative statement, 'he does not proceed from the Son,' because they feared error and so avoided offense against scripture by stating neither case directly unless occasionally they were provoked by the impudent, rash assertions of Latins who came to us arrogantly vaunting their loftiness of speech and beating the air with noisy disputations. Such foreigners wished to display their smattering of knowledge, trying

[68] Anselm dredges up a commonplace of anti-philosophical polemic—that the Academics only questioned, never established truth: Augustine had made a similar point in *Confessions* 5.19 (Augustine, *Confessions*, trans. Henry Chadwick [Oxford: Oxford University Press, 1991], 84). The African Father then went on to write three books against philosophy to expand upon it: *Against the Academics*, trans. Mary P. Garvey (Milwaukee: Marquette University Press, 1942).

[69] Medieval commentators frequently attributed this posture to Aristotle. See, for instance, a commentary on the Rule of St. Benedict: *Sancti Benedicti regula cum commentariis* 61, PL 66, col. 862.

[70] The interlocutor Nicetas directly describes schism as disaster on an individual moral level as well as for the wider church.

in their pride to obfuscate, even to smother the great wisdom of the Greeks in clouds of sophistry. But we did not yield to them, rather sent them back defeated, as they should have been. Now, however, we freely attend to your mildness, beloved servant of God, because you speak this word that can save our souls humbly and meekly, likewise listening humbly to us. So you maintain reason and attention to authoritative texts rather than contention.[71] Truly, what we have offered you here—a public assembly in the royal city—has heretofore never been granted to any earlier Latin, to any of those extolling himself in opposition to true knowledge of God. But let us go on.

"How is it that the first Council of Nicaea, where 318 fathers took part, did not treat of the procession of the Holy Spirit from the Son? Clearly the creed composed in that council and confirmed by the authority of so many fathers contains nothing of this sort. But what it does contain is locked with the key of anathema so that nothing can be added, nothing taken away without the greatest scandal to the church and danger to the soul. How then do you think that you will escape that anathema when you do not shrink from introducing the Holy Spirit's procession from the Son where it was not said before, from adding it to the faith, if you hold that the Council of Nicaea is worthy of respect for all Catholics?"[72]

Chapter 22
That we would not be rash to add something to the Gospel if it does not contradict the Gospel, just as was done at the Council of Nicaea and at many other councils.

Anselm, bishop of Havelberg, then said: "I embrace the creed of the Council of Nicaea with due veneration, and as a Catholic I embrace the twenty-two chapters of the same council that come down to us in written exemplars. But when I assert the Holy Spirit's procession

---

[71] Anselm as author seems less to shed favorable light on his namesake interlocutor than to suggest what successful discussion might be. He here allows Nicetas the magnanimity of pointing toward useful resolution of their debate.

[72] Nicetas refers to the Council of Ephesus's prohibition of accretions to the Nicene Creed: Tanner, ed., *Decrees of the Ecumenical Councils*, vol. 1, 68–69.

from the Son—a belief the Nicene documents do not prohibit—I neither teach nor add anything contrary to that creed so that I should dread its anathema. That council's statutes prohibit that we add anything contrary to its creed under threat of anathema, but they do not forbid that we add anything at all. Nor do they forbid that we teach nothing—nor is that the case, for we indeed permit the teaching of other things. You are a learned reader of the Gospel and, as you asserted before, the faith established by the Lord Jesus in the Gospel—the evangelical faith that only a sham defender would either add to or diminish—is sufficient for the salvation of the faithful. Since you do not wish to add or to erase or even to change one stroke or letter, or to explain the sense of evangelical scripture with other words meaning the very same thing, tell me then how you could ever be persuaded to accept the Council of Nicaea or any other council, when so many things necessary to the Christian faith were established in nearly all the general councils though they were nowhere in the Gospel?[73] Tell me further—if you are not willing to accept the Holy Spirit's procession from the Son for the sole reason that you do not want to seem to add anything to the Gospel not explicitly contained in it—why do you not therefore reject the faith of the Council of Nicaea as approved and accepted by the universal church, when that same faith is certainly never found so clearly and openly set forth in the Gospel? Do you believe in the Father, Son, and Holy Spirit? Do you adore the Father, Son, and Holy Spirit as one God in substance, three in persons? Do you believe in the Father, Son, and Holy Spirit as the Holy Trinity, one almighty God, a deity whole in essence and substance in the coeternal and omnipotent Trinity of one will, power, and majesty, creator of all creatures?"[74]

Nicetas, archbishop of Nicomedia, answered: "I believe, for I am a Christian, not an Arian."

Anselm, bishop of Havelberg, then said: "Do you believe that each of the persons of Holy Trinity is the one true God, complete and perfect?"

---

[73] See Matthew 5:18.

[74] Here the interlocutor Anselm queries Nicetas as if catechizing him.

Nicetas, archbishop of Nicomedia, replied: "I do so believe because I am Catholic, not Sabellian, and this is the correct faith of believers. We neither divide the substance in God as do the Arians, nor do we confuse his persons as do the Sabellians."

Anselm, bishop of Havelberg, returned: "Do not become angry, I beg you in brotherhood. Do not be offended if I question you a bit further, since I ask not so that I might watch you like a spy, ambushing you in your response, but so that I learn something from you or perhaps you learn something from me. Then we might pardon one another and come to know each other's faith."[75]

Nicetas, archbishop of Nicomedia, responded: "Ask freely what you will. I welcome it."

Anselm, bishop of Havelberg, then spoke: "Do you believe that the Son of God is the Word of God, eternal, born of the Father, consubstantial, omnipotent, and equal to the Father's divinity in all ways, born in time of the Holy Spirit and the ever-virgin Mary and having a rational soul? Do you believe that he had two births, an eternal birth from the Father and a temporal birth from his mother, that he was true God and true man, proper and perfect in each of his natures, not adopted, not as an image only, the one and only Son of God in and from two natures yet one in person, impassible and immortal in his divinity but in his humanity experiencing the true suffering of the flesh for us and for our salvation?"

Nicetas, archbishop of Nicomedia, answered: "I believe and I embrace all these things because our holy mother church so decreed in response to the heretical Nestorian belief that there are two persons in Christ, and after the heretical Eutychian belief that there is only one nature in Christ, and after very many other errors set aside concisely and clearly in your language thus far in our discussion."[76]

Anselm, bishop of Havelberg, then said: "Do you also believe the Holy Spirit is true God, whole and perfect, coequal and

---

[75] Anselm here acknowledges that his tone has antagonized Nicetas, and he effectively apologizes.

[76] Here and immediately below, Anselm elicits Nicetas's protestation that he repudiates the christological heresies of Nestorius and Eutyches outlined in his first book: *Anticimenon* 1.9.

coessential with the Father and the Son, omnipotent and coeternal through all things?" Nicetas, archbishop of Nicomedia, responded: "What you have said is indeed the catholic faith, confirmed after the Macedonian heresy and strengthened at the council of Alexandria by many orthodox fathers treating of the divinity of the Holy Spirit, understanding him in the consubstantial Trinity. Whoever does not hold this faith in its entirety reveals himself an unfaithful Christian."[77]

Anselm, bishop of Havelberg, said: "You believe well, you worship well, and you speak well. Tell me then, dear brother, for the sake of the charity we share, where in the Gospel is this faith of yours found so clearly set forth? The Gospel teaches there clearly that we believe in God the Father and in God the Son, when the Son says: *You believe in God, believe also in me* (John 14:1). You believe in the Holy Spirit, and you believe in him rightly, but nowhere in the Gospel, to my knowledge, is this belief expressed clearly and simply in words. Nevertheless, scripture directly proclaims the Holy Spirit to be God where the apostle says: *Know you not that you are the temple of God?* And immediately he adds: *and that the Spirit of God dwelleth in you* (1 Cor 3:16). For God dwells in his temple, but the Spirit of God does not dwell in the temple of God as a minister, as in another place: *Or know you not that your members are the temple of the Holy Ghost, who is in you, whom you have from God, and that you are not your own? For you have been bought at a great price. Glorify . . . God in your body* (1 Cor 6:19-20). And again: *The temple of God is holy, which you are* (1 Cor 3:17).

"You rightly worship God the Father because the Gospel teaches this: *True adorers shall adore the Father in spirit and in truth* (John 4:23). You also rightly worship God the Son because you believe in him as God and you worship him correctly as God. The Gospel suggests this: *I and the Father are one. . . . The Father is in me and I in the Father* (John 10: 30-38). For since Father and Son are truly one God, each in the other and consubstantial, not one in person, as I have said, then we must rightly adore the one God in each as in the other. But that we worship the Spirit as one to be adored and glorified together with the Father and the Son—where, I ask,

---

[77] Anselm had addressed the Macedonian heresy also in *Anticimenon* 1.9.

is this ever clearly and distinctly set forth in the Gospel? Yet any careful reader, if he diligently considers the verse, *true worshipers will worship the Father in spirit and in truth*, finds there immediately that we must worship the whole Trinity, I think. For when the scripture says, *true adorers shall adore the Father*, it immediately continues, *in spirit*, and again, *in truth*, evidently meaning that we must worship the Father in the Spirit and in Truth, that is in the Son, and we must worship the Son in the Father and the Holy Spirit, and the Holy Spirit in the Father and the Son.

"But the heretics, passing over the text of the Gospel carelessly and without restraint, foolishly wandering through it without examining the spirit and life hidden in the evangelical words, utterly failed to assert that the Holy Spirit should be worshiped. Nor did they with decent care examine the Gospel writings that show clearly whether the Spirit should be worshiped or not. See how your argument holds up, in which you claim that you so revere the Gospel that you would not dare to add anything to the faith you hold to be sufficiently established in it! Yet in this you demonstrably contradict yourself in that first you certainly felt and said that nothing should be added to the faith of the Gospel but afterwards, in Christian confession, you affirmed the faith of the holy Trinity as defined, handed down, and strengthened against heresies by the Council of Nicaea and the other councils.

Chapter 23
That faith in the Holy Trinity was fully founded in councils presided over by the Holy Spirit as *pantoskopos*, that is, the bishop over all, first author and founder of the Gospel.

"Nevertheless, you would not further so restrict the faith of the Gospel that the creed of the Nicene Council—even the other councils of the orthodox fathers at which that Holy Spirit whom you only a little while ago called *pantoskopos*, bishop of all, presided as author—might seem superfluous. The catholic faith was so strengthened and confirmed in those councils that if they had not been celebrated, the very faith that we hold, whereby we profess and believe in unity in Trinity and Trinity in unity, would not exist today, or if it did would toil and waver under innumerable

heresies. Since the Lord was aware of how many things would
have to be added for the establishment of the catholic faith after
he had told his disciples everything that was appropriate for that
time, he added: *I have yet many things to say to you, but you cannot
bear them now. But when he, the Spirit of truth, has come, he will teach
you all truth* (John 16:12-13). You remember in your brotherhood
what the Lord says in the Gospel about himself: *I am the way, and
the truth, and the life* (John 14:6). But he also says this: *When he,
the Spirit of truth, is come, he will teach you all truth* (John 16:13).
Behold, the Holy Spirit is the affection of the Father and the Son,
the binding together of both, the charity of both—the Spirit, I say,
of the Son who is Truth, the Spirit of truth teaching all the truth.
Proceeding from the Son who is Truth, the Spirit framed the Gospel
and established a faith suitable to the apostles living in their own
time. Behold, the Spirit was promised by the Son when he affirmed
that he still had much to say, but in good time! And what do you
think the same Holy Spirit, the spirit of truth, taught, except what
he knew the Son, that Truth from whom he proceeded, still had
to say? Certainly the Spirit himself taught nothing other than what
the Son said he had yet to say. Because the Holy Spirit proceeds
from the mouth of Truth, who is Christ, that Spirit first framed
the Gospel, and afterwards he took part in the councils of the holy
fathers as author and teacher of truth, as the Son had promised.
In the councils of the holy fathers he explained the faith that he
had founded more concisely in the Gospel. Proceeding from the
Son, he made known truthfully and taught more completely what
the Son still had to say. Then the whole church, spread over all
the world, could at once sustain what before the apostles alone
were unable to bear.[78]

"So, as I have said, the Holy Spirit took part in the councils of
the holy fathers, coming as promised to teach the whole truth then,
now, and always. Presiding there as the teacher of all, elucidating
faith in the Holy Trinity such as we hold between the impieties of
Arius's division of the divine substance and Sabellius's confusion

---

[78] Anselm's description of the progressive revelation of doctrine and institutions here accords with Book 1's description of the development of the faith: see
esp. *Anticimenon* 1.6-8.

of the persons, he communicated the whole truth little by little. He instituted the ecclesiastical sacraments, established as well-ordered the form of baptism that the Lord had instituted, and put in order the rite the holy church maintains for the consecration of the Body and Blood of the Lord. He set up patriarchs, metropolitans, archbishops, bishops, priests, deacons, and the other lesser ecclesiastical orders of divine ministry appropriate to the house of God. He defined unction with holy oil and the sacrament of penance, as well as the imposition of hands for holy orders. He appointed solemn Masses and other divine offices for the praise of God. Through the agency of catholic doctors he revealed for us the sacred scriptures of the Old and New Testaments as one raining on them from without. As one watering from within, he made himself known by suggesting to us, through his interior inspiration, those secret and divine things mysteriously hidden by the seal of the divine scriptures.[79] With his power as most high he powerfully demolished the heresies that crept in little by little, and through apostolic men he proclaimed ecclesiastical laws for the preservation of the Christian religion. In sum, he illuminated the entire church he had so instructed in holy teaching by the light of true knowledge, gradually teaching the whole truth. He still sheds such light and always will. For God, who never deceives us, promised this: I shall give you the Spirit *to abide with you forever* (John 14:16). And again: *Behold, I am with you all days, even unto the consummation of the world* (Matt 28:20), that is, through the indwelling grace of the Holy Spirit. So the same Holy Spirit dictated the very Gospel and those councils celebrated by the orthodox fathers. Gradually he taught the whole truth, speaking nothing contrary to that truth. Therefore you can now assuredly say that the Holy Spirit proceeds from the Son, since what the same Holy Spirit appears to have expressed about himself only dimly in the

---

[79] Anselm's figure of irrigation by the Holy Spirit derives from 1 Corinthians 12:13, as discussed in Augustine, *On the Trinity* 15.33 (Rotelle, ed., *Trinity*, 422). Here and in his emphasis on the Holy Spirit as charity Anselm follows Augustine's final book on the Trinity closely (*On the Trinity* 15.31).

Gospel, he later fully clarified in the various councils as the teacher of both of the testaments."[80]

Nicetas, archbishop of Nicomedia, answered: "You have joined together the texts of the Gospel and the sacred councils of the holy fathers appropriately, and you have credibly shown that the same Holy Spirit is the author of the Gospel and of the councils, as we also believe, thus honoring the councils with a veneration equal to our reverence for the Gospel. Truly, both we ourselves and many others of our sages do not dissent from you concerning the meaning of the Spirit's procession. But as I have often said already, to speak so of his procession has not been our practice heretofore. We do not shrink from the meaning of his procession, for we understand it rightly, but rather we recoil from unfamiliar expression of that procession. Many Greek doctors who expounded the divine scriptures, although they clearly implied to us your very understanding of the Spirit's procession in appropriate words, nevertheless did not explicitly use the term 'procession' nor did they hand it down to us in our pattern of speech."[81]

Chapter 24
That many Greek writers have said that the Holy Spirit proceeds from the Son as from the Father.

Anselm, bishop of Havelberg, then said: "Why do you say this? The famous Athanasius, archbishop of Alexandria and fiercest disputant against the Arian heresy—perfect and learned in the catholic faith, stranger to none of the Greek sages—spoke thus in his statement of the faith: 'The Holy Spirit is from the Father and the Son.' He then added, 'proceeding.'[82] Athanasius taught clearly that the Son proceeds from both when he referred the Son's procession to both just as he referred the Son's being to both, especially

[80] Anselm had addressed the increasing revelation of the Holy Spirit's role throughout Christian time in *Anticimenon* 1.6.

[81] Nicetas now shifts the basis of his resistance to *filioque* to history and practice, away from theology. He begins to agree that the substance, if not the precise expression, of Orthodox pneumatology is consonant with the Roman stance.

[82] Again see Pelikan and Hotchkiss, eds., *Creeds and Confessions*, vol. 1, 673–77.

since the Holy Spirit does not have his being from the Father and
the Son in any way other than by procession.

"Didymus too was an important doctor of the Greeks. He published many books, among them three on the Holy Trinity, and
commented on the work of Origen *On First Principles*, that is, *Peri-
archon*, leaving excellent explanations in these texts. This Didymus,
deprived of his eyes' external sight but perfectly illumined within,
showed clearly that the Holy Spirit proceeds also from the Son,
saying in his book *On the Holy Spirit* translated by our Jerome,
learned in the Greek, Latin, and Hebrew tongues: 'The Holy Spirit,
spirit of truth and spirit of wisdom, cannot hear what he does not
know from the voice of the Son, since that Spirit is himself brought
forth from the Son, that is God proceeding from God and spirit
of truth proceeding from Truth, consoler taken from consolation.'
So says Didymus.[83] Indeed, the creed of the Council of Ephesus,
with its two hundred Greek bishops, makes clear in these words
from what truth the Spirit proceeds: 'Although in substance he is
the Spirit of the Son, and we understand that his person, according to which he is Spirit and not Son, is distinct, nevertheless he
is not different from himself. For he is called the Spirit of truth,
and the Truth is Christ, while the Spirit proceeds from him even
as he does from God the Father.'[84]

Likewise Cyril, bishop of Alexandria, begins thus in his eighth
letter to Nestorius: 'To the most reverend and most God-loving,
and so forth. If the Son is a spirit in spiritual substance, or if he
is understood as such in his role as spirit and not as Son, still the
Son is not distant from the Spirit, for he is called the Spirit of
truth and the Spirit flows forth from the Son just as he does from

[83] With his reference to Didymus, Anselm seems to borrow extensively from
Peter Abelard's *Theologia Christiana*, Book 4. Abelard here incorporated and revised
much of his earlier thought, notably the work on the Trinity for which he had been
condemned at the Council of Soissons in 1121: see *Cambridge Companion to Abelard*,
224–35. From this paragraph through Anselm's discussion of John Chrysostom's
view later in this chapter, and then again in *Anticimenon* 2.26, Anselm responds to
Abelard's sources and arguments. For Abelard's use of Didymus, Cyril, and John
Chrysostom see *Theologia Christiana* 4.128–30, in Abelard, *Opera Theologica* 2, ed.
Buytaert, 329–30. On the relationship between Anselm's general argument and
Abelard's see Russell, "Anselm of Havelberg," 1:39–41.

[84] See Tanner, ed., *Decrees of the Ecumenical Councils*, vol. 1, 56–57.

God the Father.' So too John Chrysostom begins in his twenty-sixth homily on expounding the creed: 'Let the universal church rejoice. This very one is the Spirit proceeding from the Father and the Son. He divides his own gifts just as he wills.' Again in Homily 28, in another explanation of the same creedal passage, he begins thus: The Spirit is 'over the fabric of the whole church. So we must believe that the Holy Spirit is of the Father and of the Son. Again we say that this Holy Spirit is coequal to the Father and the Son and proceeds from the Father and the Son. Believe this, lest evil talk corrupt your good customs.' Yet again: 'See the sacrament of the Trinity everywhere! Behold, we believe in the Holy Spirit. This Holy Spirit proceeds from the Father and the Son and is joined with them in love.'[85]

"Augustine too, bishop of Hippo and legate of the province of Numidia in Africa—an illustrious man and the most eloquent of Africans in his explication of all the scriptures, who took part in many African councils, who wrote many books against the Manichean and Donatist heresies and published much exegesis of the Old and New Testaments, whose countless volumes are read all over the world as highest authority—that Augustine always clearly inserted into his writings much evidence about the Holy Spirit's procession from the Son. Jerome, Ambrose, Isidore, Hilary, and many other doctors in the Latin language, as well as Leo the Great, high priest of the great city of Rome, included in their writings many things about the Holy Spirit's procession from the Son. I do not set their writings before you because among the Greeks the Latin doctors were perhaps not of such great authority in those times as they would have been if they were Greek.[86] That circumstance is regrettable, yet peace was preserved between us and you, as it is said: *God is not a respecter of persons* (Acts 10:34), and *the Spirit breatheth where he will* (John 3:8)."

Nicetas, archbishop of Nicomedia, replied: "I am pleased that you wished to adduce our doctors. But I ask whether you, although

[85] Again, see Abelard, *Theologia Christiana* 4.129–30, in Abelard, *Opera Theologica* 2, ed. Buytaert, 329–30.

[86] Anselm reminds Nicetas that he here emphasizes the Greek rather than the Latin tradition.

you are a Latin, accept the authority of those whom you named and that of our other doctors."

Anselm, bishop of Havelberg, then said: "I do not exclude, disdain, reject, or judge worthy of rejection any gift of the Holy Spirit given to any faithful Christian, whether Greek, Latin, or any other race. On the contrary, I receive and embrace with an open mind every man who speaks and writes what is true and consonant with apostolic teaching."

Nicetas, archbishop of Nicomedia, then said: "I seem to have found a Latin who is truly catholic. Would that more such Latins come to us in these times! Often when they come, they act superior even to everything great and wonderful. Never do they speak to us humbly and inclusively, but haughtily, intolerably. But to return to our point, sometimes our doctors have written about faith in the Holy Trinity or about its creedal statement. Then, in the course of explaining their opinion, they may have happened to say that the Holy Spirit proceeds or flows forth from the Father and the Son. Yet they did not say this with the precise meaning of procession or flowing forth as that they attribute to procession from the Father. For what proceeds from the Father proceeds strictly speaking, and because it proceeds in a strict sense, it is also said strictly to proceed. But when we sometimes read that the Spirit proceeds or flows from the Son, not even this is said in a strict sense, for the Spirit does not properly proceed or flow forth from the Father; rather, strictly speaking, that Spirit proceeds from the Father as his first cause and origin. But if we sometimes read or say that the Spirit proceeds or flows from the Son, we do not say this in a strict sense nor is it strictly speaking the case because what is from the Son or what proceeds or flows forth from the Son is not so or does not so as from its first cause. For the Son is what he is, that is, the Son. He sends the Holy Spirit proceeding or flowing from himself, not from himself as himself, rather from the Father as his own first cause and principle. Therefore, as I have said, we do not properly say that the Holy Spirit proceeds from the Father as from his first cause.

"So the wisest of the Greeks have distinguished this procession of the Holy Spirit from the Father from his procession from the Son, ascribing the first cause of his procession strictly speaking to the Father, from whom the Son is by begetting, and from whom

the Holy Spirit is by procession. Moreover, they have ascribed the
procession of the same Holy Spirit to the Son, but not in strict
terms, since the Son is not of himself, nor is he his own cause, and
neither is he strictly speaking the first cause of the Holy Spirit in
the sense that the Spirit proceeds strictly speaking from the Son
as he does from the Father. Therefore the Father is of no other,
the Son is strictly speaking of the Father, and the Holy Spirit is
of both. Nevertheless, the Spirit is strictly speaking of the Father,
since the Father is of no other, while the Spirit is not strictly speaking of the Son, since the Son is not of no other but of the Father,
and that Son knows from the Father that the Holy Spirit is of
that same Father. And so I concede that the Holy Spirit proceeds
strictly speaking from the Father, who is of no other, but he does
not proceed strictly speaking from the Son, who is himself of the
Father. This distinction, as I have already said, is what the wisest
of the Greeks have established."[87]

Chapter 25
**That the Holy Spirit, although he proceeds from both Father
and Son, nevertheless is found in both the Latin and Greek
authors to proceed strictly speaking and principally from
the Father.**

Anselm, bishop of Havelberg, then said: "We do not deny that the
Holy Spirit proceeds strictly speaking from the Father, because our
own doctors have taught us this very thing, whether they learned
it from yours or yours from ours. Whence our Jerome says in his
Explanation of the Catholic Faith, expounding the Council of Nicaea's
'We believe in one Holy Spirit who proceeds from the Father': 'We
find in scripture that the Holy Spirit is true God, and that he is
strictly speaking of the Father.'[88] And again: 'The Son and the Spirit
are strictly speaking of the Father, and the Spirit is truly of the

---

[87] Nicetas avoids naming particular authorities among "the wisest of the Greeks,"
effectively asserting that all of the Greek sources Anselm has claimed as supporting his
view in fact understood procession in a way different from Anselm's interpretation.

[88] See again Tanner, ed., *Decrees of the Ecumenical Councils*, vol. 1, 4–5; Pelikan
and Hotchkiss, eds., *Creeds and Confessions*, vol. 1, 158–67. See also Pseudo-Jerome,
Epistolae 17, PL 30, col. 176.

Father and the Son in his procession.'[89] Therefore accept first that the Holy Spirit is strictly speaking of the Father, as scripture says: *By the word of the Lord the heavens were established, and all the power of them by the spirit of his mouth* (Ps 32:6). And the Savior says: *The Spirit of truth who proceeds from the Father* (John 15:26). Again the eminent doctor, the blessed Augustine, says in *On the Trinity*, Book 15, chapter 17: "In this Trinity the Son and no other is called the Word of God, and this for a purpose. So the Holy Spirit and no other is called the gift of God. Nor is the Word begotten from any other or does the Spirit proceed principally from any but God the Father.' Again in Book 15, chapter 17: 'And the Holy Spirit proceeds principally from him of whom the Son is born. Moreover, I have added 'principally' because the Holy Spirit is also found to proceed from the Son. But the Father granted this to him not as to one already existing but not yet having this property, rather the Father gave whatever he gave to the only-begotten Word in begetting him. The Father begot the Son in this manner, so that the good common to them might proceed from the Son also.'[90] Augustine again writes in chapter 26: 'Just as begetting from the Father, without any change from the Father's nature, attributes to the Son an essence without beginning in time, so too does procession from both attribute to the Holy Spirit, without any change from the Father's or Son's nature, being without any origin in time.' And again in the same passage: 'The Son is born from the Father, and the Holy Spirit proceeds principally from the Father. He proceeds from both Father and Son by their joint gift, without any interval of time.' And below: 'The Spirit is not begotten from both, but as Spirit of both proceeds from both.' And again in the next chapter: 'We cannot say that the Holy Spirit is not life, when the Father is life and the Son is life. Thence just as the Father, having life in himself, grants to the Son that he also have life in himself, so the Father grants to the Holy Spirit to proceed from the Son just as from the Father himself.'[91]

"According to these words of the blessed doctors Jerome and Augustine we must then concede that the Holy Spirit proceeds

---

[89] Pseudo-Jerome, *Epistolae* 17, PL 30, col. 179.
[90] Augustine, *On the Trinity*, *recte* 15.29 (Rotelle, ed., 419).
[91] Augustine, *On the Trinity* 15.47-48 (Rotelle, ed., 432–33).

strictly speaking and principally from the Father as from a first cause, because he proceeds from the Father as if in the first instance, and the Father has the Spirit from no other, rather from himself. Certainly the Father is the first cause and not the cause of the first cause. Indeed, since the Son is not of himself but of the Father, the Holy Spirit proceeds from the Son not from himself, but rather as he has this attribute from the Father, from whom he also has being by begetting. So the Father is the principal author and causal principle of procession for the Holy Spirit as he is of begetting of the Son. Even if the Spirit is not ordained to proceed strictly speaking and principally from the Son, nevertheless just as it is true that he proceeds from the Father, so is it also unambiguously true that he proceeds from the Son. We must acknowledge no inequality of his procession, since we have affirmed here that the Spirit proceeds equally from both. Although the Spirit proceeds from the person of the Father, he nonetheless also proceeds from another person, that of the Son. Yet we must not say that there are two different processions or two Holy Spirits in the way that the two persons of the Father and the Son are different. We must say rather that only one procession is from both. This procession is not first from the Father and afterward from the Son, rather the Holy Spirit's procession is one and the same, eternal and substantial, simultaneous from the Father and the Son. That Holy Spirit proceeding from both Father and Son at once and together, substantially and eternally—as one with the Father and the Son in their respective persons, that is, in their plurality of persons—constitutes the entire Trinity."

Nicetas, archbishop of Nicomedia, responded: "Now we seem able to agree, for we find that our doctors and yours never have disagreed in this opinion. If we understand their writings correctly, however, both you and we find that they have written carefully about this question. But what do you say about this, that some sages among the Greeks say that the Holy Spirit proceeds from the Father through the Son?"[92]

---

[92] On the Greek tradition that the procession of the Spirit might be "through the Son" as well as "from the Father" see Chadwick's discussion of the seventh-century Greek defender of the *filioque*, Maximus Confessor: *East and West*, 29, 69, 93, 267–69. This formulation was viewed sympathetically by the Carolingian theo-

Chapter 26
That some Greeks and even some Latins think that the Holy Spirit proceeds from the Father through the Son, and that they adduce inappropriate imagery.

Anselm, bishop of Havelberg, then said: "I am not aware that such matters have been addressed or even suggested, and so at the moment I do not know how I should respond to this except as the Apostle admonishes: *Avoid . . . novelties of words* (1 Tim 6:20). Those who say these things know what they mean. As for me, I read of notions of this sort in Book 12 of *On the Trinity* by Hilary of Poitiers, bishop and famous doctor. There this Hilary speaks to God the Father 'about the Father and the Son in your Holy Spirit, arising from you and sent through him.'[93] Again: 'Your Holy Spirit is from you and through him . . . . Let me adore you, our Father, and let me win the favor of your Holy Spirit, who is from you through your only-begotten Son.'[94] Hilary says these things, and I think we can understand them according to our prior conclusion that the Father and the Son send forth the Holy Spirit who thus proceeds from both, and the Father takes this attribute from no other while the Son has it from the Father.

"But that the Holy Spirit should proceed from the Father into the Son and thus the Spirit proceed through the Son to sanctify creation—so that he does not proceed at the same time from Father and Son alike—is entirely absurd to say or even think. Granted, some wholly ignorant people who purport to be theologians foolishly propound this notion, so revealing their stupidity. Thus they say the Son of man proceeds from the Father in his mother, and proceeds from the mother into the world, taking his being and

logian Eriugena and, as well, by the eventual Council of Florence, which in 1439 attempted an abortive suture in the East-West doctrinal argument by agreeing that, in mutual acceptance, the West would continue in the use of *filioque* while the East omitted it: Chadwick, *East and West*, 270.

[93] Hilary of Poitiers, *Trinity* 12.55, trans. Stephen McKenna, 541. In this and the immediately following citation of Hilary, Anselm seems to follow Abelard's discussion: *Theologia Christiana* 4.136, in Abelard, *Opera Theologica* 2, ed. Buytaert, 334. See also Gasper, *Anselm of Canterbury*, 24–25.

[94] Abelard, *Theologia Christiana* 12.57, in Abelard, *Opera Theologica* 2, ed. Buytaert, 543.

nature from the substance of both. So too they say that the Holy Spirit is truly of the Father into the Son, and through the Son the Spirit proceeds to sanctify creation. Men who speak thus, since they are in time, speak temporally, deceiving themselves in ascribing temporal qualities to what is eternal. For when the Son of man proceeds from the Father into his mother, he does not then proceed from his mother into the world, and when he proceeds from his mother into the world, he does not then proceed from the Father. So then those who offer this inappropriate image are consequently drawn into error and into just condemnation for it.

"Others, overreaching themselves in theological discussion even as they fall short of true theology, have framed an equally inappropriate image. They say that just as a lake is said to proceed from a spring and not from a stream but through a stream, that is, when the water of the lake comes out of the spring into the stream and arrives through the stream at a pool, so too the Holy Spirit is said to proceed properly from the Father as if from the highest source, into the Son as if into a stream, and so through the Son as if through a stream for the sanctification of men, as if into the pool of this world.[95] But I am astounded and recoil from such comparisons between the comprehensible and the incomprehensible, for these images are so far below what they would suggest that they communicate no knowledge of the truth, rather thwart minds attempting to understand. Such minds then often turn away from right faith, shut from the path of learning divine and spiritual truth by the heavy weight of physical imagery. Those who walk in faith instead set aside all such images, casting them behind and advancing in faith through their speculative intelli-

---

[95] Anselm here seems to respond to Abelard's criticism of Anselm of Canterbury's description of the procession of the Holy Spirit according to water imagery: compare *Theologia Christiana* 4.83 and 4.138, in Abelard, *Opera Theologica* 2, ed. Buytaert, 304 and 333–34; Anselm of Canterbury had attached this image to the Nile: *Incarnation*, 33–34; *Procession of the Holy Spirit*, 9, in *Anselm of Canterbury 3: Two Letters Concerning Roscelin, the Incarnation of the Work, Why God Became Man, The Virgin Conception and Original Sin, the Procession of the Holy Spirit, Three Letters on the Sacraments*, trans. Jasper Hopkins and Herbert Richardson (Toronto: Edwin Mellen, 1976), 211–14. Gillian Evans notes the community of issues and images between the two Anselms' respective works but finds no direct dependency of Anselm of Havelberg on the earlier Anselm: "Anselm of Canterbury and Anselm of Havelberg," esp. 163, 175.

gence, lifting themselves beyond themselves and climbing to the heights. So let those remain behind who walk in reason and cling to only the semblance of truth, loaded down with the burden of human ignorance and oppressed by the deep sleep of false opinion. They rightly fall behind because they set reason before faith, so are unworthy to go beyond reason with faith leading them.[96] Such ridiculous metaphors are never suggested by the wise. Instead, as we have already agreed, I think, we should embrace the catholic faith concerning the Holy Spirit's procession from the Father and the Son. But perhaps we might yet discover some unknown text that we should accept and study on account of the dignity of its author, such as the writings mentioned here of the bishop Hilary, a great authority in the church. Even if that text, I say, should seem to imply something strange, yet we should read and thoroughly explain it so that we understand its harmony with scripture and so attain to the law of charity with our catholic understanding."

Nicetas, archbishop of Nicomedia, then said: "We know that this Hilary, the bishop of Poitiers of whom you speak, took part in many Greek councils of old. He both was and is greatly esteemed among us. You expounded his writings before us carefully just now.[97] We too, if we ever found similar things in the books of our doctors, would discern their meaning in like fashion. For when exact meaning on some matter is clear in holy scriptures, prudent readers may easily direct other writings toward their true meaning. Therefore you should know in your charity, now that we have made so many arguments and adduced so many authorities, that I and indeed all the Greek sages concur in your opinion about the procession of the Holy Spirit. But you must not think that we confess this because we were bested by you in this disputation. Rather wise Greeks have always held such a view when this very question was presented humbly by wise Latins. Then the Greeks have confessed with their mouths what they believed

[96] The speaker Anselm, despite his facility with logical argument against Greeks represented here, declares himself firmly on the side of the primacy of faith characterized in Etienne Gilson's famous essay as the Augustinian perspective: *Reason and Revelation in the Middle Ages* (New York: Scribner, 1938), 3–33.

[97] The interlocutor Nicetas here tries too hard to find agreement with his opponent. Hilary had in fact been unaware of the great Nicene Council until long after it occurred. See Chadwick, *East and West*, 14.

in their hearts. Indeed, all writings about this question framed by the law of charity—from Latin and Greek sages alike—have agreed as one. But nothing that foolish Greeks and arrogant Latins speak and argue about among themselves matters to us."[98]

Chapter 27
On agreement on this question, and on removing this obstacle between the two peoples through the authority of the Roman pontiff in a general council.

Anselm, bishop of Havelberg, answered: "Let us give thanks to the Holy Spirit, who has willed that we put an end to this question in brotherly peace and acknowledgment of agreement in the presence of many men who share our view. Nothing remains now but that you teach and write without reservation even as you believe, that the Spirit proceeds from both Father and Son, and that you maintain this agreement concerning the faith with the holy Roman Church, mother of all the churches, which also teaches and writes this truth. For he who does not love the unity of the church does not love God. He who is opposed to that unity, according to the blessed Ambrose, archbishop of Milan, is surely a heretic.[99] And whoever buttresses himself with presumption and obstinacy sins without the mitigation of ignorance, so the more gravely, when reason and authority overcome him.[100] Your holiness and my humility require, since we are bishops, not only that we teach wisely what we know, but also that we patiently learn those things about which we may perhaps be ignorant."

Nicetas, archbishop of Nicomedia, replied: "I embrace your humility, beloved brother, and I acknowledge with admiration your

[98] Anselm as author allows his speaker Nicetas at least to purport that his Western interlocutor has not overwhelmed his arguments, rather that their dialogue has exposed hidden consonance between Western and Eastern beliefs.

[99] Anselm's attribution to Ambrose follows other medieval authors': see, for instance, Bernold of Constance, *De Berengarii haeresiarchae damnatione multiplici*, PL 148, col. 1459.

[100] The eleventh-century author Bernold of Constance had attributed this formulation to Ambrose and other fathers of the church in his condemnation of Berengar of Tours: Bernold, PL 148, col. 1459.

devotion to the truth of faith. I cannot but be moved when you speak. I assent to everything you have said and I affirm it with all my mind and body. But we cannot suddenly present these words, 'the Holy Spirit proceeds from the Son,' to be taught or written openly without scandal among the ordinary folk or to those less informed, since up to this point such words have not been heard openly in the Greek churches. We must rather celebrate a general council of the western and eastern churches by the authority of the holy Roman pontiff and with the approval of our devout emperors.[101] At such a council these and several other essential matters concerning God might be set forth such that neither we nor you lack understanding. Thereafter all of us in the Christian east might, in unity with the holy Roman Church and with the other churches in the west, freely accept, preach, teach, and write that 'the Holy Spirit proceeds from the Son' with common will and equal agreement, without any scandal on our part. We might then introduce it in the public singing of the Eastern church."

Anselm, bishop of Havelberg, then responded: "Would that I witness this, that I be found worthy to take part in so holy a council, where Peter as prince of apostles through his vicar, the Roman pontiff, might take his seat in the universal church entrusted to him by God and gathered together as one. There that Holy Spirit of whom we have treated might come down upon us all to teach the whole truth at that moment and forever to the end of the world, making all one in Christ with Peter and in the faith of Peter![102] Let it be so! Let it be so! Let it be so! God wills it! God wills it! God wills it! *Doxa si o Theos! Doxa si o Theos! Doxa si o Theos!*" All present then called out: "It is good! It is good! It is good! Thus let it be done! Let it be done! Let it be done!"

[101] The speaker Nicetas mentions, as potential conciliar leadership, the pope and the Byzantine emperor, with no mention of Anselm's Hohenstaufen king. Here, through his Greek interlocutor, the author issues the first medieval appeal for an ecumenical council to heal the East-West schism. See, among others, Sebastian Sigler, *Anselm von Havelberg: Beiträge zum Lebensbild eines Politikers, Theologen und königlichen Gesandten im 12. Jahrhundert* (Aachen: Shaker, 2005), 42.

[102] Anselm, in introducing the notion of a great East-West council, admits of no notion that such a council might undercut Petrine supremacy.

BOOK 3

On the Differences Between the Eucharistic Rites of the Greeks and of the Latins, in Unleavened or Leavened Bread, and On the Authority of the Roman Church

Chapter 1
The meeting in the basilica of Holy Wisdom in the presence of the Greek sages.

Anselm, bishop of Havelberg, said: "Last week, when we gathered in the Pisan district to treat of the procession of the Holy Spirit, that same Spirit who teaches all truth was present to us. He taught us clearly, through our discourse, what we must understand about him and his procession. After lengthy discussions—fraternal rather than contentious—the Spirit brought us humbly together, according to the rule of charity, in harmonious agreement. Then all your excellencies were pleased to convene us again in this sacred basilica of the Holy Wisdom, in the apse of which we are now seated.[1] Just as we must believe that the very Holy Spirit who fills the whole world is nowhere absent in his divine essence, so we must hope that he be present now in his indwelling and abundant grace in this assembly of great men. For so it is written: *Where there are two or three gathered together in my name, there am I in the midst of*

---

[1] The relocation of this second debate to Hagia Sophia both emphasizes the dialogue's importance and figuratively invokes the spirit of wisdom, which Anselm immediately below associates with Christ, and above has associated with the Holy Spirit: see *Anticimenon* 1.2; 2.13; 2.24.

them (Matt 18:20), the Lord says. I see also that still more honored persons have gathered here. I am hesitant, indeed embarrassed to speak in the presence of such great doctors, among whom I have no standing. I do not know whether you will reprove or commend what I say, given my small ability.[2] Even if I found myself only asking questions and listening to their answers among such doctors, that would not be inglorious. The Son of God himself, as the Wisdom of God, showed us just such a model of humility when he sat among the doctors both questioning and listening to them. I would much rather speak by asking a useful question than be reluctant to speak when the time is right, then not learn what I wished."

Nicetas, archbishop of Nicomedia, replied: "By the grace of God we have concluded our previous discussion in fraternal charity and with peacemaking words, so that we now face the happy prospect of further conversation, not picking apart words but inquiring into our respective opinions. Therefore the presence of these great men should not concern you, for they have gathered here not to raise accusation against you at any point, rather—with the Greeks' characteristic graciousness—to hear you speak. They heard earlier about the discussion you had with us last week, and they greatly desired then and still do wish to hear your sweet words. They desire as well to learn something new and useful in your questioning or your response. For it is written: *A wise man shall hear and be wiser* (Prov 1:5). But let there be no insult from any of us that might affront either your dignity or ours. That might rightly disturb you, providing the occasion for disagreement, so let us diligently avoid it."

Chapter 2
That we recognize that the universal church has its being in three ways—by the authority of Holy Scriptures, through universal tradition, and as a singular institution.

Anselm, bishop of Havelberg, responded: "We recognize that the universal church spread throughout the world has its being in three

---

[2] Anselm protests his lack of skill in logical argumentation. As he has shown throughout Book 2, this protestation is a polite rhetorical figure rather than a genuine expression of concern.

ways. Whatever it maintains is founded either on the authority of the holy scripture, on universal tradition, or in its unique and singular institution. The church in its entirety is subject to this authority, and in that entirety is bound by the universal tradition of the fathers, even though individual churches exist and are governed according to distinctive arrangements and ideas particular to their respective locations and perspectives.[3] Given this universality, I am amazed that the Eastern Church differs so much from Western practice in its rite of sacrifice, in the mysteries of the altar, and in the preparation of the Body and Blood of the Lord that you call the Eucharist. This rite is the universal tradition of the fathers—still more, I should say, it is the institution of our Lord Jesus Christ himself—to be maintained inviolably through all time. All Catholics must follow the law of the holy Roman Church, and she diligently uses unleavened bread in the sacrament of the altar according to ancient custom. As the mother of all churches she has shared this practice with all the Western churches.

Chapter 3
That the Greeks separate themselves from the rite of the Roman Church in a fashion contrary to catholic tradition when they instead sacrifice leavened bread.

"The Eastern Church separates itself from obedience to the sacrosanct Roman Church and from the unity of Rome's great communion when it devises something new and singular rather than holds to catholic custom, so wounding itself with the sacrilege of schism in purposefully, by the institution of its own authority, using leavened bread in the preparation of the Lord's Body.[4] I say 'purposefully' because I want you to understand that a Greek is so concerned to have leavened bread for the sacrifice of the altar that if by chance he does not have any and cannot by any means

---

[3] On the boundaries of the church Anselm borrows a Boethian formulation: see Boethius, *On the Catholic Faith*, in *Theological Tractates, The Consolation of Philosophy*, trans. H. F. Stewart and others (Cambridge, MA: Harvard University Press, 1978), 71.

[4] The speaker Anselm turns back on Nicetas the latter's assertion at the end of the prior book that schism is a grievous moral error: see *Anticimenon* 2.21.

acquire some, he would rather abstain from the ministry of the altar than offer unleavened bread in the consecration of the Lord's Body. I am, as I have said, amazed at this, and I am eager to find out the reason or authority for this custom."[5]

Nicetas, archbishop of Nicomedia, answered: "Our holy fathers who governed the patriarchate in which we now sit were learned and devout in the divine law. They ruled this imperial city in unity of ecclesiastical discipline with the entire East. We memorialize them today and rejoice in their blessing, for they left us many records of their own sacred institutions. We must believe that they lacked neither reason nor authority in their usage of leavened bread in their sacramental rite, so in reverence for them we hold to be inviolable the things that they have handed down to us, revering these practices as we ought. We do not consider it right for anyone to change these customs by any authority of office, however great, or however outstanding his holiness of life or eminence of knowledge. Therefore if the Roman Church maintains a different practice or teaches that we ought to maintain something different, it does what pleases it. According to its own judgment, though, that Roman Church only chooses what it wishes, rejects what it wishes, approves what it wishes, disapproves what it wishes, decrees what it wishes, changes what it wishes, writes what it wishes, and deletes what it wishes. It only commands what it wishes, forbids what it wishes. In all these things the Roman Church both exercises its own authority and seeks out others to follow it and imitate it, whether in good-hearted or ill-informed simplicity, and whether by habit or by compulsion of obedience. But so far we have held and still do hold to what our holy fathers decreed and handed down to us, nor do we dare dismiss that practice for any reason, for if we so presumptuously abandoned or changed it we would offend the reverent veneration we must always offer our holy fathers, so voiding the rite of that same sacrament as if it were null and empty. We would show ourselves to the whole world to be reprehensible people, completely frivolous and unstable. Instead, however, we

[5] On the origin of the East-West conflict about the material of the eucharistic host see Henry Chadwick, *East and West: The Making of a Rift in the Church from Apostolic Times until the Council of Florence* (Oxford: Oxford University Press, 2003), 200–5.

wish to hold to the knowledge and institution of our predecessors by defending it. When we are weary we may then rest in the bed of their great authority rather than reject what is familiar to us and toil to introduce new things by further inquiry."[6]

Chapter 4
That it is better to set aside error for a good reason, even if the error is longstanding, than to persist in it obstinately.

Anselm, bishop of Havelberg, responded: "No one should hesitate to give up custom for an obvious truth, because reason and truth always take precedence over custom.[7] It is better to put away even longstanding error for a good reason, in humility, rather than to persist in it out of pride and argue for it stubbornly. For no one should continue to struggle to maintain something he has once done, rather embrace gladly what he hears is better, more useful. We read that many, many good men have done this. Cyprian, the precious martyr who was long ago great bishop of mighty Carthage, practiced baptism by one immersion. In his view this was sufficient, as he noted "one faith, one lord, one immersion.'[8] But after he had accepted the better argument, he came to agree that triple immersion, after the pattern of the holy Roman Church, was the better practice. It figures the mysteries of the three days' burial both because a temporal resurrection is represented as the infant is raised up from the water the third time and because triple confession rationally predicates triple immersion.[9] Although we then celebrate triple immersion because of the mystery of the Trinity

---

[6] See Augustine of Hippo, *On Baptism, Against the Donatists* 2.13, trans. J. R. King, Nicene and Post-Nicene Fathers 4 (Grand Rapids: Eerdmans, 1956), 431.

[7] See the similar statement of Felix of Bussacone at the lesser council of Carthage over which Cyprian presided in the 250s AD: *Seventh Council of Carthage under Cyprian Concerning the Baptism of Heretics,* in *Hippolytus, Cyprian, Caius, Novatian,* Nicene and Anti-Nicene Fathers 5, trans. Alexander Roberts and James Donaldson (New York: Charles Scribner's Sons, 1903), 571. On this council and its actions see Ramsay MacMullen, *Voting about God in Early Church Councils* (New Haven: Yale University Press, 2006), 19–20.

[8] See Ephesians 4:5.

[9] Cyprian came to this conclusion at the same council: *Hippolytus, Cyprian, Caius, Novatian,* trans. Roberts and Donaldson, 572. Anselm seems to quote Hilary of

and the mystery of the three days' burial, we nevertheless accept one baptism because of the unity of the one faith and the singular substance of the one God.

"But I would rather not hear such things from your discretion because things so foreign to the holy Roman Church offend the dignity of your religion—indeed of the religion of anyone who wishes to be Christian. Be then as you have said is appropriate. Even though I have borne your posture without objection, I would meet with no such toleration from you. I am a son of the Roman Church, so unembarrassed to serve it. You know this well. Therefore you would have done honor to your discretion to speak with more reserve in order to spare me, because you know that I cannot patiently suffer the slightest injury to my mother and mistress the Roman Church.[10] Beloved brother, I too embrace with due veneration the holy fathers who have ruled the Eastern Church well. Many of them were diligent students and faithful champions of the catholic faith, although some who have ruled this imperial metropolis are known sometimes to have erred greatly in their belief."

Chapter 5
On the primacy of the Roman Church, and that it has never been tainted by any heresies at any time, rather has always been catholic.[11]

"But you hold that the authority of those in power here was so great that any of their laws is inviolable, rather than acknowledge the truth of the things they have legislated. Why do you not rather accept the laws of the sacrosanct Roman Church, which has primacy

---

Poitiers' formulation of Cyprian's reasoning: see Hilary of Poitiers, *Trinity* 8.7, trans. Stephen McKenna (New York: Fathers of the Church, 1954), 280.

[10] The interlocutor Anselm's response now turns in a direction he never broached in Book 1—loyalty to the Roman Church. Now that he has established a constructive, irenic tone with Nicetas he is willing to follow up more aggressively by adducing Roman primacy.

[11] For a lucid summary of the historical development of arguments for papal authority see Klaus Schatz, *Papal Primacy from Its Origins to the Present*, trans. John A. Otto and Linda M. Maloney (Collegeville, MN: Liturgical Press, 1996), 1–90.

through God and from God and next after God in its authority in that universal church spread throughout the world? For this we read was legislated by the 318 fathers at the first Nicene Council about the Roman Church. "We must surely know, nor must any catholic ignore, that the holy Roman Church stands above the decrees of any synod."[12] That church holds the primacy of our Lord and Savior according to his words in the Gospel to the blessed Peter the apostle: *Thou art Peter, and upon this rock I will build my church, and the gates of hell shall not prevail against it. And I will give to thee the keys of the kingdom of heaven. And whatsoever thou shalt bind upon earth, it shall be bound also in heaven* (Matt 16:18-19; 18:18). To the Lord's words is added the association of the most blessed Paul the apostle with the same city of Rome, when he received the martyr's crown with Peter on the same day, at the same time, in his glorious death under the emperor Nero. Together Peter and Paul have consecrated the holy Roman Church to Christ the Lord with their blood, setting that church over all others in the whole world by their presence and holy triumph.[13]

"Therefore, the first see is in the heavenly benefice of the Roman Church, dedicated in the martyrdom of the blessed apostles Peter and Paul. But the second see is Alexandria, and it is also consecrated to the name of the blessed Peter but by Mark, his disciple and evangelist, because Mark first preached the word of truth in Egypt when he had been sent there by Peter, and there he received his own glorious martyrdom. There the venerable Abilius

---

[12] The Nicene legislation embraced no such claim, although its sixth canon was later subjected to this interpretation: see Norman P. Tanner, ed., *Decrees of the Ecumenical Councils 1: Nicaea I to Lateran V*, vol. 1 (London: Sheed and Ward, 1990), 8–9. Rather, later western collections of canons proposed it in their presentation of the Nicene legislation. Compare, for instance, Isidore Mercator, *Collectio decretalium*, PL 130, col. 251. See also Norman Russell, "Anselm of Havelberg and the Union of Churches," *Sobornost* 1 (1979): 19–41; 2 (1980): 29–41, at 2:30 n. 2. For discussion of the fourth-century tensions about the relative authority of the great sees, see Chadwick, *East and West*, 22–23.

[13] As Russell notes ("Anselm of Havelberg," *Sobornost* 2:30–31 nn. 3-4), the speaker here seems to refer to the discussion of Petrine authority in the so-called *Decretum Gelasianum*, a late-fifth-century compilation attributed to the fourth-century pope. See *Decretum Gelasianum* 3.1-2, in Pierre Battifol, *Le siège apostolique (359–451)*, 2d ed. (Paris: Victor Lecoffre, 1924), 147.

succeeded him. The third see, at Antioch, is also honored in the veneration of the blessed apostle Peter because he lived there before he came to Rome. He appointed Ignatius as its bishop. There first the name 'Christians' was given this new people.[14] Other sees are consecrated to the memory of Peter's name—the second see in Alexandria and the third in Antioch—but the prince of the apostles has honored the first see, the preeminent and triumphant city of Rome, by the presence there of his body. He thus granted the holy Roman Church the blessing of this special privilege.[15] Rome was thus set above the others for this purpose by the Lord himself, and is preeminent among the churches in its prerogative as superior in divine law. And although Rome has indeed been afflicted by the various heresies that have arisen in the catholic faith at different times, it has always remained unshaken, founded securely as it is on a rock.[16] It cannot be torn from the simplicity of the faith by any false and sophisticated heretical arguments because Simon Bar Jona held that faith as 'the son of a dove.'[17]

"Because Rome is fortified against deceitful questions by the shield of divine wisdom wielded by the Lord, no fears or threats of emperors or any worldly powers can cause it to tremble. It is defended against all such attacks by the shield of great patience strengthened by the Lord. Therefore the Lord himself, knowing that the other churches would be grievously assaulted by heresy and that the Roman Church founded on a rock would never be weakened in the faith, said to Peter: *I have prayed for thee, Peter, that thy faith fail not, and thou, being once converted, confirm thy brethren* (Luke 22:32). The Lord spoke thus, stating directly to Peter: 'You have received this grace so that you will always be constant and

[14] Acts 11:26. Again, the speaker Anselm seems to borrow from the *Decretum Gelasianum* 3.3: in Battifol, *Le siège apostolique*, 147–48.
[15] On the tradition that all three of these great sees were Petrine see Chadwick, *East and West*, 22. As Josef Sieben (*Die Konzilsidee des lateinischen Mittelalters [847–1378]* [Paderborn: Schöningh, 1984], 158 and n. 25) and Jay T. Lees (*Anselm of Havelberg: Deeds into Words in the Twelfth* Century [Leiden: Brill, 1998], 259) point out, the speaker Anselm likely refers to commentary and accretions to the Nicene Creed the Greeks did not accept as canonical.
[16] Matthew 16:18.
[17] Jerome repeatedly offered this gloss on Peter's name: see, for instance, Jerome, *Liber de nominibus hebraicis*, PL 23, col. 839.

unmoving in the faith, although others may be shipwrecked from it. Strengthen and correct those who are wavering, and bear the pain and anxiety of all as overseer, teacher, father, and master of all.' Thus Peter, who assumed from the Lord the privilege of preserving the integrity of the faith before all others, has deservedly received the privilege of prelacy over all."[18]

Chapter 6
That the Church of Constantinople has nearly always suffered from the ferment of grave heresy.

"On the other hand, innumerable heresies have often bubbled up in the Constantinopolitan Church—if you and all those seated here give me leave to mention them, for you should never deny this truth even if sometimes it might be unspoken—such that this church abandoned the true faith. Puffed up against God and the apostolic church by strange notions, it rose up as rebelliously as it was able against the faith of Peter and his healthful teaching.[19] The loathsome Arian heresy flourished here after first sprouting up in Alexandria, then defiling almost the whole East with its poisonous ferment, even polluting some bishops of the West. This unfortunate belief about the Son of God held that there was a time when he was not, that before he was born he was not. It held too that the Son was made out of nothing that had existed before, and that he therefore had another substance or nature, and that the Son is changeable and mutable. Eusebius was the chief of the Arian heretics. After he left their first city he coveted and then seized the Church of Nicomedia, finally overtaking the Church of Constantinople, staining it with that same ferment and occupying it until his death. Here, the greatest of heresiarchs, he ruled the city of Constantinople as its bishop, took the lead, and spread the ferment of his heresy everywhere. Here he asserted that he thought that a pure man was born of the holy Virgin Mary such that he

---

[18] Anselm here assembles various characterizations of authority and leadership in a fundamentally original description and laudation of papal authority.

[19] The speaker Anselm's use of imagery of fermentation links Eastern heresy to the leavening of the eucharistic bread, as above in *Anticimenon* 1.9.

was one person in flesh and another in deity. This Eusebius did not acknowledge one Christ in both the Word of God and in the flesh, rather preached that the Word and the flesh were separately the Son of God and the Son of man.[20]

Here in Constantinople Macedonius then took charge, again wrapped up in the Arian heresy, contaminating whomever he could with the same pestilential ferment in asserting that the Holy Spirit is a creature.[21] Here the priest and archimandrite Eutyches poured forth the ferment of his heresies, believing that our Lord had two natures before they were joined, then afterward not two but one nature—making mixture and confusion.[22] Many adherents of the Arian presumption, both great and lesser folk, have lived here in Constantinople. Eudoxius, first in Antioch, and afterward a usurper of this city's see, ruled here as deceived by the Arian madness.[23] Then came the heretic Eunomius, whom Eudoxius made bishop in Cyzius, striving to suppress the diocese of Eleusis. This same Eunomius, a sophist, presumed to speak profane things against God by false logic, saying: 'God knows nothing more about his own substance than we do, nor is that which he knows known to him any more or less clearly to him than to us. But whatever we know about him, this he too fully knows. And what he knows we know in exactly the same way.'[24] More various heresies than can be numbered have always spewed with the ferment of heretical depravity in this place.

"Who could count all the heretics and all the errors of the people of this city, who have roiled the holy and immaculate church of God with this ferment of false teachings, attempting

[20] On the Arian Eusebius of Nicomedia see Henry Chadwick, *The Early Church* (Grand Rapids: Eerdmans, 1968), 133–39.

[21] Chadwick, *The Early Church*, 139.

[22] Chadwick, *The Early Church*, 201–4.

[23] Chadwick, *The Early Church*, 141–42, 147.

[24] On Eunomius see David Christie-Murray, *A History of Heresy* (Oxford: Oxford University Press, 1989), 50–51. Anselm drew this quotation from Eunomius from Cassiodorus, *Ecclesiastical History*, which he cites in the following paragraph as the work of the sixth-century author's Greek source, Theodoret: Cassiodorus, *Historia ecclesiastica tripartita* 7.19, ed. Walter Jacob and Rudolph Hanslik, Corpus Scriptorum Ecclesiasticorum Latinorum (Vienna: Hoelder-Pichler-Tempsky, 1952), 416.

to rend the robe of Christ in impious schism?[25] Those heresies have either arisen here, spreading hence widely, or have bubbled up elsewhere in the East to flow together in this city as if into the bilges of a ship. Pooled here, they have made a filthy swamp in which, sitting like slimy frogs and croaking loudly with arguments and sophistry, they have neither heard nor let others hear that faith which is the word of truth.[26] Many simple folk have been made drunk in this swamp of heresies as if by wormwood. All the filth of heretical perversity has found a dwelling here—its own nest. Here those heresies' malice and worthlessness fermented, then spread throughout the world wherever they could, not only in the spoken word but in deceitful writings. They have passed a deadly cup from this city, as from that first mighty Babylon, to emperors, kings, and princes. The emperor Constantius, son of the great Constantine, drank first from this cup of Arian heresy, as we see in his dialogue with the reverend pope Liberius written down by the bishop Theodoret, author of a history of the church. In that dialogue the holy Liberius, third pope after the Sylvester who followed Julius, displayed a wonderfully constant faith founded on a sure rock. Despite many promises and threats from the emperor recorded in that text, Liberius would take part neither in the madness of Arianism nor in the condemnation of Athanasius, incomparably great bishop of Alexandria. Because Liberius, immovable pillar and a defender of the truth, had obtained the privilege of Petrine constancy, the same emperor Constantius ordered him exiled to Thrace. Aptly was he named Liberius, because he then confessed with a free mind and free voice that truth which is Christ.[27]

"Thus the churches of Constantinople, Alexandria, and Antioch, and as well almost all the other churches established throughout the East, have labored in the catholic faith and suffered shipwreck, while the ship of Peter alone—although battered by waves of persecution and mighty wind—has nevertheless suffered no shipwreck in

---

[25] See John 19:24.

[26] The interlocutor Anselm's image of Constantinople as a virtual sewer is a marked change from the generally conciliatory tone of his responses to Nicetas in *Anticimenon* 2.

[27] Cassiodorus, *Historia ecclesiastica* 5.17, ed. Jacob and Rudolph, 237–41.

heresy.[28] Rather, however hard it has labored and still labors, Rome on its own or through its legates has driven out the ferment of malice and wickedness by which heretics have laid waste the church of God. So the blessed Peter, prince of the apostles, was commanded by the Lord, saying: *and thou, being once converted, strengthen your brothers* (Luke 22:32). Therefore the sacrosanct Roman Church, having preserved the purity of the faith, deserves by the Lord's help to be the mother of all churches. And all who rightly wish to be and indeed are called sons of God and of the church then imitate her in due humility in all the ecclesiastical sacraments. Although the various peoples have different practices and ecclesiastical customs as is appropriate to their diversity, in which they conform only incompletely to the Roman Church, nevertheless—as I have said—none should disagree with her, the most sacred mother of all, in the ecclesiastical sacraments themselves. What then do you think? Is it safe for the Constantinopolitan Church not to accept the decrees of the Roman pontiff or rather, as I might say more exactly, to despise them? If you desire neither to be nor to be called sons of the Roman Church, then you must look to this. You must judge. But if you want to be and to be called sons of the church, consider what is written: *My son, hear the instruction of thy father, and forsake not the law of thy mother, that grace may be added to thy head and a chain of gold to your neck* (Prov 1:8-9). Here I speak pure truth in pure fraternal charity. I have done so sincerely, without any ferment of deceit. Now I wish that you answer as you will in the same love, without any such ferment."

Nicetas, archbishop of Nicomedia, responded: "You have said much about the great dignity of the Roman Church, about its sublimity, but—as for what you then added about this Church of Constantinople—you might in modesty have said less. It is fitting that you as well as I show respect to those here who have patiently listened to you, that you now listen open-mindedly to me in my response to you. For the charity in which we have gathered demands this."

---

[28] See 1 Timothy 1:19.

Chapter 7
That the Greeks say that the three patriarchal seats have always been sisters, and among these they acknowledge the primacy of the Roman Church.

"I neither deny nor reject the primacy of the Roman Church, whose excellence you have expounded for me, since we read in our ancient histories that the three patriarchal sees—Rome, Alexandria, and Antioch—were sisters among which Rome held primacy as the preeminent seat of the empire.[29] So it was named the first see, and there all the others made appeal in problematic ecclesiastical cases, so that Rome might judge matters outside any clear rules. But the Roman pontiff is not therefore called the ruler of priests, nor a high priest, nor anything of the sort, rather only bishop of the first see. Boniface III, a Roman by birth and bishop of the city of Rome, obtained from the father John before the emperor Phocas that the apostolic see of the blessed Peter the apostle might be the head of all the churches, for Constantinople was at that time the first city because of the transfer of empire.[30]

Nevertheless, neither the Roman pontiff nor the bishop of Alexandria nor the bishop of Antioch might teach or institute anything in their own churches that disagreed with the faith or the harmony of the others. So that all might speak and proclaim one thing, it was decreed that two legates learned in faith and sound doctrine always be sent from the Roman Church, one to be present to the patriarch of Alexandria and the other to the patriarch of Antioch, to observe their preaching and public declaration of the faith. Likewise two legates were to be sent from Alexandria, one to be present to the Roman pontiff and the other to the Antiochene, in this same role. And again two were sent from Antioch, one to the

[29] See again Chadwick, *East and West*, 22.
[30] The speaker Nicetas draws this information from an early medieval text of which his Latin interlocutor makes extensive use below in *Anticimenon* 12ff.: here see *Book of Pontiffs (Liber pontificalis): The Ancient Biographies of the First Ninety Roman Bishops to A.D. 715*, trans. Raymond Davis, Translated Texts for Historians 6, 2nd ed. (Liverpool: Liverpool University Press, 2000), 64. This text was known only in the West; here the author supplies his Greek speaker with support for his argument he cannot realistically have had at hand.

Roman pontiff and the other to the bishop of Alexandria, in this capacity. Whatever was preached in one of these churches—because it was catholic—might then be confirmed in the authority and witness of the others. If from time to time something in the opinion of any of these churches was said that was contrary to the faith, discordant to the communion, and hostile to the truth, the legates of the others might in charity and humble admonition correct that view. If they could not correct it, and if one bishop might be so rash or presumptuous as to defend his error contentiously, the same legates might report it to the other sisters. If such a man might be recalled to the harmony of sound doctrine through canonically sent letters, that would be well, but if not, a general council might be celebrated about the matter.[31]

"But then God's will transferred the empire to this royal city so that it became premier in the orient and, in the authority of its sovereignty, was called New Rome. Then one hundred fifty bishops, convened in this city when the blessed Nectarius was established in this see, condemned Maximian the Cynic, who was contaminated by Apollinarianism. At that point I say those bishops, supported by the pious emperor Theodosius the Great, established that—just as old Rome long ago held primacy in ecclesiastical cases according to the holy fathers because of its imperial status—this younger and new Rome had primacy after it because of the dignity of empire. Just as it should be called and indeed be the second see, Constantinople should rule all the churches of Asia, Thrace, and Pontus, and should both hear and decide their ecclesiastical cases by its own authority.[32] Meanwhile the legates who as guardians of the catholic faith crossed back and forth among the Roman, Alexandrian, and Antiochene churches, safeguarding the faith by mutual, brotherly observation, were also appointed in this royal city. In the same way legates were chosen for a like ministry to those places from Constantinople, so that all might speak one belief, agreeing in the teaching of the truth."

[31] Anselm's speaker overstates the formality and regularity of this system of apocrisiaries: see Chadwick, *East and West*, 33.

[32] The author refers to the second and third canons of the First Council of Constantinople: Tanner, ed., *Decrees of the Ecumenical Councils*, vol. 1, 29–32.

Chapter 8
That the Greeks say that they take no part in the councils of the Roman pontiffs because those pontiffs have violated the unity of the Roman Empire.

"So, beloved brother, we read in our ancient histories that the Roman Church—whose primacy among these patriarchal sisters we acknowledge and to whom we attribute the high role of presiding at a general council—isolated herself from us in her loftiness when she seized the monarchical rule that was not her office, dividing the bishops and the churches of the West and of the East after the empire had been divided.[33] Therefore, if Rome celebrates a council with western bishops but without us, those bishops may receive and observe with due veneration the strictures of a council at which Rome has dictated what it judges should be said and decreed what statutes should be promulgated. But as for us—although we would not quarrel with the Roman Church about the catholic faith we share—why should we accept the decrees of a council we do not celebrate in our own times along with Rome, when its decrees are written completely without our counsel, even without our knowledge? If the Roman pontiff, sitting on high on the throne of his glory, should wish to thunder at us or cast down his commands from on high, and if he might want to judge, rather to rule us and our churches as his own will pleases and without our counsel, what sort of brotherhood or fatherhood might that be? Who could endure this with equanimity? If we did, then we would rightly be called—indeed we would be—slaves, not sons of the church. But if we were so constrained by a heavy yoke pressing upon our necks, all that remained would be that the Roman Church alone might enjoy such liberty as it wishes to establish laws for all others.[34] She herself would be without law, then neither seeming nor being the pious mother of sons but a hard and imperious mistress of slaves.

"What, then, would be the point in our knowledge of scriptures, or of our study of literature, the doctrinal instruction of our masters,

---

[33] The speaker Nicetas's specific sources are undefined.

[34] Nicetas reminds his Latin interlocutor that Christ's true yoke is easy: see Matthew 11:30.

or the noble talents of the Greek sages? The authority of the Roman pontiff alone, declared by you to be over all, voids all these things. That pontiff alone may be bishop, he alone master and teacher, he alone commissioned by himself with all responsibilities, he the sole good shepherd alone responding to God alone. But if he should desire coworkers in the Lord's vineyard, then let him boast instead of his humility, even as he maintains his primacy. Let him not despise his brothers, whom the truth of Christ has begotten in freedom, not in slavery, in the womb of mother church. *For we must all be manifested*, says the Apostle, *before the judgment seat of Christ, that every one may receive the proper things of the body according as he hath done, whether it be good or evil* (2 Cor 5:10). *All*, he says—and he who said it was an apostle but he exempted neither himself nor any mortal. *All*, he said—exempting not even the Roman pontiff. Thus we find in no creed that we are commanded to confess the Roman Church particularly. Rather we are taught everywhere to confess one holy catholic and apostolic church.[35]

"While I wish to keep peace with you, I nonetheless should say about the Roman Church that I venerate it with you but do not, like you, follow it in all things, nor do I consider that I must follow it in all things. You have expounded that church's higher authority as constraining us to accept its pattern and model, setting aside our rite without rational discussion or consideration of scriptural authority, so that we might follow Rome's lead wherever it may direct, wherever it wishes, as though we were blind men with closed eyes. Let Latin as well as Greek sages alike judge how safe or honorable this would be for us."

Chapter 9
Commendation of the Roman Church for its diligence in trying and judging ecclesiastical cases.

Anselm, bishop of Havelberg, answered: "Let it not strain your charity for me to interrupt, for you seem to me to direct many great

[35] For discussion of Nicetas's response to his Latin counterpart's assertion of Roman primacy see Francis Dvornik, *Byzantium and the Roman Primacy*, trans. Edwin A. Quain (New York: Fordham University Press, 1966), 144–47.

complaints against the Roman Church with inappropriate irony. I cannot bear this mockery, so I break in to what you are saying lest you should heap on still more to no good end. If you knew the religious practice of the Roman Church—its sincerity, equity, gentleness, humility, piety, holiness, wisdom, discretion, good will, compassion, constancy, justice, strength, discretion, moderation, purity, its charity toward all and its diligent investigation of everything in matters of ecclesiastical justice as well as its utter truthfulness in giving judgment—if, I say, you were acquainted with these things in the Roman Church through experience such as mine, you would never have said or even thought such things. Rather you would have at once, without delay, come over without waiting for our invitation and run quickly to obey such great holiness as shines in that church and such justice as it extends to others. You would not listen to anyone who wished to hold you back if you wished as much to be a lover of foreign holiness as of your own custom.

"We are indeed aware that 150 bishops gathered in this city under Theodosius presumptuously decreed that the Church of Constantinople was the second Rome, that it should be called and indeed be the second see, and that it should by its own authority rule the churches of Pontus, Asia, and Thrace, and those among the barbarians, and that also it should itself decide those legal matters brought to it.[36] We know also that 230 bishops at the Council of Chalcedon wrote to Pope Leo asking, in order to satisfy the emperors Martian and Valentine, that the metropolitan of the Constantinopolitan Church be recognized as superior to the other metropolitans of the provinces of Asia, Pontus, and Thrace.[37] But the reverend Pope Leo wrote back confirming all the acts of the synod of Chalcedon except those effected by the presumptuous ambition of the Constantinopolitans. These he struck down,

---

[36] See again the First Council of Constantinople's second and third canons: Tanner, ed., *Decrees of the Ecumenical Councils*, vol. 1, 29–32. On the discussion of Constantinople's authority in the fourth and fifth centuries see Chadwick, *East and West*, 34–35.

[37] See the Council of Chalcedon's Canon 28, Tanner, ed., *Decrees of the Ecumenical Councils*, vol. 1, 99–100.

voiding them as contrary to the statutes of the Council of Nicaea.[38] We are amazed that a man of your discretion might wish to adduce as authoritative a statute—rather a presumptive statute—decreed by 150 bishops in this city, when ecclesiastical order commands that nothing contrary to the judgment of the Roman pontiff be accepted, that nothing hold sway without his apostolic authority and confirmation. Perhaps you have read the statute of your council but have not read the blessed pope Leo's apostolic epistle in response, in which that statute is absolutely voided and exposed as contrary to the Council of Nicaea."

Nicetas, archbishop of Nicomedia, then said: "Perhaps you think that the Lord spoke to Peter alone and not to all the apostles when he said: *Whose sins you shall forgive, they are forgiven them, and whose sins you shall retain, they are retained* (John 20:23)? And again, *Whatsoever thou shalt bind upon earth, it shall be bound also in heaven, and whatsoever thou shalt loose on earth, it shall be loosed also in heaven* (Matt 16:19). But we believe that the Lord said this not to Peter only, but to all the apostles along with Peter, and to Peter and to all without distinction. Nor did the Holy Spirit sent from the Lord on Pentecost and previously promised equally to all the apostles descend on Peter alone. Rather he set them all afire together, not giving them unequal gifts differentially distributed, but offering the same gift to all equally as he had promised.[39] Therefore let us understand the power received by Peter from the Lord as not diminishing the authority of the other apostles, for they all certainly received the Holy Spirit in equal measure, without any prejudice or usurpation among them but in gentleness and meekness of heart. In that same Holy Spirit they received the same power to bind and loose. We must not attribute to Peter alone the privilege that the Lord gave to all in common. And we must beware lest we detract from others with the same prerogative of power when we ascribe the authority of all to one alone. Instead let Peter, the twelfth of the apostles, be so honored that the other eleven not be excluded

---

[38] See Leo the Great, *Letters and Sermons*, Letter 98, trans. Charles Lett Feltoe, Nicene and Post-Nicene Fathers 12 (Grand Rapids: Eerdmans, repr. 1983), 72–73.

[39] Acts 2:2-4.

from the authority of his apostolate. They received that apostolate not from Peter but from the Lord himself, even as Peter himself did, in an equal and comparable dispensation."

Chapter 10
That although the power to bind and to loose was not given to Peter alone but also to the other apostles, and although the Spirit descended not on Peter alone but also on them, Peter's ruling power is nonetheless superior to all others.

Anselm, bishop of Havelberg, then said: "I acknowledge that the Holy Spirit descended not on Peter alone but on all the apostles, nor is it said of Peter alone but for all the others: *Receive ye the Holy Ghost. Whose sins you shall forgive, they are forgiven them and whose you shall retain, they are retained* (John 20:22-23). But the Lord directed this saying particularly to Peter, so establishing him as the doorkeeper of heaven: *And I will give to thee the keys of the kingdom of heaven* (Matt 16:19), and again he said: *Feed my sheep* (John 21:17). And Peter confessed before all others: *Thou art Christ, the son of the living God*, and the Lord said: *Blessed art thou, Simon Peter, because flesh and blood hath not revealed it to thee, but my Father who is in heaven* (Matt 16:16-17). Scripture thus teaches that Peter had learned first, by heavenly inspiration, the truth that afterwards the other apostles declared abroad in open proclamation. Moreover, the Lord Jesus climbed into Peter's boat alone, not Andrew's or James's or any of the others.[40] Seated in it, he taught the crowds, revealing in this figuration the evangelical and apostolic doctrine that would soon flow forth among the throngs of the whole world from the holy Roman Church, over which he set Peter in charge as first of the apostles.

"The apostles themselves acknowledged that this power had been bestowed on Peter personally, as the book of Luke entitled Acts of the Apostles plainly reveals. For when there was a dispute at Antioch among some of the apostles as to whether or not circumcision were to be imposed on the faithful who had come from among the Gentiles, they sent a message to Jerusalem, to

[40] John 21:3.

Peter and the other senior apostles who were with him, concerning this question. When they all had gathered and a great controversy arose over the matter, Peter stood among them and—as the apostle having primacy among them—issued the judgment that circumcision should not be imposed on the Gentiles, so defining what had been doubtful by the authority conferred on him by the Lord. Peter demonstrated this authority through the vision of the cloth that had come to him, and by the conversion of Cornelius and other Gentiles.[41] James, bishop of Jerusalem, obeyed in Peter's decision with humble acquiescence, as did all apostles and elders present there.[42]

"Peter was older than the other apostles and more solid in his faith, capable of hearing the words of eternal life. Therefore he was called Bar Jona, that is, the son of a dove.[43] He was more attentive than they in the questions and answers that passed between Christ and the apostles, more effective in healing the sick by the shadow of his body. After the ascension of the Lord he took charge of the new and primitive church in Christ's stead. When Ananias and Sapphira had lied to the Holy Spirit and been destroyed by the breath of his mouth, Peter separated them from the church, from its holy fellowship.[44] He condemned Simon Magus with his money, so humbly honoring the primacy of his apostolate among the others.[45] Peter was greater in every respect, in virtues and miracles, because God worked through him. Therefore it befits none of the faithful at all to doubt that the Lord himself established Peter as ruler of the apostles. It befits them not to place his authority in question, rather to hold this belief firmly. But just as the Roman pontiff alone holds Christ's place in Peter's stead, so the other bishops hold the place of apostles under Christ and on Christ's account under Peter, then on account of Peter under the Roman pontiff as his vicar. Nor does it at all detract from any of the apostles for their respective duties to be assigned to each in humility."

[41] Acts 10:2-48.
[42] Acts 11:1-18.
[43] See above, *Anticimenon* 3.5. The speaker Anselm here repeats himself.
[44] Acts 5:1-11.
[45] Acts 8:9-24.

Chapter 11
That heresies arising in Constantinople or anywhere in the East have been destroyed there.

Nicetas, archbishop of Nicomedia, then spoke: "It may be as you say. But earlier you said that the Church of Constantinople, rather almost the entire east, has been polluted by various heresies. You said this and it was true in part, and since I am a servant of the truth I should not deny it. But say, I ask you, where have those heresies been condemned? Who has condemned them? If they have arisen here among perverse and evil men, they have also been condemned here by good and catholic men. After the emperor Constantine the Great was converted to the faith and wrote laws pleasing to God for the Christian people, Rome along with all the west and Constantinople along with all the East hastened to the faith as a result of the emperor's decrees. Because this new and heretofore unknown faith was suddenly proclaimed publicly and because the study of the liberal arts flourished in this city—and because many skilled in logical argument and discriminating in dialectic excelled here in discursive reasoning—those learned men began to examine the Christian faith through that discourse.[46] But they fell short in their investigation and rational consideration. Pressing their investigations too far and professing themselves to be wise, they became fools.[47] They emptied themselves into their own thoughts as they investigated without humility what they should have piously and humbly believed. Even as they strained to the height of human knowledge in the arrogance of their reason, they fell into the pit of faithlessness.[48] Many became heretics and created for themselves many sects. They confused and mangled the Christian faith, splitting it into many divergent heresies. But then the church of the East, seeing that such men abused secular

[46] When the Greek speaker here takes up the role of the liberal arts he refers obliquely to the renaissance of the liberal arts ongoing in Europe in his time. This discussion in *Anticimenon* sheds light on the author's own vision of the liberal arts as formed in the cathedral school of Liège.

[47] See Romans 1:22.

[48] Nicetas now echoes the speaker Anselm's criticism of the Greeks in *Anticimenon* 2.21.

learning and that heretical leaders bubbled up at various times and places, celebrated many councils after sending synodal letters everywhere and gaining the support of pious emperors. The first such council was at Nicaea in the province of Bithynia. There the Arian heresy was condemned and the creed for all catholics was drafted, then ratified by the inviolable authority of the Holy Spirit and of 318 fathers.[49]

"Afterward, as various other heresies followed, many other councils were celebrated for the destruction of the different heresies and for building up the catholic faith. In the church of Chalcedon and here in Constantinople as in Ephesus, Antioch, and Alexandria, general councils have been solemnly held for the condemnation of heretics and for strengthening the faith and unity of all the churches. Thus, as I have said, if heresies have arisen here, they have also been destroyed here. Clearly the church of God increased more and more in the knowledge of the scriptures through the occasion of these heresies, and the faith grew stronger with their extinction. But after the catholic faith was defined and then perfected, the holy fathers rightly forbade that anyone should dare to argue further about the faith in public, since we must add or take away nothing else. When the truth has been found and anyone wishes to seek further, what else can he find but falsehood? Of course one may question humbly in order to discern something previously unclear about the faith, providing he does not contentiously cast doubt on anything defined by the holy fathers as a secure boundary of faith. This no mortal may revise, as the gravest anathemas forbid.[50]

"So stop reproaching us, as you have wished, about heresies. All wise men know that the truth and power of the good prevail over the lies and offenses of the wicked. Tell me, I ask you, where those heretics are now? They are not here, nor are their names heard anywhere in the East, rather catholics throughout the Ori-

---

[49] Here and frequently below, in adverting to the ecumenical councils of late antiquity, Anselm's interlocutors use the language of the *Book of Pontiffs*, with its emphasis on the number of conciliar participants: see here *Book of Pontiffs* 34, trans. Davis, 15.

[50] After the First Council of Nicaea, ecclesiastical councils regularly anathematized alterations in the creed. See, for instance, the seventh canon of the Council of Ephesus, Tanner, ed., *Decrees of the Ecumenical Councils*, vol. 1, 65.

ent offer God fitting homage with clear, sound faith. Perhaps in the city of Rome such heresies have not arisen because wise, discriminating men and scholars of scripture were not there as they are among us. The empty knowledge by which the heretics among us were misled is indeed blameworthy, and so too the rusticity of Roman knowledge is greatly to be praised, according to which they have said neither one thing nor the other about the faith but have listened to others in simplicity before speaking and teaching, because they were themselves untaught.[51] But this lack of knowledge seems to have resulted from negligence in the study of the faith, from the dullness of stupidity, or perhaps from the heavy obstacle of worldly occupation. For the learned to think or speak is either entirely good or bad, but for the unwise or unlearned to think or speak is neither."

Chapter 12
That the head of the church on earth must be one—namely Rome—and not two or more as the Greeks say, and that the heresies of the Greeks have been destroyed by the authority not of the Greeks but of the Roman pontiffs.

Anselm, bishop of Havelberg, replied: "The Apostle says: *Christ is the head of the church. But the head of Christ is God* (Eph 5:23; 1 Cor 11:3). So Christ as head of the church granted his place on earth to Peter, foremost of the apostles, when he ascended into heaven. When Peter followed Christ into martyrdom he assigned Clement as his successor in the vicariate. Thus Roman pontiffs in succession have held Christ's place as head of the church on earth as he is its head in heaven. Do not then seek to make two or more heads for the one body of the church, for that is unseemly, disgraceful, unnatural, the opposite of perfection, a corruption in any body at all. When you say that 140 fathers gathered in this city decreed that Constantinople should have primacy over all the churches in the East as the new and younger Rome, and that it may by its own authority settle ecclesiastical cases, what do you do but

---

[51] The speaker Nicetas ironically praises Roman lack of theological sophistication.

raise up two heads in the one body of the one church, setting up
altar against altar, as if building another sacrificial platform like
the Manicheans?[52] Those heretics, dividing themselves from the
church in their perversity, long ago built their own such platform
as a separate place of sacrifice. In place of Easter they celebrated
the day on which Mani was killed in their rite at that platform or
altar raised by five steps, adorned with precious linens, heavily
ornamented, and set in an open space before their worshipers.[53]

"When you in the East hold so strongly to your different sacrificial rite and so oppose the Roman Church, you likewise raise up
the horn of singularity.[54] But if you think that you do so rightly
because of the transfer of empire, you demonstrably rest your
argument on human rather than divine judgment. If you say that
the head of the church is here because of the authority of this city,
because it is the seat of royal power, you can declare that Antioch
is a third head of the church for the same reason, because it too
has been a seat of royal authority. Similarly you can raise a fourth
head of the churches in Babylon as capital city of Egypt and seat of
royal power—that is, if you can add it to your empire and subject
it to the laws of the Christians. Yet again you can establish a fifth
head of churches in the great city of Baghdad, which they say is
the seat of the kingdom of the Persians, if you can conquer it and
subject it to ecclesiastical laws.[55] And so we can adduce the same
reasoning for establishing heads of churches in the respective seats
of the other kingdoms, finding then not one Peter, foremost of
the apostles, but many Peters and many foremost apostles. You
can see that that would be absurd. Let all those here judge after
hearing both you and me.

---

[52] As the author is aware, there were 150 participants in the First Council of
Constantinople: *Anticimenon* 3.9. The count here differs, probably through simple
scribal error.

[53] Augustine had offered a similar titillating description of the Manichean rite:
Augustine, *Against the Epistle of the Manicheans Called Fundamental* 8, trans. Richard Stothart, in *St. Augustin* (sic): *The Writings against the Manicheans and against
the Donatists*, Nicene and Post-Nicene Fathers 4, ed. Philip Schaff (Grand Rapids:
Eerdmans, 1956), 132–33.

[54] See Lamentations 2:17.

[55] Here alone Anselm makes reference, deeply ironically, to the Muslim East.

"It is certain, then—doubtful to no one sane of mind—that just as there is one church, so the church has one head, and this head is that Roman pontiff whom not only the authority of a human empire but also the majesty of the divine judgment sets before all as their ruler. All who wish to be saved in obedience to that church and in the faith of Peter must imitate its model and custom, especially in the ecclesiastical sacraments. So says blessed Ambrose, archbishop of Milan: 'He who disagrees with the Roman Church is clearly a heretic.'[56] But because you have said that heresies that arose here have also died here, and you have said that this was done by the authority of the holy fathers of the East gathered in the Nicene Council and in many other councils, I wonder about your discretion, because you ascribe to the members the role of the head. You assign to those who sat at these councils what clearly pertained to him who presided. None of the holy fathers present at these councils—neither any one of them nor all together—would usurp that authority to themselves as a council. They would rather acknowledge all authority of any council as inhering in the Roman pontiff, whether presiding in his own person or affirming its actions through his legates. For example, this ecclesiastical rule, well known to them, commands: "Councils should not be celebrated contrary to the judgment of the Roman pontiff.'[57] We must then realize that heresies have arisen here because of Greek error, but that they have been destroyed by the authority not of the Greeks but of the Roman pontiffs.

"Pope Sylvester, a Roman in origin, summoned the council at Nicaea celebrated with 318 bishops gathered under Constantine Augustus. There the whole faith was explained by apostolic authority. Arius, Photius, Sabellius, and their heretical followers were condemned. Victor and Vincent, priests of the city of Rome, presided over that council on behalf of the Roman pontiff Sylvester,

---

[56] See above, *Anticimenon* 2.27. Anselm again seems to borrow from a later source attributing this statement to Ambrose: Bernold, PL 148, col. 1459.

[57] Anselm seems here to import this canon from Cassiodorus's reference: Cassiodorus, *Historia ecclesiastica* 4.9, ed. Jacob and Hanslik, 165. Anselm's subsequent summary of the actions of ancient councils and popes is largely drawn from Cassiodorus's work, itself—as he emphasizes below in *Anticimenon* 3.21—largely translated from Greek sources.

and they were the first signatories to its statutes. The same pope
Sylvester gathered 277 bishops in the city of Rome and again condemned Calixtus, Arius, and Sabellius. Pope Innocent, of Alban
origin, condemned the heretics Pelagius and Celestius. This Pelagius said that the child of a Christian mother need not be born
again through baptism. Pope Leo, a Tuscan, decreed a council in
Chalcedon under the emperor Martian. There 630 bishops were
gathered, and there catholic faith was expounded by apostolic
authority such that we believe Christ to have two natures, that
is, God's and man's. The archimandrite Eutyches and Nestorius,
bishop of this city, were condemned with Dioscorus, archbishop of
Alexandria, at Chalcedon. Paschas, bishop of Heraclius, and Luke,
bishop of the church of Ausculum, as well as Boniface, a priest of
the holy Roman Church and vicar of the lord Pope Leo, presided
at this council and signed its statutes on that pope's behalf. Pope
Felix, a Roman, condemned Acacius, bishop of Constantinople,
and Peter, bishop of Alexandria, at a council in his see because they
were Eutychians. Pope Gelasius, an African, found Manicheans
in the city of Rome and deported them into exile, burning their
books outside the basilica of St. Mary. After the synod had been
held here, and letters had been sent throughout the East, he again
condemned Acacius and Peter.[58]

"Pope Agapitus, a Roman, was received in glory when he
came to Constantinople before the emperor Justinian Augustus,
in whose presence he refuted and condemned Anthymius, bishop
of this city, who was misled by the Eutychian heresy to deny that
Christ has two natures. The emperor then sent Anthymius into
exile. Pope Theodore, a Greek, condemned Pyrrhus, bishop of
Constantinople, who had earlier come to Rome and been condemned for those heresies in which he was involved, but like a
dog returned to the vomit of the heresy in which he was condemned.[59] The same pope, after sending legates here, condemned
Paul, bishop of this city, because he wished to confess neither
one nor two wills or operations in Christ the Lord. Pope Martin,

---

[58] Anselm's rapid summary of councils and popes is, again, drawn from Cassiodorus, *Historia ecclesiastica*, esp. Book. 5, ed. Jacob and Hanslik, 212–302.

[59] See 2 Peter 2:22.

a Tuscan, condemned Cyril of Alexandria and Sergius, Pyrrhus, and Paul, patriarchs of Constantinople, who presumed to invent novelties contrary to the pure faith, in a patriarchal synod at the Lateran held with 105 bishops. Martin then sent copies of that condemnation through all the East and West in the hands of orthodox men.[60]

"Pope Donus, a Roman, found Nestorian monks from Syria in the city of Rome in the monastery called Boezanas. He scattered them among various other monasteries and established Roman monks in that place. Agathon, a Sicilian, sent his legates to Constantinople to unite churches at the request of the pious emperors Constantine, Heraclius, and Tiberius. These envoys were the bishops Abundantius of Paternense, John of Regitanum, and John of Ostia, and the priest Gregory of Ravenna, the priests Theodore and Gregory, the deacon John, and the subdeacon Constantius. These men entered the city and were received there with great honor on the Lord's day, when they were summoned to the church of the Holy Mother of God near the palace of Blachernae in such great dignity that the emperor in his piety directed that caparisoned horses bring them with his compliments. These men, presiding over a synod of 150 bishops in the basilica of Trullus and representing the blessed Pope Agathon in the presence of the emperor in his royal splendor, condemned Macarius, patriarch of Antioch, and his followers, who claimed there is one will and operation in Christ. The emperor then sent Macarius into exile in Rome. The same council also established that we speak of two wills and two operations in Christ. On the same occasion John, bishop of Ostia, celebrated public Masses in Latin on the octave of Easter in the presence of the emperor and the patriarchs, and all acclaimed the pious emperors and their victories in Latin as with one voice.[61]

"Behold, then, you see that any heresies arising here or elsewhere have been struck down and destroyed by the rock of faith

---

[60] For this material after the conclusion of Cassiodorus's account in the late fourth century the author Anselm depends heavily on the *Book of Pontiffs* 59–77, trans. Davis, 54–73.

[61] *Book of Pontiffs* 80–81, trans. Davis, 76–80.

through Peter the apostle. Not only because of those councils mentioned here but also as a result of many others celebrated throughout the East as well as many councils of the Africans in which various heresies have been condemned, the Roman Church possesses two holy privileges, divinely constituted: a faith purer than all other churches' and the power of judgment over all. Since she thus is preeminent in power, who then would be so imprudent as to choose not to accept her authority and her formal decrees, or not to follow her rite in the ecclesiastical sacraments? Let her great authority then suffice for you to set aside the rite of leavened bread and adopt unleavened bread in the sacrifice of the altar, and conform in this as in the other sacraments to the holy and immaculate Roman Church like a son devoutly obedient to his mother."[62]

Nicetas, archbishop of Nicomedia, answered: "In the archive of this church of Holy Wisdom we preserve the ancient histories of the Roman pontiffs and the statutes of the councils.[63] There we find the things you have stated concerning the authority of the Roman Church. We would be greatly embarrassed to deny what we have before our eyes as recorded by our fathers. But neither the Roman pontiff himself nor his emissaries would have condemned anyone in the East without the consent, approbation, and support of established orthodox bishops throughout that region. In their zeal for the faith these bishops condemned heresies and confirmed the correctness of catholic belief, sometimes with and sometimes without the support of the Roman Church. But since you pretend so much authority for that oft-mentioned church of Rome, tell me, I ask, which of the Roman pontiffs established that unleavened bread must be used in the sacrifice of the altar, such that we might be forced to accept it or be justly condemned?"

---

[62] Curiously, this is the speaker Anselm's first direct reference to the Greeks' leavening of the host, to which most of this book's specific debate is addressed.

[63] The Greek speaker, demonstrating his historical knowledge, now elicits his counterpart's historical commentary.

Chapter 13
That the Greeks say they use leavened bread in the sacrifice of the altar by the authority and institution of the Roman pontiffs Siricius and Melchiades.[64]

Anselm, bishop of Havelberg, replied: "I confess that I have found this written nowhere in the ecclesiastical books found among us."[65]

Nicetas, archbishop of Nicomedia, then said: "Clearly Pope Melchiades, an African, established this practice when he directed that sacrificial offerings on the Lord's day throughout the churches be made with bread explicitly said to be 'fermented' and consecrated by a bishop. And Pope Siricius, a Roman, established that no priest celebrate weekly Mass unless with bread consecrated by the bishop of that place and specified as 'fermented.'[66] If the authority of Roman pontiffs suffices for you against me, it should also suffice for me against you. You argue with me for your rite of sacrifice with unleavened bread, as the Roman Church now practices through long custom. But I set before you what is written about those Roman pontiffs' ancient custom of unleavened bread. If you condemn me as one who distorts custom, I will then judge you to distort apostolic institution. But to violate an institution is graver and more presumptuous than to offend custom, for the former is confirmed in the authority and argument of its author while the latter is upheld only in the usage of one place or another. The catholic Roman pontiffs Melchiades and Siricius established the sacrifice of leavened bread, as is clear to anyone who reads the deeds of the Roman pontiffs and their various mandates.

[64] This translation preserves the manuscripts' Hellenized spelling of the name of the pope usually called Miltiades in English histories.

[65] As Jay T. Lees notes, manuscript evidence does not support the PL's attribution of this statement to the speaker Anselm, although the context does not argue against it: *Anselm of Havelberg: Deeds into Words in the Twelfth Century* (Leiden: Brill, 1998), 267 n. 316.

[66] See *Book of Pontiffs* 33, 40, trans. Davis, 14, 31. The speaker Nicetas again seems to refer to a work to which he would have had no access, but which the author Anselm knew well. The latter, in so informing Nicetas, allows his interlocutors effectively to debate the same text. The interlocutor Anselm will recur to these details below in *Anticimenon* 3.15.

Besides, as I believe and as is implied in the custom of those who acted on the same authority, the Roman Church was in concord with the Greeks in ancient times, and the Greeks with the Roman Church. Both sometimes used leavened bread and sometimes unleavened bread in the ministry of the altar according to the convenience of those making the offering. Nor was any Greek or Latin scandalized when he wished to communicate in either fashion. We can be the surer of this because we read that, when a great number of Greeks and Latins lived together in the city of Rome, not only Latins but many Greeks were heads of the holy Roman Church. Pope Anacletus was a Greek, as were his successors Evaristus, Telesphorus, Hyginus, Eleuther, Anterus, Xystus, Eusebius, Zosimus, John, likewise John the son of Plato, and Zacharius the son of Polienus—we know of all these and there were many more, whom I now forget, who headed the Church of Rome and were Greek in their origin, eminent in the practice of Christian religion and the soundness of their doctrine.[67]

"Do you imagine that these Greek prelates and their Latin subjects had daily conflict about sacrificing unleavened or leavened bread, so that the Greek pontiffs offered only leavened bread and the Roman Church never communicated with them through it, or that the Roman Church with its Latin priests used only unleavened bread, so that even as pontiffs of Rome they likewise withdrew themselves from the communion with their Roman subjects in offering unleavened bread? Who would believe this, even dare assert it? How could these prelates be catholic if their catholic subjects would not communicate with them? Or how could their subjects be catholic if catholic prelates would not offer them communion? How could such a church rightly be called a church, in which there were no concord of communion among pontiffs or subjects?[68] No, I think rather that we must believe, as I have said, that in ancient times everyone used unleavened or leavened bread indifferently according to the judgment of those who presided or

[67] Anselm had discussed Greek influence in Rome in *Anticimenon* 2. Prologue.
[68] Here, in Nicetas's speech, the author Anselm reveals his phenomenological interest. His emphasis on practice in an essentially theological discussion is distinctive among medieval authors.

offered it, without any scandal among those so communicating, whether they were Greeks or Latins. Thus within the walls of great Rome near the church of the blessed Caesarius there is to this day a congregation of Greek monks, and outside the walls near the Latin Way in the Roman countryside, in the place called Grottaferrata, another congregation of Greek monks. As far as I know they offer leavened bread without any scandal to the Roman pontiff, or even the Latins among whom they live, and with whom they too take communion."[69]

Chapter 14
That we may believe that the apostles and their successors used unleavened and leavened bread indifferently; and that the Western Church little by little abandoned the one completely, and the Eastern Church the other.

"I also think that we must believe that the apostles of Christ did the same, when in the rite of the nascent church they used sometimes unleavened, sometimes leavened bread. For they traveled through many regions preaching the Gospel, and when they stopped at some church of Christians and wished to offer the holy sacrifice to the Lord for the communion of the brethren, we must well believe that they made no special effort to acquire the one or the other, either leavened or unleavened bread—or for that matter made an issue of it in their inquiry.[70] Rather they offered whatever was at hand, leavened or unleavened, in simple devotion. And I think that this form of sacrifice or communion was handed down from ancient times, indeed from the apostles, as much in the Roman Church as in all the other churches, although no particular passage of scripture may tell us exactly this. But gradually the Roman Church gave up leavened bread and adopted only the one form,

---

[69] The author Anselm relates, again in his speaker Nicetas's voice, a detail of contemporary practice he—in his several sojourns in Italy—is likelier than a Greek interlocutor to have known. Anselm had noted above that he was an eager *voyeur* of Greek religious communities in the East: see *Anticimenon* 1.10. It is difficult to imagine that he would not have been equally interested in Grottaferrata.

[70] The Greek speaker now projects the author's phenomenological interest into the early days of Christianity.

unleavened bread, according to its own authority. Meanwhile the Eastern Church gradually abandoned unleavened bread in exclusive favor of the other, that is, leavened bread. But neither the ancient Greek nor the ancient Latin sages considered their counterparts despicable on this account, although their practices differed. Instead they esteemed and encouraged each other mutually in peace and charity. Making no judgment against each other, they celebrated councils together as opportunity arose.

"Then certain Latins in more recent times, some three hundred years ago, exalted themselves excessively and rashly, as we read in the accounts in our chronicles, that is, our books of annals.[71] And their foolishness has provoked many scandals between Latins and Greeks. In those times a certain Charles, king of the Franks, furiously seized the Roman empire and caused himself to be named patrician of the city of Rome. At that time, in violation of the dignity of the empire, he divided—rather tore apart—imperial unity, creating many scandals between Latins and Greeks not only by the division of imperial authority but also in the diversity of ecclesiastical standards.[72] Hence the Latins blaspheme our leavened bread, judging it unworthy for the sacrifice of the altar and calling us heretics in self-exaltation rather than in truth. They retire from their altars, refusing to communicate with us. Provoked, we have responded likewise, and are careful never to use their unleavened bread, which we judge unworthy of the sacrifice of the altar. We called them unleavened heretics in just retribution rather than in prideful arrogance. Retiring from our altars, we too refuse to communicate with them, falling into the same state. To whatever degree we sin in this, we do so under grave provocation.

"But if the Romans wanted to rein in such reproaches and walk with us in fraternal charity rather than tread upon us from the power of their lofty station, we would rejoice greatly. We would restrain our own blunt reaction, passing no judgment on the Latins

[71] The Greek interlocutor names no specific sources, and indeed the author Anselm here probably constructs Nicetas's position from Latin sources the historical Greek cannot have known.

[72] The speaker Nicetas points specifically to the controversies of the Carolingian period as the origin of the current hostility about ritual practice.

or excluding anyone who disagreed with us in this from the bond of our communion. We would thus offer the Latins due reverence, greeting them with due honor as the Apostle enjoins, in charity and willingness of heart.[73] This proverb is true: 'where absurd provocation leads, inappropriate response follows.'[74] But we must always note—and we must not easily forget—that the authority of the Greeks was once so great among the Latin sages that the very names of ecclesiastical offices or ceremonies were established in Greek, so called even today in the Roman Church all through the West: patriarch, metropolitan, archbishop, bishop, chorbishop, priest, deacon, subdeacon, acolyte, exorcist, canon, cleric, abbot, monk, church, monastery, cenobite, hermit, basilica, baptism, exorcism, catechumen, epiphany or theophany, hypopantes, parasceve, pentecost. Thence clearly we must acknowledge that the authority of the Greeks was considered important, because the Latins of long ago—as wise as they are now or perhaps more so—in their ancient times chose these names for ecclesiastical offices and ceremonies."

Chapter 15
That the authority of many Roman pontiffs should have more weight than that of two, that a synod may void the statutes of a synod, and that Popes Melchiades and Siricius do not seem to have instituted anything about the eucharistic host, but about the blessing-bread.

Anselm, bishop of Havelberg, then said: "If you judge that we must obey what the popes Melchiades and Siricius ordained concerning leavened bread because of their authority in this regard, then we should the more rigorously obey what we see done in daily practice by more Roman pontiffs, what we customarily celebrate respectfully in all the churches, not only in Rome but throughout nearly the whole world. I have had to say these things because of you Greeks alone, and those who live in Pontus, Thrace, and certain places in Asia, and that nation of the Ruthenians who—virtual

---

[73] See 1 Timothy 1:5.
[74] The saying Anselm quotes is unrepresented in published proverb collections—as indeed are most of the aphorisms he seems to understand as commonplaces.

idiots ignorant of all divine scriptures—imitate your rite by custom alone, simply and thoughtlessly, because they are your close neighbors and so bear the yoke of this empire as slaves and in fear.[75] But it was appropriate, was it not, for many other popes acting in the authority of the apostolic see they too ruled, to improve prior practice for good reason, in accordance with the growth of the church as it rose from day to day into a higher level of understanding?[76] If you consider that the authority of the apostolic see rests in two popes you must also recognize that it inheres in many more, for the authority of many holy fathers who spoke and did good is greater than that of two who discharged the same authority, even if they were good, and spoke and did good. Besides, as you know, a synod sometimes supersedes an earlier synod in reexamining an issue—sometimes out of necessity, sometimes for convenience, sometimes according to the tenor of the times. This befalls entirely at the discretion of those presiding, whom then as now God has willed to have charge of his church, and to whom he has entrusted the keys of discernment and power for every holy task, so long as the foundation of the catholic faith is preserved unshaken.

"Further, as I think, this practice established by the pontiffs Melchiades and Siricius seems not to have been about leavened hosts, rather about the blessing-bread they required be distributed among all the churches on each Lord's day.[77] I offer no disagreement about what you have said about the harmony of the ancient Latin and Greek sages, who perceived no scandal, as you have pointed out, in the offering of either unleavened or leavened bread. But I consider that we must follow the judgment of my predecessors, especially of the Roman pontiffs, in this discussion. Their judgment should please me more than my own, for it was their place to judge of me and my opinion. So we should rightly imitate not only the diligence of their teaching but their modesty in learning."

---

[75] The speaker Anselm here harshly, backhandedly responds in kind to Nicetas's earlier accusation that Rome is a cruel "mistress of slaves": see *Anticimenon* 3.8. The Ruthenians inhabited Ukraine.

[76] Anselm here adverts to his notions of the growth of doctrine and ecclesiastical institutions across time as set forth in Book 1: see esp. *Anticimenon* 1.6-8.

[77] See again *Book of Pontiffs* 33 and 40, trans. Davis, 14 and 30.

Chapter 16
That Constantinople and all the Eastern Church have been under obedience to the Roman Church and rightly should now be, so following its sacramental rite.

"Moreover, because you complain of later, even recent rudeness of Latins to Greeks, you should not be surprised that all the histories demonstrate that you were in ancient times under the obedience of the Roman Church, that is the Latin Church, but that you have for a long time since then shown contempt for the sweet yoke of its obedience. You have denied the subjection your antecedents humbly showed the Roman Church, purporting your own discretion and your own wisdom in lofty matters. Therefore you should not be surprised if those who grieve that you have, to an evil end, separated yourself from its obedience, are outraged at you and reprove your rites.

"As for what you boastingly say, that the Latins use Greek terms for ecclesiastical dignities and ceremonies, I ask whether you think that the Latins should be apologetic to the Greeks that the latter might frame these terms for them because they were as Latins ignorant, so lacking in Latin eloquence that they did not know how to invent them on their own? Do not imagine this, I beg you. Rather, the ancient Greeks frequently visited Rome in its splendor as mistress and head of the world and its empire. Like the other nations of the world, the Greeks were subject to the Roman pontiff, obeying him with due reverence. They accepted his counsel in the ordering of ecclesiastical titles and solemnities as in many other things offered in the holy and praiseworthy humility of the Roman Church because those Greeks were as wisely humble as they were humbly wise. Italy was in ancient times called Greater Greece, as the ancient histories tell, and in the city of Rome spoken language saw lively use of both tongues. Latins used Greek and the Greeks used Latin in turn, and neither tongue was strange to the inhabitants of Rome. As a result certain things in the church are called by Latin terms and others in Greek. So it is established in the Roman rite that in solemn Masses on the highest feast days the lessons and the Gospel should be recited both in Latin and in Greek, because of the presence of each people, those learned

in either tongue.⁷⁸ Would that the Greeks of our times might be
as humble and obedient to the Roman Church as they heretofore
were! How gladly, how joyfully, I say, the Roman Church even
today would admit their counsels and attend to their discretion
in its wonted humility! For the Roman Church has never been so
proud or envious as to insist arrogantly and contentiously on its
own institutions of any sort, or to disparage or resist the institutions of others if their practices were indeed good.

"The Roman Church often changes its institutions in favor of
better practices, and has humbly taken up as models the good
institutions of others. So bells were first used in the Church in
Campania near the city of Nola, so that they were then called
nola or *campana*.⁷⁹ The Roman Church accepted this convention
as good, never showing contempt for it because it considered it
alien, not its own. But the Greeks, secure in their own discretion
and confident of their own judgment, wise in their own eyes and
sufficient in themselves, are always wont to boast about their own
discoveries of whatever sort. They spitefully disparage the institutions of others, however good, claiming that what they do is good
because it is their practice and that what they do not do is not
good because it is not theirs. But the Apostle says: *Not that we are
sufficient to think any thing of ourselves, as of ourselves, but our suffi-
ciency is from God* (2 Cor 3:5). Yet he also says about himself, both
humbly and boldly: *I think that I also have the spirit of God* (1 Cor
7:40). Therefore the Latins sometimes use Latin terms, sometimes
Greek for the ecclesiastical orders, such as the Greek *episcopus* for
the Latin *pontifex*, the Greek *presbyter* for the Latin *senior*, that is,
a priest, the Greek *diaconus* for the Latin *minister*. So the care of
translators shifts terms from Greek into Latin or from Latin into
Greek, or from Hebrew into Latin or Greek."

Nicetas, archbishop of Nicomedia, responded: "Enough has
been said on both sides about the authority of the Roman Church.
But you have asserted that apostolic authority ordained the practice

⁷⁸ See again *Anticimenon* 1. Prologue.
⁷⁹ The Rule of St. Pachomius had noted this etymology. See the Latin version
probably known to Anselm: Pseudo-Jerome, *Regula sancti Pachomii a sancto Hieronymo in latinam sermonem conversa* 2, PL 50, col. 278.

of unleavened bread after careful consideration of the better argument, and handed down this commandment to all the churches of the world. Now I would like to hear why this was done, so that the usage of leavened bread established by the popes Melchiades and Siricius was eliminated and the usage of unleavened bread established and promulgated. For if the argument you promise is compatible with the authority you likewise postulated, it seems we must indeed believe what you are trying to assert. And if, as I have said, argument and authority are mutually supportive, we must then all assent to your claims, laying aside the leavened bread that those two pontiffs seemed to have established in order that we conform to that greater number of pontiffs who ordained otherwise and take up the usage of unleavened bread."

Anselm, bishop of Havelberg, replied: "I will not easily accede to what you say, when you so readily suppose me now to believe that the Roman Church once used leavened bread and later, setting that practice aside, took up unleavened bread. Rather, because you have adduced the institution of the popes Melchiades and Siricius, I must answer you what I think of this assertion. I am not misled by any false reasoning, rather preserve the authority of these great fathers. Now pay close attention why we must use our unleavened rather than your leavened bread in the sacrifices of the altar."

Chapter 17
That in the Lord's Supper Christ consecrated unleavened bread, and that nowhere does the Old Testament command that leavened bread be sacrificed, rather unleavened bread.[80]

"Our Lord Jesus Christ himself, who came into this world to make sinners whole and revealed himself as the model of all truth, as we must believe, used unleavened bread in that first consecration of his most sacred body, which he then distributed to his disciples, establishing this as the model they should follow in commemorating him. The Lord said as he offered them the sacrament: *Take, this is my body*, and so he spoke at the institution of the sacrament: *Do*

---

[80] Anselm apparently builds his argument directly from scriptural sources without following intermediate authorities.

this for commemoration of me (Luke 22:19). He said this on account
of the error of certain men who do not think that the same body
is consecrated in the sacrifice of the altar as he consecrated in the
Paschal Supper and gave to his disciples. Those men attend too
much to the phrase that follows, *in my commemoration,* supposing
the Lord to have instituted this rite only *in commemoration,* and not
that we must celebrate the sacraments of the altar in the reality of
his own body.[81] *This,* he said, *is my body, this do. This* means that
very body, not only as a commemoration but in its bodily reality.
Do this, that is, consecrate it, and because he said *in my commemoration* he wished us to understand that the sacrament of his true
body should only be celebrated by the faithful in memory of his
passion and for the health of their souls. For the Apostle says: *As
often as you shall eat this bread and drink this chalice you shall show
the death of the Lord until he come* (1 Cor 11:26). So we must believe that Christ used only unleavened bread in the great Paschal
Supper, offering his disciples what he had consecrated as his own
body, for he said of himself: *I am not come to destroy the law, but to
fulfill* (Matt 5:17).

"Moreover the Law says in Exodus, called Hellesmoth in Hebrew: *The first month, the fourteenth day of the month in the evening,
you shall eat unleavened bread until the one and twentieth day of the
same month in the evening. Seven days there shall not be found any
leavening in your houses. He that shall eat leavened bread, his soul shall
perish out of the assembly of Israel, whether he be a stranger or born
in the land. You shall not eat any thing leavened. In all your houses
you shall eat unleavened bread* (Exod 12:18-20). Therefore, because
according to the commandment of the Law leavened bread was
to be found in no house of Israel in those seven days, but only
unleavened bread, and because Christ came not to abolish the Law
but to fulfill it, clearly he used unleavened bread, consecrating it in

---

[81] Various early fathers, including Ignatius of Antioch, had written against the
Gnostic position that the Eucharist was symbolic, and Anselm perhaps refers to their
texts, although he is certainly aware of the contemporary discussion about the Real
Presence in the Eucharist opened by Berengar of Tours in the late eleventh century:
see John Marenbon, *Medieval Philosophy: An Historical and Philosophical Introduction*
(London: Routledge, 2007), 118–19. Anselm may have cited Bernold of Constance's
record of Berengar's condemnation: see above, *Anticimenon* 2.27.

the Paschal Supper, so fulfilling the ancient Passover and inaugurating the new Passover. How might it have been leavened, when leavening was forbidden among all the houses of Israel in those seven days according to the law, banned and prohibited both for strangers and natives under the certain penalty of condemnation? But perhaps you wish to frame the following conjecture, that acting in his omnipotence he created for himself a new leavened bread to complete this sacrament—but that is well known to be contrary not only to the Gospel but also to all probability.

"Does this reasoning not seem sufficient for you? Christ as author of this sacrament—he whom we must follow in all things—should suffice for you as model and example. If Christ's authority is insufficient for some person who inquires of another, then I want to avoid that man as *a heretic after the first and second admonition* (Titus 3:10), as the Apostle warns. But may you take note of this in charity, that nowhere does the Old Testament prescribe or even permit that leavened bread be offered in sacrifice to the Lord, rather absolutely forbids everywhere that it be offered as disagreeable to God. So, for example, we read in Leviticus (2:11), called Vaicra in Hebrew: *Every oblation that is offered to the Lord shall be made without leaven, neither shall any leaven or honey be burnt in the sacrifice to the Lord* (Lev 2:11). Likewise in Leviticus: *This is the law of the sacrifice of peace offerings . . . . If the oblation be for thanksgiving, they shall offer loaves without leaven tempered with oil, and unleavened wafers anointed with oil, and fine flour fried* (Lev 7:11-12). Likewise: *This is the law of consecration. When the days which he had determined by vow shall be expired, he shall bring him . . . an oblation to the Lord, one he lamb . . . without blemish, and one ewe lamb of a year old . . . for a sin offering, and one ram without blemish for a victim of peace offering, a basket also of unleavened bread tempered with oil, and wafers without leaven anointed with oil* (Num 6:13-15). Again: *This is the law of the sacrifice and libations . . . . The priest shall take a handful of the flour that is tempered with oil . . . and he shall burn it on the altar for a memorial of most sweet odor. . . . And the part of the flour that is left, Aaron and his sons shall eat, without leaven, and he shall eat it in the holy place. . . . And therefore it shall not be leavened, because part thereof is offered for the burnt sacrifice of the Lord. It shall be the most holy* (Lev 6:14-17). Likewise in Exodus: *Thou shalt not sacrifice the blood of my victim upon leaven* (Exod 23:18). Again: you shall offer *unleavened bread and a cake without leaven, tempered with oil, wafers . . . anointed with oil* (Exod 29:2). Likewise also *twelve loaves* baked of *fine flour . . . set one against the other upon the most clean table before the Lord . . . and every Sabbath they shall be changed* (Lev 24:5-8). No one doubts that this scripture refers to unleavened bread.

"So you see it has been established both by clear reasoning and solid authority that we must use unleavened rather than leavened bread in the sacrifice of the altar. For everywhere we abhor the ferment of dishonesty, excluding it from sacrifice, and everywhere we approve the *unleavened bread of sincerity and truth* (1 Cor 5:8), in the offering of which God is appeased, showing the people his favor."

Nicetas, archbishop of Nicomedia, then said: "You have aptly adduced the reasoning that you promised, supporting it with great authorities. I dare not deny what is clearly true, lest I blush with embarrassment and abandon all appearance of serenity in favor of shamefaced confusion. Then I might be caught in untruth even as I toil contentiously against the truth, for he who speaks the truth does not struggle while the liar reveals his character. Let what you say then stand for the moment. But on the other hand, we read thus in the Gospel: *eulogēsen arton*, that is, 'He blessed bread' (Luke 24:30). When the text says *artos*, it then seems to indicate mere bread, common bread, that is, leavened bread such as men use everywhere, and which they name by the usual term *artos*, that is, 'bread.' Whenever people specifically mean unleavened bread they do not use this word *artos* for 'bread,' rather the specific term *azymos*. The Greek *a* means 'without' in Latin, and *zumos* means 'leaven.' So I understand simply leavened bread, in its usual meaning, when I read in the Gospel: *eulogēsen arton*, that is, *he blessed bread*. For why should I write or read there *eulogēsen azumon* when the evangelist placed *eulogēsen arton* there, clearly indicating ordinary bread? You seem to have shown persuasively in what you have adduced to the contrary in the Old Testament that leavened bread is never permitted in the sacrifice. Nor can I at all deny this, for I heartily acknowledge that the texts support your assertion. But it seems to me that in the same Old Testament book of Leviticus we find the oblation of leavened bread, where the children of Israel hear through Moses: *You shall count therefore from the morrow after the Sabbath, wherein you offered the sheaf of the firstfruits, seven full weeks. Even unto the morrow after the seventh week be expired, that is to say fifty days, and so you shall offer a new sacrifice to the Lord. Out of all your dwellings, two loaves of firstfruits, of two tenths of flour leavened, which you shall bake for the first fruits of the Lord* (Lev 23:15). Here leavened bread plainly seems worthy of sacrifice to the Lord, unless there might be some other explanation by which we might understand it otherwise than it seems to be written."

Anselm, bishop of Havelberg, then said: "In my view we must interpret divine scripture so that it never contradict itself, rather always be harmonious. This should be the strong inclination of the prudent reader—that he know he has rightly understood the scripture of divine law when he brings it into harmony with other scripture and with the law of charity. The oblation described here, in which two loaves of the bread of the first fruits are offered from two tenths of the leavened fine flour, pertains in no way to the right order of sacrifices offered especially to the Lord, because it takes place neither at the altar nor in any holy place, nor in the holy of holies. Nor does it take place according to the rite of other oblations. Rather when the priest receives the bread of the first fruits of the leavened fine flour from one who offers it, and then lifts it up in thanksgiving for the fruits of the earth in the presence of the Lord, he then sacrifices it not according to the formal rite of other offerings, but in informal practice. So, dearly beloved, consider this carefully and you will see that I have spoken truly. You will find that nowhere in the Law is leavened bread offered to the Lord in sacrifice, instead always unleavened bread or the purest fine flour without any leaven. So we must believe too that the Son of God himself—because he knows best how God the Father must be appeased—used unleavened bread in the consecration of his most sacred Body according to the form of oblation established by the Lord everywhere in the Old Testament, by which he wills that he is appeased to favor his people. The Son would not destroy the figuration of the Law in its offering unleavened bread, rather would fulfill it by completing the truth of that Law in the consecration of his true Body."

Chapter 18
That leaven is nowhere in the divine scripture understood as
good, and that it is unsuitable even for careful handling.

"Thence in all of divine scripture leaven is nowhere understood to
signify goodness, as is our unleavened bread. So the Lord in the
Gospel of Luke says (12:1): *Beware ye of the leaven of the Pharisees,
which is hypocrisy* (Luke 12:1). And again in the Gospel according
to Matthew: *Take heed and beware of the leaven of the Pharisees and
Sadducees* (Matt 16:6). And the Apostle says: *Purge out the old leaven,
that you may be a new paste, as you are unleavened. For Christ our
Pasch is sacrificed. Therefore let us feast, not with the . . . old leaven
of malice and wickedness, but with the unleavened bread of sincerity
and truth* (1 Cor 5:7-8). Moreover, if you consider the matter correctly, your leavened bread is in no way as suitable for handling
with reverence as that unleavened bread we use as handed down
to us through Moses, that one in all the house of God who kept
the faith and ordered all things according as their exemplar on
the mountain, and finally through Christ himself. When leavened
bread is handled, broken, and distributed it falls apart easily into
many crumbs and can never be held together, however carefully
and attentively, as is required.[82] Because the tiniest particle of a
crumb, so to speak, is the true and real Body of the Lord, even its
slightest neglect incurs the Lord's grave curse, as is written: *Cursed
be he that doth the work of the Lord deceitfully* (Jer 48:10). Besides,
God the Father chose our unleavened bread in the Old Testament
as well as the New. God the Son both approved and consecrated it
for the holy consecration of his Body. This bread is strong, sincere,
valid, pure, uncorrupted, neither hollow nor porous, not soft, not
easily broken up into tiny crumbs but manageable and suitable in
every way for consecration, breaking, and distribution in complete
meticulousness. Among us religious Latins the hands of deacons
prepare this bread from select grains and from the purest fine flour
in a place consecrated for future hosts and accompanied by the
chanting of psalms. It is kept under diligent care until the time
of the sacrifice. In consideration of such reason and authority as

---

[82] Again Anselm as speaker stresses the author's practical bent.

well as the convenience of this sacramental host, all Greeks living throughout the East should clearly agree to use unleavened rather than leavened bread."

Chapter 19
That because of their time-honored usage of leavened bread, Greeks cannot embrace the usage of unleavened bread unless first a general council has been held to accept either species of bread indifferently, lest there be scandal to either Greeks or Romans.

Nicetas, archbishop of Nicomedia, responded: "I see that, as I have been taught, the Eastern Church has used leavened bread from the beginning, and I know this usage has been handed down from our predecessors. I revere the longstanding custom of this great church, so I neither dare to judge the practice rashly nor see how it can easily be changed. Yet, as for me, I think that it should be changed. No Greek sages, I declare, disagree with me in this conclusion. Therefore, if it happened that I were in a place where no leavened bread whatsoever were available but unleavened bread was ready at hand, and I wished to sing Mass, offering the Lord the sacrifice of the altar, I would certainly not shrink from unleavened bread, rather would confidently consecrate it for offering as an immaculate sacrifice to God. I would faithfully communicate and would present it to other Greeks for their communication if they were present and it were a day of public communion, whether on Easter or any other solemn feast in which the church as a whole is accustomed to communicate according to the rule that no Christian person is then permitted to abstain from the communion of the altar unless he is banished as public penance. But because there are more of the faint-hearted than of people earnest and well instructed in the faith, and because the common people who do not understand the process of such discernment are easily scandalized, this would be worthwhile—for all Latins and Greeks to strive diligently in the Lord to celebrate a general council at a suitable place and time, convening as one body, and for all to adopt in uniformity, universally, either the rite of unleavened bread or of leavened bread universally.[83] Or if neither one nor the other might be accepted universally without some scandal, even great scandal to the other party or people, they might at least agree in this—that neither this side nor that rashly condemn the other for the usage of leavened or unleavened bread to which it is respectively accustomed, rather offer each other mutual peace. In that case holy charity might not so be brought down, so weakened in one people that it brings peril to the other.

"Indeed, it appears according to the authorities and the logical argument we have set forth, as according to the very rite of the sacrament, that we ought to offer an unleavened host. But the Greeks' usage of leavened bread has been so long maintained that it could not be changed without great scandal to many, even to the entire people. Therefore it would be well to allow what has been done among us for a long time, especially since leavened and unleavened bread are alike bread, although differing in form still in substance no different in being leavened or unleavened. So the integrity of the faith is preserved if either is offered nearly universally. That living bread who came down from heaven may aptly be figured in either. So the ruinous scandal of discord might be removed from the midst of either nation, while no danger to the right faith will arise whether we offer either unleavened or leavened bread. As I have said, the host of our savior, the Lord Jesus Christ, may be rightly made from either for the salvation of those believing in it and those faithfully offering it—if not for the salvation of those wickedly disputing about it. For it is written: *God is not the God of dissension, but of peace* (1 Cor 16:33), and this is proclaimed from heaven by angels: *on earth peace to men of good will* (Luke 2:14). The sacred host, whether of leavened or unleavened bread, is made of many grains gathered into one, so signifying the people of the whole church gathered into one and the same fraternal charity.[84]

---

[83] Nicetas renews his call for the great East-West council first offered in *Antici-menon* 2.27.

[84] Cyprian had used this image in his letter to Caecilius: Cyprian of Carthage, *Epistle 62, On the Sacrament of the Cup of the Lord* 13, *Hippolytus, Cyprian, Caius, Novatian*, trans. Roberts and Donaldson, 362. Anselm as author generously places this beautiful and affecting image in the mouth of his Greek interlocutor, whose call for concord is thereby the more appealing.

He who separates himself from the charity that is in Christ Jesus communicates by this host at his great peril, however secure he may think himself.

"The rash perversity of the unfounded judgments by which we tear at each other seems to me a greater sin than the differences in sacramental practice occasioning that disagreement, for these rites make no matter to the Lord, as I said earlier. But as for head-strong prejudice by those in evil discord, that is never allowed for any Christian. Discord offends God. It is filled with sin, while the offering of the host pleases God with its salvation-bringing devotion. Discord stands in accusation of those who sharply condemn others, while the host brings forgiveness to those who are healthily saved. The former provokes by offending God our judge, and the latter pleases our merciful God by propitiating him. The former sends us to hell, the latter to heaven. Through the former we are separated from God but through the latter made part of his body. In the former we are earthly and in the latter heavenly. So whatever our difference in this sacred oblation, we must all come together in the unity of charity. Just as charity compensates a multitude of sins in sacred oblation, so that same oblation compensates our sins in true charity. Just as the salvation-bearing host works its salvation in charity, so that perfect love knows no scandal in different modes of sacrificing the host. For when charity is absent, all other goods are made empty, and when it is present those same goods become rich favors.

"Therefore, if there were a general council for the sharing of all these considerations, with the most pious emperors supporting it, and if a person of my insignificance might be present at that council, I would confidently say these same things in the presence of all. In stating my view I would fear neither Greek nor Latin. With due humility and reverence I would call upon the Roman pontiff, pointing out how—with his help—we who have always been one in our catholic faith might again have unity in the observance of the sacraments, so removing all occasion for enmity and discord. I hope that he might patiently hear me as I offered this humble counsel just as Peter, although he was foremost of the apostles, humbly listened long ago to Paul's frequent chastisement. In that reproach we commend Paul's firmness as a confident, just rebuke and we praise Peter's patience in his gentle bearing. In this instance I would be far inferior to Paul, but the pontiff ought not to be inferior to Peter. Then the Roman pontiff might be a Latin to the Latins and to the Greeks a Greek, so *all things to all men* (1 Cor 9:22). He might gain all, settling all matters on which we disagree by the humble authority of his apostolic see, either taking away the one practice and instituting the other universally or, removing all scandal, authorizing both indifferently."[85]

Anselm, bishop of Havelberg, then said: "We have said enough on this question, but there remains something I wish to bring to your careful attention."

Chapter 20
On the mixing of wine and water in the chalice, which the Greeks do one way and the Latins another.

"Tell, if you will, why in the sacrifice of the altar you Greeks do not offer wine and water poured and mixed together? Why do you consecrate pure wine without water? After you have consecrated the pure wine of the oblation, then afterward you mix simple, unblessed water with the most sacred Blood in the chalice. You communicate in this way. Why, I ask, do you do this?"[86]

Nicetas, archbishop of Nicomedia, responded: "We do not read that Christ, in that great supper of his which is particularly called the Lord's Supper, consecrated water mixed with wine in the chalice. We do as he did, following his model. We have no other reason than that we imitate the Savior in this practice."

Anselm, bishop of Havelberg, then said: "Although the Gospel says nothing explicit about the water as to whether it was added or not, nevertheless it is reasonable given the custom of the Jews and the Palestinians, who always drink wine mixed with water, that we understand Christ himself to have sacramentally consecrated

[85] Here in the specificity of the speaker Nicetas's appeal to the Roman papacy for irenic leadership, the author Anselm comes closer than in any other passage of *Anticimenon* to inviting papal initiative in ecumenism.

[86] This issue had emerged in the previous century, in Humbert's legation to Constantinople in 1054: see Chadwick, *East and West*, 226.

wine mixed with water. But if you say that it is rash to claim that he mixed wine with water in the Lord's Supper because we do not read this, I argue in the same way that it is rash to say that he did not add water to the wine because also we do not read in the Gospel that he did not. If it seems to you unsafe to say something because scripture fails to mention it, why do you not find it similarly unsafe to deny something because scripture does not deny the same thing? As for me, I do not claim that wine mixed with water was in the Lord's cup because I am contentious, but neither should you contentiously deny this, especially since the authority of the Gospel neither affirms the one nor denies the other. In these ambiguous matters we must claim nothing rashly, nor rebut anything with indignation. When you make a claim, then, beware of rashness, and when you rebut it beware of indignation. Just as rashness arguing for one position is presumptuous, so is wrath in rebutting it quarrelsome. We must guard against both in all discretion if we wish to seek out truth.

"Because the Gospel states clearly that blood and water came from the Lord's side on the cross in his redemption of our salvation, we seem rightly to offer wine and water offered as mixed in the chalice in our memorial of the Lord's passion, for the remission of our sins.[87] We do so too that water may be present in the blood of the new and eternal testament, for water signifies the people saved and redeemed in the communion of that same blood of the new and eternal testament as the one Body of the church incorporated, united, made holy, and offered up in its Head, that is, in Christ. For it is written that many waters are many peoples.[88] For this reason we Latins offer wine and water mixed in one cup, to signify in the wine the Blood of Christ and in the water the people of Christ, that is, the church, so that they may be consecrated together as mixed together in one body rather than divided. When you offer only pure wine without water in the chalice you do not then sanctify the church as the Body of Christ with Christ its Head,

---

[87] John 19:34.
[88] Revelation 17:15. Abelard had cited this passage in his discussion of the Eucharist, in one of the shorter variants of his systematic theology: Peter Abelard, *Epitome theologiae christianae*, PL 178, col. 1742.

but offer Christ alone consecrated as Head of the church without his members. This practice seems to lack all reason. Surely the wine and water are rightly meant to be consecrated not individually but together."

Nicetas, archbishop of Nicomedia, then replied: "As you have said, many waters are many peoples. But we, imitating the exact model of the Lord's Supper, offer only pure wine in the cup for consecration as the blood of the new and eternal testament through divine operation and power in the ministry of the priest. Afterward we reasonably and appropriately mix in water so that the people may be sanctified through this union, though not by their own agency, now that they are united with the sacred blood. Thus we devoutly celebrate the consecration of the Blood of Christ in the consecration of wine, pure and by itself. But we do not thereby neglect the salvation of the Christian people, for we mix in the water afterwards so that the water signifying the people is made holy by participation in the same sacrament. Indeed, we find it less appropriate for that which sanctifies and that which is sanctified to be consecrated equally in one and the same act of consecration. So it suffices if the water, that is, the people, is made holy by participation in the divine consecration and not by sharing in the same act of consecration. We are not sanctified from the beginning with Christ, rather through the Holy Spirit and the imparting of the Holy Spirit. Then through the holy sacraments of Christ and the church we begin to be sanctified by participation and communion."

Anselm, bishop of Havelberg, then said: "But I would not wish you to separate head from members, or members from head, for the Apostle says: *Christ is the head of the church* (Eph 5:23). If by this separation you remove Christ, where, I ask you, is then the church's Head? Or how can the church exist where its Head, that is, Christ, is not? Or how can Christ be called the Head of a church where his members are not? Look to it then, my brother, that you do not think of him as a head to be separated from his members by some figment of false reasoning, or the members from their head, for this is to do away with Christ and the church, and to confuse everything. Surely divine scripture says much about the Head, that is, Christ, that is not appropriate to the church. Similarly it says

many things of the person of the church that are not appropriate
to the head. But that scripture does not therefore at all mean to
separate the one from the other. Just as Eve was made from the
side of the sleeping Adam, so the church was made from the side
of Christ suffering on the cross.[89]

Therefore in the oblation and consecration of the most sacred
Body and Blood of the Lord celebrated as a memorial of his passion,
the water that flowed from Christ's side should be present with his
Blood.[90] That water is a figure of the church, refreshing and baptizing the church as it sanctifies it. Our humanity thus lives as renewed
by these two substances flowing as one from the Lord's side, so that
if it incurs the stain of sin after baptism it might still have water of
forgiveness in which to be washed, and so be renewed from day to
day. If we offer wine without water, the Blood of Christ begins to
lack us like a head without members. And if we offer water alone,
then the people seem to lack Christ, like members without a head.
But when the two are mixed, then the mystery of Christ and the
church is complete in its spiritual interpretation, because Christ
and the church are shown to be one body, not two, that is, the
wine and the water—the Blood of Christ taken by his children in
communion and the water of sacred purification and renewal they
then receive. So they drink in Christ's Blood, the price of Christian
salvation, and pass into the unity of his Body, the church, by their
spiritual purification and quickening.[91]

"You ought not then to wonder that the two liquids, water and
wine, are transformed for the spiritual growth of our souls when
they are consecrated by divine operation. Every day the many liquids we consume become our blood for the sustenance of our bodies. Therefore surely wine and water are appropriately first mixed
for our mystical understanding, but after their consecration we
drink only blood because we have before been baptized by water
and afterward we drink it in a spiritual sense in our hunger and

[89] Genesis 2:21-22.

[90] John 19:34.

[91] In this and the following paragraph Anselm is again indebted to Cyprian,
Epistles 62.2-14, *Hippolytus, Cyprian, Caius, Novatian*, trans. Roberts and Donaldson, 359–62. Cyprian was in fact addressing those who used water alone in the
sacrament—not wine alone.

thirst. Who might presume to receive communion in the sacrament
of the Lord's Body and Blood unless first he were reborn in the
water of baptism? To do so would not be to communicate but to
act outside right order, so to place oneself outside the communion
of Christians. No one who drinks this cup is incorporated with
Christ unless he is first buried with Christ as his member through
baptism. So we rightly mix water with wine before their consecration, and in consecrating the two together we partake of them
only as Blood after this consecration, because before we must be
baptized in water and afterward we must be nourished and filled
with the Blood of Christ. You, though, seem to act improperly
when you keep the water from like consecration in consecrating
wine alone. When you do so you treat only one element of the
two that should be joined as one, regarding it as separate when
the other is removed. In that oblation you offend him whom you
should please even as you rightly strive to make your sacrifice, and
you make no attempt to distinguish what you offer from what you
should offer. To separate wrongly what should be joined is a great
sin. And you dangerously, wrongly, separate the substances joined
on the cross to flow mystically from the Lord's side. You do so as if
to institute some better practice on your own authority, contemptu-
ously changing what has been divinely established."

Nicetas, archbishop of Nicomedia, responded: "I make no attempt to divide those members of the church rightly and divinely
joined together with Christ as its head, rather to join them appropriately, so that the members gathered by the sanctification of
the Head may also be sanctified, so fitted for worthy sanctification
in their union with Christ. I can adduce many reasons for which
we must do this."

Anselm, bishop of Havelberg, then said: "Always making objec-
tions, though, goes on forever. You have a subtle gift for framing a
new perspective and your Greek eloquence is fluent in its defense.
But in such things modest, sober wisdom is worth more than any
sharp discretion that, too probing, strives to go beyond the bounds
established by the holy fathers.[92] The Apostle warns *not to be more*

<hr>

[92] Anselm here cuts off discussion for no particular reason, as if acknowledging
that both sides have cogent arguments and neither clearly has won the day.

wise than it behoveth to be wise, but to be wise unto sobriety (Rom 12:3).
What is so false that it may not seem true when it is spoken? Or
what is so true that it may not seem false when it is spoken? But
let astute wisdom rather than persuasive eloquence accompany
your speech, lest you seem to utter falsehood rather than truth.
I know without any doubt that I have spoken the truth because
we know and believe without doubt, as the Gospel testifies, that
blood and water flowed together from Christ's side on the cross in
redemption of salvation for us and for all of humankind. For that
reason we offer wine and water together mixed and consecrated
in one cup for the remission of all sins, and therefore we so teach
the rite of this offering. Our imitation of the model of Christ's
Passion suffices for us. We do not wish that model trammeled by
any new practices. Whatever we do, in these or other ecclesiastical
sacraments, we do according to the image preceding it, according
to the truth as it appeared in Christ. We consider that nothing is of
ourselves, rather that all things are from God, by whom all things
are sanctified in the sacraments and in truth."

Nicetas, archbishop of Nicomedia, answered: "Your reasoning
pleases me, as do your authority, your truth, your ritual practice,
your humility, your affability, and the well-ordered maturity of
your words. Above all else I desire to see a general council, so that
when we all come to agreement we may all speak the very same
thing in our Lord Jesus Christ. Just as the host is made—whether
leavened or unleavened—from many grains of pure wheat, and
as from many grapes together the wine is pressed, so from many
throngs of Greeks and Latins let us constitute one church, one
in heart and in perspective, lest your unleavened or our leavened
bread be a judgment of damnation on us on the Lord's day for
our mutual conflict, since either form of bread is instituted for
our salvation.[93] For you as well as for ourselves we must then
fear dangerous contention more than difference in the exercise of
this obligation."

---

[93] See Acts 4:32. Nicetas alludes again to Cyprian's sacramental imagery for
ecclesiastical union, completing the figure of grains into bread with its analogue,
grapes into wine. See again Cyprian, *Epistle 62*, chap. 13, *Hippolytus, Cyprian, Caius,
Novatian*, trans. Roberts and Donaldson, 363.

Chapter 21
On difference between the Greeks' and the Latins' rituals of baptism.

Anselm, bishop of Havelberg, then said: "I find you wise and discreet in all your words, and for that reason I ask that you be patient enough to answer me a bit further, to explain to me something that amazes and disturbs me. As I understand it your custom is that when a Greek wishes to marry a Latin wife, as happens frequently—especially among persons of imperial rank—first you anoint the woman with holy oil poured into a vessel, then you bathe her whole body with it. Finally, when she has thus crossed over into your rite and law, you conclude her marriage. But I would like to know exactly why you do this, if in fact you do, for it seems some form of rebaptism. If that is the case, then you are judging us Latins or even other Christians, however they may have been baptized under the invocation of the Holy Trinity, as requiring rebaptism. But this is clearly a heresy like that of the former sect of the Arians. We must then celebrate no councils with you, rather against you, and you must be condemned without any question or hearing.[94] Whatever you do or say about it, this practice is utterly abominable, detestable, and execrable to both God and man. By it you take the name of the Lord in vain, presuming to violate the invocation of Holy Trinity, in which we are baptized in the name of the Father and of the Son and of the Holy Spirit.

"We read in the history of the venerable Greek bishop Theodoret translated into Latin by Cassiodorus through Epiphanius the rhetorician that a certain Eusebius, bishop of Nicomedia, overwhelmed by the leaven of Arian heresy, rebaptized the emperor Constantine the Great according to the Arian dogma. This book relates: 'Constantine had fallen ill and left the city of Constantinople for the hot springs. While he was staying at Nicomedia, heavy with fatigue and pondering the uncertainty of his life, he received the grace of holy baptism.'[95] The same Constantinopolitan emperor,

---

[94] The speaker Anselm here acknowledges the other side of conciliarism—indeed, of ecumenism—that is, its definition of heterodoxy in the course of affirmation of orthodoxy. Here he threatens more than argues.

[95] Cassiodorus, *Historia ecclesiastica* 3.12, ed. Jacob and Hanslik, 154.

as we find in the *Ecclesiastical History* of the Palestinian bishop Eusebius of Caesarea, had been baptized before, in the early days of his conversion at Rome, in the Lateran palace by the blessed pope Sylvester.[96] Either of these histories, Eusebius's or Cassiodorus's, is rightly called ecclesiastical because of the truth it reveals about the church in various periods. In fact it was Constantius Augustus, son of the great Constantine, who was leavened by that heresy and so rebaptized by that Eusebius, bishop of Nicomedia. He demanded that the venerable pope Liberius return from exile, commanding him to consent to his and other heretics' rebaptism, but the blessed pope in no way cooperated. Although he publicly opposed the heretic Constantius in this matter, nevertheless Liberius ignored many heretical beliefs among many people for this emperor's sake. Constantius Augustus commanded that Liberius's successor, the pope Felix, be beheaded because he had proclaimed that emperor heretical for his second baptism by the bishop Eusebius of Nicomedia at the villa of Aquilone.[97] And if such heretical corruption remains among the nation of the Greeks, that is, rebaptism in the Greek rite of those who come to them already baptized in the name of the Holy Trinity, how then, I ask you, can they be called Christians? Whoever accepts rebaptism denies the power of the Holy Trinity according to which all catholic baptism is done, and he has been judged already."

---

[96] In fact, Eusebius made no such claim in either his *Ecclesiastical History* or his *Life of Constantine*. The claim that Sylvester had baptized Constantine and so cured him of leprosy, then received from the emperor dominion over the western regions of the Roman Empire he might then hand down to subsequent popes, was central to the *Donation of Constantine*, the famous eighth-century forgery important in the papal-imperial politics of Anselm's day. Eusebius had known, with Cassiodorus, that the emperor was baptized only on his deathbed outside Nicomedia by the Arian bishop who shared the name Eusebius: Eusebius of Caesarea, *Life of Constantine*, chaps. 61-64, trans. Averil Cameron and Stuart G. Hall (Oxford: Clarendon Press, 1999), 177–79.

For the *Donation of Constantine* and the related *Constitution of Constantine*, with details of the emperor's illness and baptism by Pope Sylvester, see Johannes Fried, *Donation of Constantine and* Constitutio Constantini: *The Misinterpretation of a Fiction and Its Original Meaning* (Berlin: Walter De Gruyter, 2007), esp. 138–42, 151–53.

[97] Anselm has corrected Cassiodorus's attribution of rebaptism to Constantine against the *Book of Pontiffs* 27–28, trans. Davis, 29–30.

Nicetas, archbishop of Nicomedia, answered: "If the Latins fully understood the rites of the Greeks they would not slander us so easily, nor be so easily scandalized concerning them. But it is no surprise that they judge incorrectly, since they do not know the truth about this rite. May we Greeks, orthodox in our faith, never accept that any Christian be baptized a second time in the name of Holy Trinity! To do this or to preach that it should be done is to fall into heresy. In truth, however, we do have certain rituals of purification by unction with sacred oil. When foreigners come to us—whether they are men or women wishing to pass over into our rite and our society—we anoint them with sacred oil because we do not know if they have earlier received the sacrament of unction. But by no means do we rebaptize those who we are aware have already been baptized, nor do we even anoint those who, we have no doubt, have been already anointed, so sanctified by unction with chrism through the laying on of hands and complete in the Christian religion. But this ritual is not intended as repetition. Rather, we do it because we do not know whether it has been done."[98]

Chapter 22
On the concord of the Greek and Latin sages.

Anselm, bishop of Havelberg, then said: "I give thanks to God, who has removed this scandal from me and taken away that reproach to the name 'Christian' of which I have heretofore suspected the wise nation of the Greeks."

Nicetas, archbishop of Nicomedia, responded: "If the faith and rites we maintain in the law of God are pleasing to you in your discretion, then we greatly rejoice. We seem to differ somewhat not in great matters but in small things. Although these latter concerns do not stand in the way of the salvation of souls, they hinder our fraternal charity. Therefore we must work concertedly,

[98] On the Byzantine rite of unction of foreigners see Chadwick, *East and West*, 231. Anselm seems to have been the only twelfth-century Westerner concerned about this matter—understandably, given his role in the courts of German monarchs interested in Byzantine marriage alliances.

as I said before, to gather a general council at an appropriate place and time where all these matters separating us may be reformed in one concord. Then Greeks and Latins may be made one people under their one Lord Jesus Christ—in one faith, one baptism, and one sacramental rite."[99]

Anselm, bishop of Havelberg, then said: "To question is the bastion and subterfuge of heretics, but when you express your desire for a general council you yearn for that which is indeed catholic. Therefore I join you in calling for a general council in which your wisdom, eloquence, holiness, maturity, discretion, gentleness, modesty, devotion, constancy, and piety—indeed, your perfection—may shine forth before the whole church for the salvation and instruction of all. My own humility, moderation, insignificance, devotion, indeed my own profound desire, will never cease to seek this happy prospect."[100]

All who were present then shouted: "*Doxa soi, o Theos, doxa soi, ō Theos, doxa soi, ō Theos*, three times, meaning 'Glory be to God.' They also cried *Kalos dialogos*, that is, 'a good dialogue.' And *Holographi, holographi*, that is, 'Write it all down, write it all down. Here it ends. Thanks be to God.'"

---

[99] Nicetas renews the call for an East-West council he has offered in *Anticimenon* 2.27 and 3.19.

[100] Anselm here joins in the call to ecumenical council, as he did at the conclusion of the previous book: *Anticimenon* 2.27.

Bibliography

MANUSCRIPTS

Berlin. Staatsbibliothek Preussischer Kulturbesitz. Ms. theol. fol. 80.

EDITIONS AND TRANSLATIONS OF ANSELM OF
HAVELBERG'S WORKS

Anticimenon

Baluze, Etienne and others, eds. *Antikeimenon*. In *Spicilegium sive collectio veterum aliquot scriptorium qui in Galliae bibliothecis delituerant*. Volume 1, 161–207. Paris, 1723.

D'Achery, Jean Luc, ed. *Antikeimenon*. In *Spicilegium sive collectio veterum aliquot scriptorium qui in Galliae bibliothecis delituerant*. Volume 13, 88–252. Paris, 1677.

Migne, Jacques-Paul, ed. *Dialogi*. Patrologiae latinae cursus completus. Volume 203. Columns 1139–1248. Paris, 1841–64.

Salet, Gaston, translator. *Dialogues, Livre I: Renouveau dans l'Église*. Sources Chrétiennes 118. Série des texts monastiques d'occident 18. Paris: Éditions du Cerf, 1966.

Apologetic Letter

Antry, Theodore J., and Carol Neel, translators. In *Norbert and Early Norbertine Spirituality*, 29–62. Mahwah, NJ: Paulist Press, 2007.

Letters

Bernard, Auguste, and Alexandre Bruel, eds. *Recueil des chartes de l'abbaye de Cluny*. Volume 5, 526–27. Paris, 1894.

Jaffé, Philippe, ed. In *Monumenta Corbeiensia*. Bibliotheca rerum germanicarum 1, 339–41. Berlin: Weidmann, 1864.

Litany of the Saints
Winter, Franz, ed. *De ordine pronuntiandae letaniae ad Fridericum Magdeburgensem archiepiscopum.* In Winter. "Zur Geschichte des Bischofs Anselm von Havelberg." *Zeitschrift für Kirchengeschichte* 5 (1882): 144–55.

EDITIONS AND TRANSLATIONS OF OTHER PATRISTIC AND MEDIEVAL WORKS*

Abelard, Peter. *Opera theologica.* Volume 2: *Theologia Christiana.* Ed. Eligius M. Buytaert. Corpus Christianorum, Continuatio Medievalis 12. Turnhout: Brepols, 1969.

Alberigo, Giuseppe and others, eds. *Conciliorum oecumenicorum generalium decreta.* Volume 1: *The Oecumenical Councils from Nicaea I to Nicaea II (325–787).* Turnhout: Brepols, 2006.

Anselm of Canterbury. *Anselm of Canterbury, Volume 3: Two Letters Concerning Roscelin, the Incarnation of the Work, Why God Became Man, The Virgin Conception and Original Sin, the Procession of the Holy Spirit, Three Letters on the Sacraments.* Translated by Jasper Hopkins and Herbert Richardson. Toronto: Edwin Mellen, 1976.

Antry, Theodore, and Carol Neel, translators. *Norbert and Early Norbertine Spirituality.* New York: Paulist Press, 2007.

Augustine of Hippo. *Against the Academics.* Translated by Mary P. Garvey. Milwaukee: Marquette University Press, 1942.

——. *City of God against the Pagans.* Edited and translated by R. W. Dyson. Cambridge: Cambridge University Press, 1998.

——. *Confessions.* Translated by Henry Chadwick. Oxford: Oxford University Press, 1991.

——. *Expositions on the Book of Psalms.* Translated by Philip Schaff. Nicene and Post-Nicene Fathers 8. Grand Rapids: Eerdmans, 1956.

——. *Tractates on the Gospel of John 11–27.* Translated by John W. Rettig. Washington, DC: Catholic University of America Press, 1988.

——. *The Trinity.* Edited by John E. Rotelle. Translated by Edmund Hill. Brooklyn, NY: New City Press, 1991.

——. *Writings against the Manichees and against the Donatists.* Edited by Philip Schaff. Nicene and Post-Nicene Fathers 4. Grand Rapids: Eerdmans, 1956.

Barber, Malcom, and Keith Bate, editors and translators. *The Templars: Selected Sources.* Manchester: Manchester University Press, 2002.

* Editions in the series Patrologiae Latinae cursus completus, ed. Jacques-Paul Migne (Paris, 1841–64), are listed as PL.

Benedict of Nursia. *Rule of St. Benedict*. Edited and translated by Timothy
Fry. Collegeville, MN: Liturgical Press, 1981.

———. *Sancti Benedicti regula cum commentariis*. PL 66, columns 215–932.

Bernold of Constance. *De Berengarii heresiarchae damnatione multiplici*. PL
148, columns 1453–60.

Boethius. *On the Catholic Faith*. In *Theological Tractates, The Consolation of
Philosophy*. Translated by H. F. Stewart and others, 52–71. Cambridge,
MA: Harvard University Press, 1978.

*Book of Pontiffs: The Ancient Biographies of the First Ninety Roman Bishops
to AD 715*. Rev. ed. Translated by Raymond Davis. Translated Texts for
Historians 6. Liverpool: Liverpool University Press, 2000.

Cassiodorus. *Historia ecclesiastica tripartita*. Edited by Walter Jacob and
Rudolph Hanslik. Corpus scriptorum ecclesiasticorum latinorum 71.
Vienna: Hoelder-Pichler-Tempsky, 1952.

Cyprian of Carthage. *Epistles, Treatises, Seventh Council of Carthage*. Translated by A. Cleveland Coxe. In *Fathers of the Third Century*. Ante-Nicene
Fathers 5. New York: Charles Scribner's Sons, 1903.

Eusebius of Caesarea. *Ecclesiastical History*. 2 volumes. Translated by Roy
J. Deferrari. New York: Fathers of the Church, 1953–55.

———. *Life of Constantine*. Translated by Averil Cameron and Stuart G.
Hall. Oxford: Clarendon Press, 1999.

Gregory of Nazianzus. *Discours 27–31*. Edited and translated by Paul Gal-
lay. Sources Chrétiennes 250. Paris: Éditions du Cerf, 1978.

———. *St. Gregory of Nazianzus: Select Orations*. Translated by Martha Vin-
son. Washington, DC: Catholic University of America Press, 2003.

Hilary of Poitiers. *Trinity*. Translated by Stephen McKenna. New York:
Fathers of the Church, 1954.

Hincmar of Reims. *Opuscula et epistolae quae spectant ad causam Hincmari
Laudunensis*. PL 126, columns 279–648.

Idung of Prüfening. *Cistercians and Cluniacs: The Case for Cîteaux, a Dialogue
between Two Monks, an Argument on Four Questions*. Cistercian Fathers
33. Kalamazoo,2 MI: Cistercian Publications, 1977.

Isidore Mercator. *Collectio decretalium*. PL 130, columns 41–1178.

Julius I. *Epistola ad Antiochenos*. PL 8, columns 879–907.

Jerome. *Dialogus adversus Pelagianos*. PL 23, columns 491–590.

———. *Homiliae Origenis in Jeremiam et Ezechielem*. PL 25, columns
583–786.

———. *In Hieremiam prophetam*. Edited by Siegfried Reiter. Corpus scriptorum ecclesiasticorum latinorum 59. Vienna: F. Tempsky, 1913.

———. *Liber de nominibus hebraicis*. PL 23, columns 815–904.

Leo the Great. *Letters and Sermons*. Translated by Charles Lett Feltoe. Nicene and Post–Nicene Fathers, 2d series 12, 1–216. Grand Rapids: Eerdmans, 1894.

Libellus de diversis ordinibus qui sunt in ecclesia. Rev. ed. Edited and translated by Giles Constable and Bernard S. Smith. Oxford: Clarendon Press, 2003.

Otto of Freising. *The Two Cities: A Chronicle of Universal History to the Year 1146 A.D.* Translated by Charles Christopher Mierow. New York: Columbia University Press, 1928.

Pelikan, Jaroslav, and Valerie Hotchkiss, eds. *Creeds and Confessions of Faith in the Christian Tradition*. Volume 1. New Haven: Yale University Press, 2003.

Photios. *On the Mystagogy of the Holy Spirit*. Translated by Holy Transfiguration Monastery. Astoria, NY: Studion, 1983.

Pseudo-Augustine. *Dialogus quaestionum 65 Orosii percontantis et Augustini respondentis*. PL 40, columns 733–52.

———. *Quaestiones veteris et novi testamenti 127*. Edited by Alexander Souter. Corpus scriptorum ecclesiasticorum latinorum 50. Vienna: F. Tempsky, 1908.

Pseudo-Jerome. *Epistolae*. PL 30, columns 13–308.

———. *Regula sancti Pachomii sancto Hieronymo in latinum sermonem conversa*. PL 50, columns 271–304.

Rupert of Deutz. *Altercatio monachi et clerici, quod liceat monacho praedicare*. PL 170, columns 537–42.

———. *In Apocalypsim*. PL 170, columns 825–1214.

Tanner, Norman P., ed. *Decrees of the Ecumenical Councils*. Volume 1: *Nicaea 1 to Lateran V*. London: Sheed and Ward, 1990.

SECONDARY WORKS

Angold, Michael, ed. *The Cambridge History of Christianity*. Volume 5: *Eastern Christianity*. Cambridge: Cambridge University Press, 2006.

———. *Church and Society in Byzantium under the Comneni, 1081–1261*. Cambridge: Cambridge University Press, 1995.

———. *The Fourth Crusade: Event and Context*. London: Pearson, Longman, 2003.

Backmund, Norbert. *Geschichte des Prämonstratenserordens*. Grafenau: Morsak, 1986.

———. *Die mittelalterlichen Geschichtsschreiber des Prämonstratenserordens*. Bibliotheca Analectorum Premonstratensium 10. Averbode: Praemonstratensia, 1972.

———. *Monasticon praemonstratense: id est historia circariarum atque canon-iarum candidi et canonici ordinis praemonstratensis.* 2 volumes in 4 parts. Straubing: C. Attenkofer, 1949–52. 2d ed., Part 1. Berlin: Walter de Gruyter, 1983.

Barber, Malcolm. *The New Knighthood: A History of the Order of the Temple.* Cambridge: Cambridge University Press, 1994.

Barmann, Lawrence F. "Reform Ideology in the *Dialogi* of Anselm of Havel-berg." *Church History* 30 (1961): 379–95.

Battifol, Pierre. *Le siège apostolique (359–451).* 2d ed. Paris: Victor Lecoffre, 1924.

Berman, Constance Hoffman. *The Cistercian Evolution: The Invention of a Religious Order in Twelfth-Century Europe.* Philadelphia: University of Pennsylvania Press, 2000.

Berschin, Walter. "Anselm von Havelberg und die Anfänge einer Geschichts-theologie des hohen Mittelalters." *Literaturwissenschaftliches Jahrbuch,* n. s. 29 (1988): 224–32.

Bierlein, Raymond Eugene. "Anselm of Havelberg: His Life and Works." M.A. thesis, Western Michigan University, 1971.

Bischoff, Guntram G. "Early Premonstratensian Eschatology: The Apoca-lyptic Myth." In *Spirituality of Western Christendom.* Edited by E. Ro-zanne Elder, Kalamazoo: Cistercian Publications, 41–71.

Bomm, Werner. "Augustinusregel, *professio canonica* und Prämonstratenser im 12. Jahrhundert. Das Beispiel der Norbert-Viten, Philipps von Har-vengt und Anselms von Havelberg." In *Regula Sancti Augustini.* Edited by Gert Melville and Anne Muller, 239–94.

———. "Anselm von Havelberg, *Epistola apologetica*—Über den Platz der 'Prämonstratenser' in der Kirche des 12. Jahrhunderts: Vom Selbst-verständnis eines frühen Anhängers Norberts von Xanten." In *Studien zum Prämonstratenserorden.* Edited by Irene Crusius and Helmut Flache-necker, 107–83.

Braun, Johann Wilhelm. "Anselm von Havelberg." In *Deutsche Literatur . . . Verfasserlexicon.* Edited by Kurt Ruh. Volume 1, columns 384–91. Berlin: Walter de Gruyter, 1978.

———. "Studien zur Überlieferung der Werke Anselms von Havelberg I: Die Überlieferung des *Anticimenon.*" *Deutsches Archiv für Erforschung des Mittelalters* 28 (1972): 133–209.

Bredero, Adriaan H. "The Announcement of the Coming of the Antichrist and the Medieval Concept of Time." In *Prophecy and Eschatology.* Studies in Church History, Subsidia. Edited by Michael Wilks, 3–13. Oxford: Blackwell, 1994.

218 Anselm of Havelberg

Brooke, Christopher. *The Age of the Cloister: The Story of Monastic Life in the Middle Ages*. Mahwah, NJ: HiddenSpring, 2003.

Buytaert, Eligius M. "The Greek Fathers in Abelard's 'Theologies' and Commentary on St. Paul." *Antonianum* 34 (1964): 408–45.

Bynum, Caroline Walker. Docere verbo et exemplo: *An Aspect of Twelfth-Century Spirituality*. Harvard Theological Studies 31. Missoula, MT: Scholars Press, 1979.

——. *Jesus as Mother: Studies in the Spirituality of the High Middle Ages*. Berkeley: University of California Press, 1982.

Chadwick, Henry. *The Early Church*. Grand Rapids: Eerdmans, 1968.

——. *East and West: The Making of a Rift in the Church, from Apostolic Times until the Council of Florence*. Oxford: Oxford University Press, 2005.

Christiansen, Eric. *The Northern Crusades: The Baltic and the Catholic Frontier 1100–1525*. Minneapolis: University of Minnesota Press, 1980.

Christie-Murray, David. *A History of Heresy*. Oxford: Oxford University Press, 1989.

Constable, Giles. *The Reformation of the Twelfth Century*. Cambridge: Cambridge University Press, 1996.

——. *Three Studies in Medieval Religious and Social Thought: The Interpretation of Mary and Martha, the Ideal of the Imitation of Christ, the Orders of Society*. Cambridge: Cambridge University Press, 1995.

Crusius, Irene. ". . . *ut nulla fere provincia sit in partibus Occidentis, ubi ejusdem religionis congregationis non inveniantur . . .* : Prämonstratenser als Forschungsaufgabe." In *Studien zum Prämonstratenserorden*. Edited by Irene Crusius and Helmut Flackenecker, 11–32.

——, and Helmut Flackenecker, eds. *Studien zum Prämonstratenserorden*. Veröffentlichungen des Max-Planck-Instituts für Geschichte 185. Studien zur Germania Sacra 25. Göttingen: Vandenhoeck & Ruprecht, 2003.

Dräseke, Johannes. "Bischof Anselm von Havelberg und seine Gesandtschaftsreisen nach Byzanz. *Zeitschrift für Kirchengeschichte* 21 (1901): 160–85.

Dvornik, Francis. *Byzantium and the Roman Primacy*. Translated by Edward A. Quain. New York: Fordham University Press, 1966.

Eberhard, Winfried. "Ansätze zur Bewältigung ideologischer Pluralität im 12. Jahrhundert: Pierre Abélard und Anselm von Havelberg." *Historisches Jahrbuch* 105 (1985): 353–87.

Edyvean, Walter. *Anselm of Havelberg and the Theology of History*. Rome: Catholic Book Agency, 1972.

Elm, Kaspar, ed. *Norbert von Xanten: Adliger, Ordensstifter, Kirchenfürst.* Cologne: Wienand, 1984.

Evans, G. R. "Anselm of Canterbury and Anselm of Havelberg: The Controversy with the Greeks." *Analecta Praemonstratensia* 53 (1977): 158–75.

———. "Unity and Diversity: Anselm of Havelberg as Ecumenist." *Analecta Praemonstratensia* 67 (1991): 42–52.

Fried, Johannes. *Donation of Constantine and* Constitutum Constantini: *The Misinterpretation of a Fiction and Its Original Meaning.* Millenium Studies 3. Berlin: Walter de Gruyter, 2007.

Froese, Walter. "The Early Norbertines on the Religious Frontiers of Northeastern Germany." Ph.D. thesis, University of Chicago, 1978.

Fulton, Rachel. *From Judgment to Passion: Devotion to Christ and the Virgin Mary, 800–1200.* New York: Columbia University Press, 2002.

Funkenstein, Amos. *Heilsplan und natürliche Entwicklung: Formen der Gegenwartsbestimmung im Geschichtsdenken des hohen Mittelalters.* Munich: Nymphenburger, 1965.

Gasper, Giles E. M. *Anselm of Canterbury and His Theological Inheritance.* Aldershot: Ashgate, 2004.

Gaussin, Pierre-Roger. *L'Europe des ordres et des congrégations: Des Bénédictins aux Mendiants (VIe–XVIe siècle).* Saint-Etienne: Centre Européen de Recherches sur les Congrégations et Ordres Monastiques, 1984.

Gilson, Etienne. *Reason and Revelation in the Middle Ages.* New York: Scribner, 1938.

———. *The Spirit of Medieval Philosophy.* Translated by A. H. C. Downes. New York: Scribner, 1940.

Grundmann, Herbert. *Religious Movements in the Middle Ages: The Historical Links between Heresy, the Mendicant Orders, and the Women's Religious Movement in the Twelfth and Thirteenth Century, with the Historical Foundations of German Mysticism.* Translated by Steven Rowan. Notre Dame: University of Notre Dame Press, 1995.

———. *Studien über Joachim von Floris.* Beiträge zur Kulturgeschichte des Mittelalters und der Renaissance 32. Leipzig: Teubner, 1927.

Hampe, Karl. *Germany under the Salian and Hohenstaufen Emperors.* Translated by Ralph Bennett. Totowa, NJ: Rowman and Littlefield, 1973.

Heneghan, John J. *The Progress of Dogma according to Anselm of Havelberg.* New York: Paulist Press, 1943.

Jaeger, C. Stephen. *The Envy of Angels: Cathedral Schools and Social Ideals in Medieval Europe, 950–1200.* Philadelphia: University of Pennsylvania Press, 1994.

Kamlah, Wilhelm. *Apokalypse und Geschichtstheologie: Die mittelalterliche Auslegung der Apokalypse vor Joachim von Fiore.* Historische Studien 285. Berlin, 1935; repr. Vaduz: Kraus, 1965.

King, Peter. "Chapter 3: Metaphysics." In *The Cambridge Companion to Abelard.* Edited by Jeffrey E. Brower and Kevin Guilfoy, 65–125. Cambridge: Cambridge University Press. 2004.

Ladner, Gerhart B. *The Idea of Reform: Its Impact on Christian Thought and Action in the Age of the Fathers.* Cambridge, MA: Harvard University Press, 1959.

Lawless, George. *Augustine of Hippo and His Monastic Rule.* Oxford: Clarendon Press, 1987.

Lawrence, C. H. *Medieval Monasticism: Forms of Religious Life in Western Europe in the Middle Ages.* London: Longman, 1984.

Lees, Jay T. *Anselm of Havelberg: Deeds Into Words in the Twelfth Century.* Studies in the History of Christian Thought 79. Leiden: Brill, 1998.

———. "Anselm of Havelberg's 'Banishment' to Havelberg." *Analecta Praemonstratensia* 63 (1986): 5–18.

———. "Charity and Enmity in the Writings of Anselm of Havelberg." *Viator: Medieval and Renaissance Studies* 25 (1994): 53–62.

Lubac, Henri de. *Medieval Exegesis.* Volume 1: *The Four Senses of Scripture.* Translated by Mark Sebanc. Grand Rapids: Eerdmans, 1998.

MacMullen, Ramsay. *Voting about God in Early Church Councils.* New Haven: Yale University Press, 2006.

McDonnell, Ernest W. "The 'Vita Apostolica': Diversity or Dissent." *Church History* 24 (1955): 15–31.

McGinn, Bernard. *Visions of the End: Apocalyptic Traditions in the Middle Ages.* New York: Columbia University Press, 1979.

Marenbon, John. *Medieval Philosophy: A Historical and Philosophical Introduction.* London: Routledge, 2007.

Melville, Gert, ed. Secundum regulam vivere: *Festschrift für P. Norbert Backmund, O.Praem.* Windberg: Poppe-Verlag, 1978.

———. "Semantik von *ordo* im Religiosentum der ersten Hälfte des 12. Jahrhunderts. Lucius II., seine Bulle vom 19. Mai 1144, und der 'Orden' der Prämonstratenser." In *Studien zum Prämonstratenserorden.* Edited by Crusius and Flackenecker, 201–23.

Melville, Gert, and Anne Müller, eds. Regula sancti Augustini: *Normative Grundlage differenter Verbände im Mittelalter.* Paring: Augustiner-Chorherren-Verlag-Paring, 2002.

Morrison, Karl F. "Anselm of Havelberg: Play and the Dilemma of Historical Progress." In *Religion, Culture, and Society in the Early Middle Ages: Studies in Honor of Richard F. Sullivan.* Edited by Thomas F. X.

Noble and John J. Contreni, 229–56. Kalamazoo MI: Medieval Institute Publications, 1987.

———. "The Exercise of Thoughtful Minds: The Apocalypse in Some German Historical Writings." In *The Apocalypse in the Middle Ages*. Edited by Richard K. Emmerson and Bernard McGinn, 352–73. Ithaca: Cornell University Press, 1992.b

Munz, Peter. *Frederick Barbarossa: A Study in Medieval Politics*. London: Eyre and Spottiswoode, 1969.

Neel, Carol. "Philip of Harvengt and Anselm of Havelberg: The Premonstratensian Vision of Time." *Church History* 52 (1993): 483–93.

Newman, Martha G. *The Boundaries of Charity: Cistercian Culture and Ecclesiastical Reform, 1098–1180*. Stanford, CA: Stanford Univesity Press, 1996.

Ngien, Dennis. *Apologetic for* Filioque *in Medieval Theology*. Milton Keynes: Paternoster, 2005.

Nichols, Aidan. *Rome and the Eastern Churches: A Study in Schism*. Collegeville, MN: Liturgical Press, 1992.

Nicholson, Helen. *The Knights Templar: A New History*. Stroud: Sutton, 2001.

Oppl, Ferdinand. "*Amator ecclesiarum*. Studien zur religiösen Haltung Friedrichs Barbarossas." *Mitteilungen des Instituts für österreichische Geschichtsforschung* 88 (1980): 70–93.

———. "Aspekte der religiöse Haltung Kaiser Friedrich Barbarossas." In *Barbarossa und die Prämonstratenser*. Edited by Karl-Heinz Ruess, 25–45.

Penth, Sabine. *Prämonstratenser und Staufer: Zur Rolle des Reformordens in der staufischen Reichs- und Territorialpolitik*. Historische Studien 478. Hussum: Matthiesen, 2003.

Petit, François. *Spiritualité des Prémontrés aux XIIe et XIIIe siècles*. Études de théologie et d'histoire de la spiritualité 10. Paris: J. Vrin, 1947.

Rauh, Horst Dieter. *Das Bild des Antichrist im Mittelalter: Von Tychonius zum deutschen Symbolismus*. Beiträge zur Geschichte der Philosophie und Theologie des Mittelalters, n.s. 9. Münster: Aschendorff, 1973.

Roby, Douglass. Transitus et stabilitas: *Understanding Passage from One Religious Order to Another in Twelfth-Century Monastic Controversy*. Ph.D. thesis, Yale University, 1971.

Rose, Valentin, and Fritz Schillman, eds. *Verzeichnis der lateinischen Handschriften der königlichen Bibliothek zu Berlin*. 3 volumes. Berlin: A. Asher and Co., 1901; repr. Hildesheim: Georg Olms, 1976.

Ruess, Karl-Heinz, ed. *Barbarossa und die Prämonstratenser*. Schriften zur staufischen Geschichte und Kunst 10. Göppingen: Gesellschaft für staufische Gesschichte, 1989.

Russell, Norman. "Anselm of Havelberg and the Union of Churches." *Sobornost* 1 (1979–80): 19–41; *Sobornost* 2 (1980): 29–41.

Schatz, Klaus. *Papal Primacy: From Its Origins to the Present.* Translated by John A. Otto and Linda M. Maloney. Collegeville, MN: Liturgical Press, 1996.

Schimmelpfennig, Bernard. *The Papacy.* Translated by James Siebert. New York: Columbia University Press, 1992.

Schreiber, Georg. "Anselm von Havelberg und die Ostkirche." *Zeitschrift für Kirchengeschichte* 60 (1941): 354–411.

———. "Studien über Anselm von Havelberg zur Geistesgeschichte des Hochmittelalters." *Analecta Praemonstratensia* 18 (1942): 5–90.

Sieben, Hermann Josef. *Die Konzilsidee des lateinischen Mittelalters (847–1387).* Paderborn: Ferdinand Schöningh, 1984.

———. *Studien zur Gestalt und Überlieferung der Konzilien.* Paderborn: Ferdinand Schöningh, 2005.

Sigler, Sebastian. *Anselm von Havelberg: Beiträge zum Lebensbild eines Politikers, Theologen und königlichen Gesandten im 12. Jahrhundert.* Aachen: Shaker, 2005.

Smalley, Beryl. *The Study of the Bible in the Middle Ages.* Notre Dame: University of Notre Dame Press, 1964.

Southern, R. W. "Aspects of the European Tradition of History Writing, 2. Hugh of St. Victor and the Idea of Historical Development." *Transactions of the Royal Historical Society,* 5th series 21 (1971): 159–79.

———. *Western Society and the Church in the Middle Ages.* New York: Penguin, 1970.

Spörl, Johannes. *Grundformen hochmittelalterlicher Geschichtsanschauung: Studien zum Weltbild der Geschichtsschreiber des 12. Jahrhunderts.* 2d ed. Darmstadt: Wissenschaftliche Buchgesellschaft, 1935.

Tierney, Brian. *Foundations of the Conciliar Theory: The Contribution of the Medieval Canonists from Gratian to the Great Schism.* Cambridge: Cambridge University Press, 1955.

Töpfer, Bernhard. *Das kommende Reich des Friedens.* Berlin: Akademie-Verlag, 1964.

Van Engen, John H. *Rupert of Deutz.* Berkeley: University of California Press, 1983.

Vlasto, A. P. *The Entry of the Slavs into Christendom: An Introduction to the Medieval History of the Slavs.* Cambridge: Cambridge University Press, 1970.

Vogüé, Adalbert de. *Les règles monastiques anciennes (400–700).* Typologie des sources du moyen âge occidental 46. Turnhout: Brepols, 1985.

Weinfurter, Stefan. "Norbert von Xanten als Reformkanoniker und Stifter des Prämonstratenerordens." In *Norbert von Xanten: Adliger, Ordensstifter, Kirchenfürst.* Edited by Kaspar Elm, 159–85.

———. "Reformkanoniker und Reichsepiskopat im Hochmittelalter." *Historisches Jahrbuch* 97–98 (1978): 158–93.

———. "Vita canonica und Eschatologie: Eine neue Quelle zum Selbstverständnis der Reformkanoniker des 12. Jahrhunderts aus dem Salzburger Reformkreis (mit Textedition)." In *Secundam regulam vivere: Festschrift für P. Norbert Backmund, O.Praem.* Edited by Gert Melville, 139–67. Windberg: Poppe, 1978.

Wentz, Gottfried, ed. *Das Bistum Havelberg.* Germania sacra. Part 1. Volume 2. Berlin: Walter de Gruyter, 1933.

Williams, Rowan. *Arius: Heresy and Tradition.* Rev. ed. Grand Rapids: Eerdmans, 2001.

Winter, Franz. *Die Prämonstratenser des zwölften Jahrhunderts und ihre Bedeutung für das nordöstliche Deutschland: Ein Beitrag zur Geschichte der Christianisierung und Germanisierung des Wendenlands.* Berlin, 1965; repr. Darmstadt: Scientia Verlag Aalen, 1966.

———. "Zur Geschichte des Bischofs Anselm von Havelberg." *Zeitschrift für Kirchengeschichte* 5 (1882): 138–55.

Wolf, Gabriel Markus. Trado meipsum ecclesiae: *Die Feiern der Einkleidung in den Praemonstratenser-Orden als Spiegel praemonstratensischer Spiritualität.* Windberg: Poppe-Verlag, 2005.